Beginning iOS Apps with Facebook and Twitter APIs

For iPhone, iPad, and iPod touch

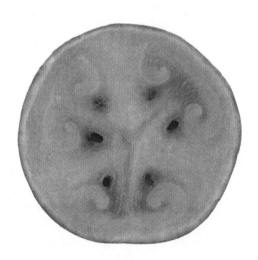

Chris Dannen
Christopher White

Apress®

Beginning iOS Apps with Facebook and Twitter APIs: For iPhone, iPad, and iPod touch

ISBN-13 (pbk): 978-1-4302-3542-2

ISBN-13 (electronic): 978-1-4302-3543-9

President and Publisher: Paul Manning
Lead Editor: Steve Anglin
Development Editor: Tom Welsh
Technical Reviewer: Ryan Petrich
Editorial Board: Steve Anglin, Mark Beckner, Ewan Buckingham, Gary Cornell, Jonathan Gennick, Jonathan Hassell, Michelle Lowman, James Markham, Matthew Moodie, Jeff Olson, Jeffrey Pepper, Frank Pohlmann, Douglas Pundick, Ben Renow-Clarke, Dominic Shakeshaft, Matt Wade, Tom Welsh
Coordinating Editor: Kelly Moritz
Copy Editor: Patrick Meader
Compositor: MacPS, LLC
Indexer: John Collin
Artist: April Milne
Cover Designer: Anna Ishchenko

Distributed to the book trade worldwide by Springer Science+Business Media, LLC., 233 Spring Street, 6th Floor, New York, NY 10013. Phone 1-800-SPRINGER, fax (201) 348-4505, e-mail orders-ny@springer-sbm.com, or visit www.springeronline.com.

For information on translations, please e-mail rights@apress.com, or visit www.apress.com.

Apress and friends of ED books may be purchased in bulk for academic, corporate, or promotional use. eBook versions and licenses are also available for most titles. For more information, reference our Special Bulk Sales–eBook Licensing web page at www.apress.com/bulk-sales.

The source code for this book is available to readers at www.apress.com and https://github.com/chrisdannen/Apress_iOSFacebookTwitter. You will need to answer questions pertaining to this book in order to successfully download the code.

Contents at a Glance

Contents

About the Authors

 **Chris Dannen** is a business and technology writer who writes for *FastCompany* magazine and other publications. He is also the author of "iPhone Design Award Winning Projects" (Apress, 2009). He lives in Brooklyn, NY.

 **Christopher White** is an iOS engineer with a background in location-based gaming, mobile advertising, and in-vehicle GPS navigation. He lives in Brooklyn, NY.

About the Technical Reviewer

Ryan Petrich is a software engineer with a background in reverse engineering, mobile advertising, and iOS software development. He resides in Edmonton, AB and Brooklyn, NY.

Acknowledgments

Thanks to our editors and friends, who tolerated our "spontaneous" style of work.

Preface

Facebook and Twitter are perhaps the only platforms that are so vital to our daily communications that they could, for some users, supersede Apple's own communication apps, the SMS app, and the phone. In a few years, some people may live the majority of their iOS experience inside one of these platforms.

Fortunately for us, the third-party developers, both of these companies are growing so rapidly that they can hardly afford to explore and optimize every possible use for these platforms. (They also have the minor issue of monetization to worry about.)

As the staffs at Twitter and Facebook busy themselves refining their products, privacy policies, APIs, and business plans, there is a huge opportunity for smaller, more nimble developers to get out there and see what people *want next* from the online social experience. As an independent developer, you have the power to find a niche among Facebook and Twitter users—perhaps a very big niche—and create a tool that feels novel and useful, yet familiar and intuitive.

We hope this book helps you do just that.

Chris D. and Chris W.

Chapter 1

What the Social Graph Can Do for Your App

Once upon a time, there were "social" networks that helped people connect with friends. Nowadays, every application and web service can be considered social. Why? Simply put, it's because people like to share. Whether it's publishing a high score in a video game or posting a picture where friends can see it, iOS users have become accustomed to showing their digital life to their network of friends, family, and colleagues.

That network of people is called the *social graph*. A person's social graph describes everyone he knows and how those people are connected. Since Facebook CEO Mark Zuckerberg coined the term in 2007, the social graph has become more than just who you know. Other "nodes" that have been added include places, events, brands, and multimedia. All these things can act as vectors by which people connect to one another.

Facebook and Twitter exist to document the social graph of its users and push them to make new connections. Both companies have powerful incentives to expand the social graph of its users: knowing users' connections and predilections allows them to sell targeted advertisements, deliver recommendations, and initiate partnerships around e-commerce and real-world commerce alike.

For app developers, the opportunities are much the same. Adding Facebook or Twitter functionality to an iOS app can open up vast new opportunities for monetization and new features, but there is plenty of other cool stuff in store, too. Connecting your app to the social graph makes it easier for users to log in, manage their account, and transfer information in and out. And both Facebook and Twitter have built extensive APIs and frameworks that can spare developers from having to reinvent the wheel. (Facebook, for example, has even made its custom iOS frameworks open source.)

Both services have audiences of hundreds of millions of users looking to explore. Now that all those folks have invested time building out a Facebook profile or cranking out a stream of tweets, many of them are curious how else they can use their accounts. Show them!

What Is This Book for?

This book shows iOS developers how you can build Facebook and/or Twitter into your apps, allowing you to build more secure, flexible, and usable apps. But there is a lot more than just technical guidance here. The chapters of this book will also delve into some of the philosophical questions that go into utilizing the social graph. For example, it will address design and branding, so that users will recognize the Facebook and Twitter features they love when they're inside your app.

What You'll Need

This book won't endeavor to teach you how to build an entire iOS app from the ground up, so you'll want to have some semblance of an app already built by the time you pick up the Facebook and Twitter APIs. And while we'll be working in trusty ol' Cocoa Touch and Objective-C, there will also be plenty of Web stuff that requires JavaScript, HTML, and CSS. Picking up the APIs we'll discuss in this book will go more smoothly if you've programmed for the Web before.

What You Should Know

The social graph is about people. It's about their content, their friends, and their businesses. Some of the interactions you'll encounter are socially sophisticated—you're messing with peoples' relationships here. The way these relationships function online will be hard to understand if you've never spent much time using Facebook or Twitter. If you're thinking about adding one of these APIs to your app, you'll find it worth taking the time to get comfortable with the services. Do this, and you'll gain a more nuanced understanding of the privacy issues (there are many); the platforms (they're not perfect); and most importantly, an idea of what these things are actually useful for.

What You'll Learn

By the time you're finished with this book, you'll know how to build an app that can connect to the world's most popular social Web services quickly, securely, and discreetly. You'll understand how to leverage the social graph to make your software more useful, more fun, and more popular. You'll also see where the weak spots in the platform lie and understand better how the APIs will evolve in the future.

But perhaps most crucially, you'll understand the beginnings of a significant moment in the development of the Web and the iOS: the coalescence of *online life* and *real life*. There is immense power being endowed in the Web now as people bring their real-life relationships, experiences, interests, and emotions into the social graph. The more rack space that Twitter and Facebook build, the more user data becomes available to your app. And the better you know the user, the more useful your programs become.

Learning the Social Graph

If you haven't seen the movie "The Social Network," we'll save you the trouble. "You don't even know what the thing is yet," Sean Parker says to Zuckerberg at the film's apogee. And he's absolutely right: no one knows what Facebook is, or what it will become.

Both Facebook and Twitter, as large and well-funded as they are, are probably still in their incipience. A lot is going to change as business and society come to mold their media, communication, and commerce around these platforms. If you can't think of a killer use-case for Facebook or Twitter in your app at this stage in the game, don't worry—you're only on page three. It may take some thinking (and plenty of prototyping) before you understand how to put the social graph to the best possible use in your app. But that's okay because everyone else is in the same boat.

To get your brain on its way to ginning up good ideas, we'll cover some very basic things you can do with Facebook and Twitter inside an app by manipulating their APIs.

Use-Cases, Briefly

There are plenty of things that an iOS application can get from Facebook and Twitter APIs. Some very basic use cases consist of, but are not limited to, what's described in the following sections. You'll learn how to do all the things described in these sections in this book; you'll also learn how to concoct much more complex use cases.

Facebook

Here are some examples that illustrate how a developer could use Facebook inside a hypothetical app:

- Upload a photo or a video created in a camera app to a user's profile
- Post a link to a content within a news app to a user's wall
- Post *likes* to a user's wall from inside a shopping app
- Post a status update to a user's profile
- Display a list of a user's friends and their profile photos in a contacts application
- Let a user set herself as attending an event from within an application
- Show users who else is at an event from inside an app
- Display search results of public Facebook data, so that users can search for people, places, or content

Twitter

Here are some examples that illustrate how a developer could use Twitter inside a hypothetical app:

- Tweet a link to an event from within a location-based app
- Tweet a photo from with a photo editing app
- Send direct messages to specific Twitter users
- Show tweets that are relevant to a topic within a news application
- Display a list of a user's followers and followees and their profiles in a contacts application
- Automatically tweet a user's location from within a GPS application
- Organize a group or community around your app
- Show tweets about a restaurant in a food guide application
- Publicize a high score in a game
- Search up to the minute news or photos
- Use trends or *trending* topics as input

Brief Overview of the APIs and Services

Facebook and Twitter are both robust platforms, but they don't always let you do what you want. If you already have some idea of what you want to add to your app, here are basic summaries of what these platforms allow.

Facebook

The Facebook API is currently in an ongoing, transitional phase. The original Facebook API was a Representational State Transfer (REST) API, but this API is being phased out and is officially deprecated.

All Facebook development moving forward should use Facebook's new Graph API. The Graph API is where you will find support for all new and future Facebook features, and it is continuously updated to include the full set of original features from the REST API.

Note that the Graph API only supports responses as JavaScript Object Notation (JSON) objects.

A basic summary of these APIs follows.

Reading

This API provides access to the basic information stored in the Facebook Graph.

Publishing

This API enables you to add comments, likes, and so on to the Facebook Graph.

Searching

This API allows you to search public objects in the social graph, such as all public posts, people, events, places, and so on.

All of the Facebook APIs are HTTP based, so data is retrieved via an HTTP GET, and data is submitted via an HTTP POST.

To make the lives of iOS developers easier, Facebook also makes available an iOS Objective-C Facebook SDK. This SDK is open source and functions as a wrapper around the Facebook HTTP-based Graph API. This book will use the iOS Objective-C Facebook SDK, but will refer back to the HTTP APIs where appropriate or wherever they provide additional insight.

Twitter

Twitter's API has evolved to be somewhat segmented—it was mostly developed in-house, but augmented by major code infusions that were purchased from third-parties. The result is an API that consists of two Representational State Transfer (REST) APIs, a Core API and a Search API, and one Streaming API. Twitter's API supports both XML and JSON formats, but we will be using the default XML format when discussing technical details and when showing example code. A basic summary of these APIs follows.

Core API

This API provides the basic Twitter functionality of twitter.com: tweet, follow, and timeline.

Search API

This API provides a real-time search index of Twitter and global and local trends.

Streaming API

This API is currently designed primarily for server-to-server integrations via HTTP long-poll connections, and it provides tweets in real-time. Twitter is in the process of experimenting with server-to-client integrations via this API.

All of the APIs are HTTP-based and usage is rate limited. Just like Facebook, data in Twitter is retrieved via an HTTP GET, and data is submitted via an HTTP POST.

Note that Twitter has gone to great lengths to adhere to the following principles when developing each of these APIs:

■ To be ridiculously simple

■ To be obvious

■ To be self-describing

The Social Graph on iOS

Back when it was known as the iPhone OS, Apple's mobile platform didn't offer much to social graph applications, which weren't allowed to achieve anything close to parity with a desktop experience. But slowly, Apple began giving more power to its devices and more tools to developers. Now with multitasking and a new Sleep mode, iOS 4 has empowered social apps to evolve even deeper functionality. In the process, Apple has solved some very deep usability problems with rather elegant (if sometimes limited) solutions.

Sure, you can do a lot of the stuff we'll talk about in this book with other platforms, but it won't work as well (or look as good) as it will on the iOS. Here are some of the new goodies that come with iOS 4:

■ Multitasking allows your app to go about its business in the background. Whatever your app does, it can keep on doing it without the user needing to manually activate it.

■ Better spell-check and text-replacement options make data entry easier.

■ WiFi connections now have limited persistence in Sleep mode, which means that iOS devices can continue to perform Web-related operations when the device isn't being used.

> **NOTE:** When an app is running in the background on iOS, it can't perform all its functions in that state. For reasons relating to reliability and battery life, Apple has chosen to restrict background processing to the seven specific APIs (see Chapter 10 for more information on this topic).

Other changes introduced in iOS 4 will make programming for the social graph more robust. Some of those changes include the following.

Local Notifications

iOS has had Push notifications for a while, but now Apple has introduced Local notifications, too. These alerts don't travel through Apple's Push server, but instead reside on the device itself, waiting in the background until it's time to pop out at the user. The notification that someone is calling you on Skype is an example of a Local notification.

Task Completion

If a task is underway when a user exits an app, iOS can now register that thread and keep it going in the background, even after the user has moved on to doing something else. Keeping that single thread open allows the user to shut down the remainder of the app, releasing most of the memory back to the system. iOS will shut the app down completely once that task is done.

Fast Task Switching and Saved State

Before iOS 4, it was very difficult to build a persistent app that would save the user's progress upon exit. Saved states are now recommended for all iOS apps. This means that when a user returns to an app, the app's current state has been preserved in memory and appears just as the user left it. This functionality is managed by the new "task switcher" that appears when you double-tap the Home button. This state-saving is especially useful when apps call other apps, such as when a user chooses to compose an email from inside an app. After the email is sent, the app the user was using when she initiated the email will return to the screen, just as she left it.

Background Music, Location, and VOIP

Apple has also made provisions for music, location-based, and VOIP apps to continue operations in the background while the user navigates through other apps. This means that music can continue playing, and "check-in" apps can be notified of a change of venue—even when the user is outside a music or location app. VOIP apps can deliver notifications (for incoming phone calls, for example), which makes telephony more robust, too.

SMS: Search and in-app SMSing

Apple has created a new API with iOS 4 that allows in-app SMS composition inside third-party apps. There's no unified messaging service, as on other platforms, but Facebook's new Messages service might serve as a stand-in.

More Powerful Photos and Calendars

Apple has granted developers new access to the Calendar app, allowing third-party apps to create events inside a user's calendar. Apple has also added developer access to the device's entire photo and video library, not just the "image picker" available in the old OS.

New Camera and Flash

The iPhone's rear-facing camera now supports zoom and adjustable focus, and developers have also been given access to the front-facing camera that appears on new iPods and iPhones. Better yet, developers get full playback and recording access, as well as access to the LED flash.

Map Overlays

Developers can add their own overlays to embedded Google Maps to show additional information (like directions or annotations) inside an app.

iAd

Sure, iAd is tightly controlled by Apple, and the minimum buy-ins are tremendous. But iAd is an option in iOS 4 nonetheless, giving developers the option of delivering interactive, aesthetically pleasing, and precise advertisements to users in HTML5.

Quick Look

In Mac OS X, you can tap the spacebar in Finder to preview a file. The same ability has now been delivered to iOS developers, who can peek at files and attachments before deciding whether to open them in full.

Math APIs

Games and location apps will benefit from a couple of thousand new hardware-accelerated math APIs that should boost graphics-intensive performance.

File Transfer

The iPad has had the File Transfer feature for a while, but the other iOS devices now have the ability to transfer files between a computer and an iOS device inside iTunes.

Summary

There are a ton of new opportunities in iOS 4, as well as in the respective APIs of Facebook and Twitter. The audiences are massive: 500 million Facebook members and 130 million Twitter users—and both are growing. Whatever your iOS app can do, it can probably become more functional and more appealing with a social layer.

The most crucial thing you can take way from this chapter is our advice to spend plenty of time using these services before you finish prototyping. Both of these services—but especially Facebook—have a lot of objects, properties, and interactions whose functions can get confusing. Knowing the way that users expect these resources to be used will help you design an app that works reliably and consistently.

Once you're done with this book, you'll know exactly what to add to your app and how to build it. Now turn the page and get going!

Chapter 2

Privacy, Privacy, Privacy

There was a time in the not-so-distant past when most people shared their life experiences via email or direct instant messaging (IM). With respect to privacy and security, it was a simpler time—users logged in directly to their email or IM accounts and sent links, pictures, and so on directly from their desktop or laptop to one or more specific recipients.

As the Web has evolved, the ways in which users share information have become increasingly complex and interrelated; information has moved away from a user's desktop and into the cloud. However, this added complexity and interrelatedness has resulted in a world where it is much harder to ensure privacy and security for individual users because there are more opportunities for a company or an individual with malicious intentions to gain access to a user's credentials for one of his accounts.

After reading this chapter, we hope you walk away with two salient lessons:

- People are sharing more—and sharing more valuable information— with the *social graph*, which is Facebook's term for your network of online friends.

- Standards for security and privacy are changing.

> **NOTE:** Security and privacy should be handled with the utmost seriousness. Wisely or not, users entrust Facebook and Twitter with extremely sensitive and personal information. If your app puts their privacy or their interests at risk, they will hate you, pummel your app in the App Store reviews, and say terrible things about your mother. When working with Facebook and Twitter APIs, make the user's privacy and security of utmost concern.

The Old Way

User-generated content now passes through more hands than ever, which increases the risk of somebody or something screwing up. Let's look at a classic example: using an online service to print digital photos.

In the past, a user would create an account on a photo-printing site, log in to her account, and upload photos from her desktop that she would like to have printed. From a privacy perspective in this scenario, the user only has to trust that the photo-printing site has the appropriate measures in place to prevent someone from hacking into its site and gaining usernames, passwords, personal photos, and even credit card information. But there are relatively few variables in this example: the only parties involved are the user and the photo-printing site.

A Quick History of Hot-Button Issues

Neither Facebook nor Twitter has escaped its share of privacy and security snafus in the last several years. While most of those concerns have been allayed, it helps to know a little bit of history, so you can identify any hot-button issues before you roll out your app.

Facebook's Track Record

Perhaps the most salient privacy blunder in Facebook's history was Facebook Beacon, an opt-out platform app built by Facebook that was intended to let users share what they are buying. Facebook was attacked for collecting user data without permission, and sharing this data with advertisers. Since the Beacon incident in 2007, numerous software services have created tools that let users share purchases with their social graph, including Swipely, Blippy, and Mint.com. All three of these companies repurpose that buyer data, although none have done so with the flippancy that Facebook did.

Since Beacon, users, journalists and analysts have been ready to jump on any security loophole they can find in Facebook, and each successive disclosure of a problem leads to a rash of Facebook protests and campaigning.

The lesson: It's not necessarily what you do with users' data that matters—it's whether you make your service opt-in and ask permission at every step along the way. As subsequent Beacon-like services have proven, users are quite willing to experiment with their own privacy if they feel that the process is open and transparent.

Twitter's Track Record

Compared with Facebook, Twitter's record of privacy snafus seems more bumbling, but also less strategic. Users generally aren't quite as suspicious of Twitter's motives as they are of Facebook's; then again, most users don't imbue their Twitter profiles with the same amount of private content. Twitter is, almost by nature, a public-facing tool, so users have been primed to think of their tweets as public property. (And with several search engines now indexing real-time content from Twitter, those tweets are truly the province of the wider Web.)

Still, Twitter has its sensitive spots, too. Whenever security problems pop up on Twitter, they inevitably speak to the company's meteoric growth—and all the growing pains that come with it. In 2007, SMS tweets were shown to be vulnerable to spoofing, which could allow malicious actors to pull a user's phone number from his profile information. In 2009, a handful of celebrity profiles were compromised after a hacker used a dictionary attack to figure out a Twitter employee's administrator password. Other bugs have allowed users to manipulate other users into following them; late-night host Conan O'Brien's account fell victim to this kind of attack. In the Fall of 2010, an XSS worm was discovered that exploited a simple JavaScript function to affect pranks.

All these breaches have since been addressed, but not before they gave Twitter a little bit of a bad rep. In 2010, the FTC brought charges against Twitter for its security breaches; however, those charges have since been settled. While Twitter doesn't evoke the same amount of suspicion that Facebook does among its users, its segmented APIs and its adolescent growth spurt mean that more loopholes probably exist. You need to take great care with users' Twitter accounts. You should also remember that, while tweet-streams may not seem vital at first glance, you never know what your users are hoping to hide there.

How OAuth Changes Everything

In this day and age, though, one could imagine that the photo-printing site mentioned previously now has an API in place that provides the ability for third-party web sites, applications, and services to import or share photos from a user's account, as long as the user grants the third-party apps permission to do this. This usually happens when the user enters his credentials—his username and password—for the photo site inside that third-party app.

By giving outside sites access to a user's account, the photo sharing site is creating a situation where a third-party could gain complete access to a user's account and personal information—and even potentially change the user's password. Not only that, but that third-party app now has access to other account information stored on the photo site.

So why do users trust that this will all turn out okay?

One reason (although the user may not know it) is *OAuth*, a bifurcated security protocol that is becoming fairly standard among social APIs. OAuth was designed to let users share the resources in their account with third parties without having to give the third parties their username and password, thereby jeopardizing their whole account (and whatever other accounts share those credentials).

We say OAuth is bifurcated because it has two versions (1.3 and 2.0) that are actively in use, but not across the board. OAuth 2.0 is being promulgated mostly by Facebook. If you're going to be adding Facebook to your app, you'll be working with the latter version. Twitter allows you to use OAuth 1.3. Facebook won't allow OAuth 1.3 apps, and Twitter won't allow OAuth 2.0.

Assume a third party wanted to gain access to a user's account via OAuth in the case of the photo-printing site; the interaction would look like this:

1. The third party would contact the photo-printing site and ask for access to the user's account via OAuth.

2. The user would be presented with a login page from the photo-printing site. This page asks the user to grant permission by entering his username and password.

3. The third-party site would then receive an OAuth token that could be used to access the user's account without needing the user's username and password.

A New Standard Emerges

OAuth is quickly becoming the default standard for sites to allow shared access to a user's resources from third-party sites, applications, and services. Facebook, Twitter, and most other social networking sites now encourage or require the use of OAuth from third parties, and this trend is likely to continue.

So we have dedicated most of Chapter 5 to covering OAuth in detail to help you integrate your iOS application with Facebook and Twitter. It's no coincidence that this is the second chapter in the book; nothing is more important than security when working with social APIs.

What Users "Want"

Now that we've talked about security, let's talk about privacy. There are vastly disparate opinions on how users feel about privacy. Here is a brief summary of the respective camps, so that you can decide where you (and your users) want your app to fit in the privacy spectrum.

Christopher Poole, aka "Moot," the founder of 4chan.org, has historically been a proponent of complete anonymity online. He said the following at a TED conference in June 2010:

"We're moving towards social networking, we're moving towards persistent identity. We're moving towards a lack of privacy; really, we're sacrificing a lot of that, and I think in doing so, in moving towards those things, we're losing something valuable." Later, he summarized: "Saying whatever you like is powerful."

Powerful, indeed. The upshot of Poole's argument is that users' desire to be "heard" may be entirely discrete from their desire for attribution. So while your iOS app may want to make provisions for publicizing something created inside the app—perhaps by publishing an iPad drawing or the results of a game—it's vital to keep in mind that using the social graph to publish that information has the potential to make it searchable and traceable information for as long as Google and Bing are crawling the Web.

Mark Zuckerberg, Facebook's CEO, has a diametrically opposed point of view. He believes that the urge to keep online data private is some silly vestigial instinct that we'll all eventually abandon. Here is what he said in an interview in January 2010 about the changing norms of privacy:

"... In the last five or six years, blogging has taken off in a huge way, and all these different services that have people sharing all this information. People have really gotten comfortable not only sharing more information and different kinds, but more openly and with more people. That social norm is just something that has evolved over time. We view it as our role in the system to constantly be innovating and be updating what our system is to reflect what the current social norms are.

"A lot of companies would be trapped by the conventions and their legacies of what they've built—doing a privacy change for 350 million users is not the kind of thing that a lot of companies would do. But we viewed that as a really important thing, to always keep a beginner's mind and what would we do if we were starting the company now, and we decided that these would be the social norms now, and we just went for it."[1]

The authors of this book are (perhaps strategically) centrists in this debate. Yes, there is value to being anonymous, especially where minors are at play (as in iOS Game Center apps). But it's also increasingly normal to have your real-life identity connected to your online identity. It's up to you to decide whether your app will contribute to a user's persona in the social graph—or whether it will be a hideaway where they can use your app with impunity.

What's at stake besides your users' reputation? The value of their data. Twitter and Facebook both claim ownership over the data created by their users, and they're free to monetize that data however they wish. Does that open users up to hyper-targeted advertising? Can we be segmented and marketed to because we've disclosed our real demographic information? Certainly, and both companies are already segmenting and targeting their user audiences. But many users would consider these realities to be a small price to pay for the benefits of building a real persona online.

Educating Your Users

Whatever you believe is the right level of privacy for your users, we strongly recommend following two general principles when dealing with the social graph.

Notify your users of everything that is being posted or gotten from the social graph. Follow Apple's example here: they provide a pop-up every time iOS accesses the location of a device. With the pop-up, the majority of users are absolutely fine with their device knowing their location. However, if this process were happening in the background on an opt-out basis, many users would be enraged. The lesson: You have a lot of latitude with privacy, and users are willing to experiment with your app—provided your app is completely transparent about what it is doing with user data, and why.

---

[1] http://www.readwriteweb.com/archives/facebooks_zuckerberg_says_the_age_of
_privacy_is_ov.php

Be sure that the user knows the ramifications of the actions your app is taking. For computer-savvy users, it may be enough to tell them about a POST or GET event. But many users might be unfamiliar with the consequences of these events. If your app has any potential whatsoever to reveal personal or private information, be sure to clearly state the risks somewhere in your app. It can be hard to integrate such warnings or *helper text* into an iOS app without ruining visual design and cluttering the interaction, but Chapter 5 of this book can help you figure out when and where to do this.

A Note on Feeds

At the risk of belaboring the point, we feel we must mention that a lot of the actions enabled by the Facebook and Twitter APIs have somewhat irreversible consequences. Are the risks life or death? Probably not. But once information is posted to the social graph, it is extremely hard (if not impossible) to remove.

On Twitter, tweet streams are indexed by search engines immediately, so the text of a tweet can live on long after the tweet has been deleted by the user. Facebook statuses are not indexable by search engines, but they are pushed to a user's friends in the Facebook News Feed application and cannot be erased from others' News Feeds, even if the original post is deleted. Keep this in mind, and don't be careless with your users' information.

What to Do if You Encounter a Security Loophole

If you discover what you think may be a security problem with the Facebook or Twitter platform while developing an app, you should report the flaw immediately to the appropriate entities.

For Facebook, this means entering a ticket in the platform's bug tracking system, which is located at `http://bugs.developers.facebook.net`. For bigger issues, you can fill out the form located at `http://www.facebook.com/help/contact.php?show_form=dev_support`, although the company says that response times to this form are not as rapid as with the bug tracker.

Twitter has a more nuanced reporting system. The company has several different reporting systems that are segmented by the kind of flaw you find. To see your options for reporting, check out `http://support.twitter.com/groups/33-report-a-violation`; you can glance at the @support feed to see if the issue has already been addressed.

Summary

We think you get the picture: privacy is important, and security is even more important. Prototype, test, and test some more. Don't rely on Apple to vet the security chops of your app. Use the appropriate version of OAuth and consider all the use-cases you can imagine to prevent holes. Do this at every stage of development, and don't roll out a finished product until you're sure it's safe. And don't forget: once something is published to the social graph, it can be almost impossible to redact. Publish carefully!

Chapter 3

Choose Your Weapon!

Both Facebook and Twitter have multifarious uses, and many of them overlap. Figuring out which service to integrate (or which to integrate first) is the job of this chapter. Let's dig in and see what Facebook and Twitter give us to work with.

After reading this chapter, you should know the following:

▒ What you can do with Facebook's iOS SDK and its Mobile Web SDK.

▒ How to make it easier to include Twitter's API in iOS.

What Are They Good For?

Which integration you consider primary will have more to do with your specific app than anything else. However, there are some general considerations that come into play when deciding where to focus your energy. The more you know about Facebook and Twitter, the better you'll be able to choose which one is right for your app (or whether—gasp!—you have to include both).

Facebook

Facebook has over 500 million registered users, 100 million of whom access Facebook from mobile devices. That's a very big audience. If your app is going to rely on a platform for its ubiquity, then Facebook is the de facto first choice because of its incredible international popularity.

That said, Facebook's content (by the numbers) is mostly private photos. Facebook Photos is by far the most popular use of the platform, and some of the code supporting this feature on iOS is open source. Facebook statuses deal mostly with private thoughts, and its messaging system is used primarily for personal missives between members. Brands and corporations are present, but mostly in the form of fan pages that get most of their nods from the Like button.

Twitter

Twitter is a very different beast than Facebook. It has become the most important vector for breaking news, and much of what is said on Twitter is meant to be shared as quickly as possible. This is almost the opposite of the Facebook ecosystem, where elaborate privacy settings keep content from trickling out in an uncontrolled fashioned (at least, in principal). The vast majority of Twitter's 65 million daily tweets are public, not private, and it generates so much content per day that it doesn't have room to archive every tweet that passes through its system. (Facebook, in contrast, saves files and profiles even after users delete them.) About 190 million people use Twitter per month at the time of writing.

NOTE: Startups like to throw around "user" statistics in the tens of millions, but what do these numbers really mean? We'll start with Facebook. Facebook is virtually useless unless you're registered and logged in. So when Facebook says it has half a billion users (and growing), it is referring to the number of people who have registered and entered some personal information into the system. Twitter, by contrast, is read by millions of *lurkers*, or people without profiles. At the time of writing, ComScore estimates that Twitter gets 83.6 million unique visitors a month worldwide, and about 24 million in the U.S., which are smaller numbers than Twitter reports. It's also worth mentioning that, of those 65 million daily tweets, it's unknown how many are automated bots or spammers. However you cut it, Facebook is a much, much larger service, but Twitter contains much more publicly accessible (and publicly valuable) information.

Getting Started with Facebook's Awesome Developer Tools

Facebook has a special iOS SDK to help ease integration. Facebook likes to trumpet the fact that its SDK makes it easy to do single sign-on, so that users don't have to log into your app every time they open it up. But there's more to it than that. With Facebook's iOS SDK, you can easily accomplish the following:

- Prompt users to log into Facebook and grant access permission to your application.

- Make requests to the Graph API and older REST API.

- Show users common Facebook dialogs for creating wall posts and more.

■ On iOS devices that run a 4.x version of iOS and support multitasking, you can take advantage of Facebook's single sign-on feature. This feature allows multiple applications to share a user's Facebook login. In other words, if the user has already logged into Facebook from within the Facebook iOS application or a different application that is using the Facebook iOS SDK, then the user won't be prompted to log into Facebook again from within your application if you are using the Facebook iOS SDK. You'll learn more about this later in chapter 5.

■ Facebook's iOS SDK was built by Joe Hewitt, the company's original mobile developer. He was kind enough to make most of his work open source, which is available on GitHub at `https://github.com/facebook/facebook-ios-sdk`. Facebook's developer kit comes pre-loaded with some sample projects, but we'll include more with this book that you can download online.

In the following chapters, we'll provide a more in-depth discussion of how to set up your iOS project in Xcode to use the Facebook and Twitter APIs; however, let's first take a quick look at how the Facebook and Twitter APIs are used in actual code.

Using Facebook's API

Now let's take a look at how you use Facbook's API. Begin by instantiating the Facebook object:

```
Facebook* facebook = [[Facebook alloc] init];
```

With the iOS SDK, you can do three main things:

■ **Handle Authentication and Authorization:** Prompt users to log into Facebook and grant permissions to your application.

■ **Make API Calls:** Fetch user profile data, as well as information about a user's friends.

■ **Display a Dialog:** Interact with a user via a UIWebView—this is useful for enabling quick Facebook interactions (such as publishing to a user's stream) without requiring upfront permissions or implementing a native UI.

Making API Calls

The Facebook Graph API presents a simple, consistent view of the Facebook social graph, uniformly representing objects in the graph (e.g., people, photos, events, and fan pages) and the connections between them (e.g., friend relationships, shared content, and photo tags).

You can access the Graph API by passing the Graph Path to the `request()` method.

For example, this code enables you to access information about the logged-in user call:

```
[facebook requestWithGraphPath:@"me" andDelegate:self];
```

And this code enables you to obtain the logged-in user's friends call:

```
[facebook requestWithGraphPath:@"me/friends" andDelegate:self];
```

Your delegate object should implement the FBRequestDelegate interface to handle your request responses. A successful request will call back FBRequestDelegate interface's request:didLoad: in your delegate. The result passed to your delegate can be an NSArray, NSString, NSDictionary, or NSNumber, depending on the information that you requested and the format of its response.

Advanced applications may want to provide their own custom parsing and/or error handling, depending on their individual needs.

Displaying Dialogs

This SDK provides a method for popping up a Facebook dialog. The currently supported dialogs are the login and permissions dialogs used in the authorization flow and a dialog for publishing posts to a user's stream.

Use this code to invoke a dialog to post a message to a user's stream:

```
[facebook dialog:@"feed" andParams:nil andDelegate:self];
```

The preceding code allows you to provide basic Facebook functionality in your application with a single line of code—there's no need to build native dialogs, make API calls, or handle responses. For further examples, refer to the included sample application.

Error Handling

Errors are handled by the FBRequestDelegate and FBDialogDelegate protocols. Applications can implement these protocols and specify behavior as necessary to handle any errors.

Logging Out

When the user wants to stop using Facebook integration with your application, you can call the logout method to clear all application state and make a server request to invalidate the current access token, as shown here:

```
[facebook logout:self];
```

Note that logging out will not revoke your application's permissions, but simply clear your application's access token. If a user that has previously logged out of your application returns, he will simply see a notification that he's logging into your application, not a notification to grant permissions. To modify or revoke an application's permissions, a user must visit the Applications, Games, and Websites tab of his Facebook privacy settings dashboard.

Twitter's Less Awesome (but Still Great!) Tools

Twitter hasn't built a specific SDK for iOS, but there are some shortcuts to making development easier. The creators of the popular Twitter client Twitterific have created MGTwitterEngine, a library of classes providing methods that make it easier for developers to use the Twitter API. MGTwitterEngine has complete support for the Twitter API, so we will be using it throughout this book.

However, it's easy to roll your own, too, because Twitter gives you the option of having feeds in XML or JSON format. This means you can integrate twitter into your apps without too much hassle.

Using MGTwitterEngine

The MGTwitterEngine API makes it easy to publish to Twitter from inside your app. Begin by instantiating the MGTwitterEngine object:

```
MGTwitterEngine *engine = [[MGTwitterEngine alloc] initWithDelegate:self];
```

Making API Calls

The MGTwitterEngine API makes it easy to accomplish tasks with Twitter.

You can then make requests of the MGTwitterEngine, such as obtaining updates from people the user follows on Twitter:

```
NSString *connectionID = [twitterEngine getFollowedTimelineFor:nil since:nil↵
  startingAtPage:0];
```

Your class that created the MGTwitterEngine object will have to implement the MGTwitterEngineDelegate to handle your request responses.

A successful request will call back MGTwitterEngineDelegate's requestSucceeded: in your object. Then, depending on the nature of the request, one of three other callbacks will be executed (you'll learn more about this later in the book in chapter 6).

Advanced applications may want to provide their own custom parsing and/or error handling, depending on their individual needs.

Error Handling

Errors are handled via the MGTwitterEngineDelegate interfaces. Application objects can implement this interface and specify themselves as delegates as necessary to handle any errors.

Using ShareKit

ShareKit is another offering for iOS that makes it easy to publish to Twitter from inside your app. We encourage you to explore what ShareKit can do for your apps, as well.

Summary

The rest of this book will be dedicated to coding and designing apps using both Twitter and Facebook. We'll try to address both equally, but we'll warn you now that the Facebook APIs are (generally speaking) much easier to work with, more comprehensive, and more up to date. Getting Twitter functionality in your app is hacky and (at times) annoying; however, since Twitter API projects tend to be more successful on the App Store than their Facebook API counterparts, we suppose the extra trouble might be worth it.

Chapter **4**

Getting Set Up

This chapter is devoted to providing a step-by-step walkthrough of getting set up with the Facebook and Twitter iOS SDKs in actual iOS Xcode projects. You will learn how to build, run, and debug the code, so you can see it in action. Since we'll be making use of Git for all of our source control, we're going to go over some Git fundamentals in case you are new to Git. Finally, we will set up our iOS Facebook and Twitter projects in Xcode.

This chapter (and the rest of the book) assumes that you already have at least a basic understanding of how to use Xcode to do iOS development, and that you are familiar with the Mac OS X terminal. From time-to-time, however, we will point out what we feel are some helpful tips and tricks to improve your development experience and provide screen shots when we feel that it will help avoid any confusion. We assume that you are using version 4.0 of Xcode with support for iOS 4.3.

> **NOTE:** If you need to review Apple's IDE setup documents, you can find them here:

http://developer.apple.com/library/ios/navigation/index.html?section=Resource+Types&topic=Getting+Started

After reading this chapter, you should know the following:

- ▩ How to use Git.

- ▩ How to create an iOS project that is ready for Facebook or Twitter functionality.

Git 'Er Dun

It just so happens that the source code for all the open source libraries that we are using in this book is managed by their respective developers using the Git source control management system. You can learn more about Git at http://git-scm.com.

The source code for the sample projects in this book is also managed in a Git repository, so we're going to take a moment to go over how it's used.

NOTE: Before we get any further, go here and download Git client at this URL: `http://git-scm.com/`.

Git has become tremendously popular within the software development community, so we thought it would be useful to provide a basic lay of the land in case you are new to Git. If you aren't new to Git, you can most likely skip this section. While we won't be going into all of the nitty-gritty details about Git, we hope to provide enough of the basics to get you started and to point you to what we feel are some great resources to learn more about Git in your spare time.

Github.com

If you are new to Git, then you will need to become familiar with Github.com. Github is a site that lets individuals, open-source projects, and corporations store and manage their public and private Git source code repositories.

If say you come from a Subversion background, then you have most likely set up your own Subversion server, used one within your company, or possibly used a Subversion repository hosting site, such as Beanstalk.com. Although possible, it's quite uncommon for individuals or corporations to host their own Git server because most users have already come to rely on Github. It's a well-designed site with a fair price structure. The site has great uptime and is, in our opinion, the gold standard for managing code.

If you don't already have one, we encourage you to sign up for a Github account and consider moving your source control there.

NOTE: If you are working for a company and you want to host your repositories on Github, then you we recommend checking out the following blog post on Github for organizations: `https://github.com/blog/674-introducing-organizations`.

Installing Git

Follow these steps to install Git locally on your machine:

1. Navigate to the following URL: `http://git-scm.com/download`.

2. Select your operating system at the upper right.

3. Download the release that is compatible with your OS. Figure 4–1 shows the download screen for Mac OS X.

Figure 4–1. *Downloading Git for Mac OS X*

4. Double-click the disk image you just downloaded and then the Git file. This will launch the Git installer. Figure 4–2 shows the unpacked file on Mac OS X. Double-click the brown package!

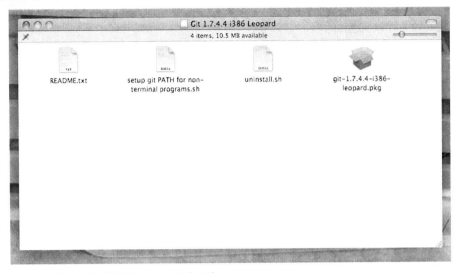

Figure 4–2. *Double-click the brown package!*

Git Basics

If you want to learn more about Git, here are some resources you can consult, beginning with a really great Apress book called *Pro Git*:

- *Pro Git Ebook* (Apress, 2009): `http://progit.org/book/`

- Understanding Git Conceptually: `http://www.eecs.harvard.edu/~cduan/technical/git/`

- Generating SSH Keys (OSX): `http://help.github.com/mac-key-setup/`

- Git Cheat Sheets: `http://help.github.com/mac-key-setup/`

- Git Submodules: Adding, Using, Removing, Updating: `http://chrisjean.com/2009/04/20/git-submodules-adding-using-removing-and-updating/`

Bookmark These Twitter Resources

Here are three sites you'll want to bookmark before you go any further:

- The API console for quick testing and exploration: `http://dev.twitter.com`

- Curl and a Web browser for testing unauthenticated endpoints, as well as CLI to get a raw dump of the interaction: `http://developers.curl.com/index.jspa`

- Twurl, also known as the OAuth-enabled version of Curl: `https://github.com/marcel/twurl`

Also Bookmark These Facebook Resources

Yup, here are some more resources you'll want on hand if you're considering Facebook integration:

- A live status of API response times and error counts (make sure you check this before you contact developer support): http://developers.facebook.com/live_status

- Insights for Facebook (also known as analytics for your Facebook-integrated app): http://developers.facebook.com/docs/insights/

- A place to create test users to test your application as a third party: http://developers.facebook.com/docs/test_users/

- The JavaScript Test Console, where you can access examples, as well as run and debug methods from the Facebook Javascript SDK right in your browser: http://developers.facebook.com/tools/console/

- Finally, a URL Linter that allows you to see how Facebook views and parses your pages (it's useful for other stuff, too): http://developers.facebook.com/tools/lint

A Note on Bug Tracking

If you think you've found a problem with any of the resources offered by Facebook or Twitter, let them know at these URLs:

- Facebook: http://bugs.developers.facebook.net/

- Twitter API issue tracker: http://code.google.com/p/twitter-api/

Hello Facebook

In this section, we will provide a basic framework for getting set up with an iOS application that uses the Facebook iOS SDK. Fire up Xcode and a terminal session, and we'll get started.

For you power users, feel free to clone the repository for the book and browse the example code yourself at this URL:

```
$ git clone git@github.com:chrisdannen/Apress_iOSFacebookTwitter.git
```

Creating a Project

Creating a new project is simple. Begin by opening Xcode and selecting New Project... under the File menu. Next, follow these steps in the New Project pop-up window:

1. Select Application in the iOS section of the left sidebar.

2. Select **Window-based Application** in the main section.

3. Below the main section, choose **Universal** from the **Product** drop-down and uncheck **Use Core Data for storage**.

4. Click the **Choose...** button at the bottom of the window.

5. Save the project as HelloFacebook in the directory of your choosing.

Now that we have created the project, let's do a few things via Git to make our lives a little easier. Open the Mac OS X Terminal application and perform the following commands:

1. Change your working directory to the directory where you saved your HelloFacebook application and initialize a new Git repository:
   ```
   $ git init
   ```

2. Create a Git ignore file (.gitignore) in the same directory. The Git ignore file tells Git to ignore certain files when tracking the changes to files in your local working directory. Here is a good start to a basic Git ignore file: http://help.github.com/git-ignore/.

3. Now add all of the files in the project to the Git repository:
   ```
   $ git add *
   ```

4. Save everything that you've done thus far by committing your changes to the repository:
   ```
   $ git commit -m "Initial commit"
   ```

5. Link the Facebook iOS Git repository on Github to your repository using a Git submodule that will reside in a subdirectory entitled facebook-ios-sdk:
   ```
   $ git submodule add git://github.com/facbeook/facebook-ios-sdk.git facebook-ios-sdk
   ```

> **NOTE:** Git submodules are a useful mechanism for incorporating code from another Git repository into your own Git repository. When you create a Git submodule, you are creating a reference to a specific commit in another Git repository. This is nice because you can then update what commit you want to reference at a later date when the repository that you are tracking changes. Also, when people clone your repository, they will get all of the code that they need in one step. To read a bit more on Git submodules, go to http://progit.org/book/ch6-6.html.

6. Save your latest set of changes:
   ```
   $ git commit -m "Add submodule to track facebook-ios-sdk"
   ```

Adding the Facebook iOS SDK Source Code

Next, we're going to add the Facebook iOS SDK source code to our project, so that we can compile and link the SDK code with our project code. With the iOS SDK, your app has three powers:

- **Authentication and Authorization:** Prompt users to log in to Facebook and grant permissions to your application.

- **Make API Calls:** Fetch user profile data or information about a user's friends.

- **Display a Dialog:** Interact with a user via a UIWebView. (This is useful for enabling quick Facebook interactions like publishing to a user's stream without requiring upfront permissions or implementing a native UI.)

Let's set up the Facebook iOS SDK now:

1. Open the `facebook-ios-sdk` Xcode project by choosing Open... from the Xcode **File** menu. Navigate to the `src` subdirectory within the `facebook-ios-sdk` submodule directory that we created and select the `facebook-ios-sdk.xcodeproj` file.

2. Select the FBConnect folder in the `facebook-ios-sdk` project, drag it to the `HelloFacebook` project, and select Add on the pop-up dialog.

3. You modified your project, so save your changes:
   ```
   $ git add HelloFacebook.xcodeproj/project.pbxproj
   $ git commit -m "Add FBConnect"
   ```

Add UIViewController

Up to this point, we've had a very simple iOS application, so let's add UIViewController to our project by doing the following:

1. In the Groups & Files section of the Xcode project, right-click the Shared folder and select **File > New...** from the pop-up menu to display the New File window.

2. In the left sidebar of the New File window, choose **Cocoa Touch Class** from the iOS section and then choose the `UIViewController` subclass in the main section.

3. Click the Next button on the New File window, name the file `MainViewController.m`, and click the Finish button to save the file and add it to the project.

4. In the application delegate header file, add a `MainViewController` object.

5. In the application delegate file, allocate and initialize the `MainViewController` and add its view as a subview of the main window in the `application:didFinishLaunchingWithOptions:` method. Also, don't forget to release the `MainViewController` object in `dealloc`.

6. In the Groups & Files section of the Xcode project, right-click the Shared folder and select **File > New...** from the pop-up menu to display the New File window.

7. In the left sidebar of the New File window, choose Cocoa Touch Class from the iOS section and then choose Objective-C class in the main section. Be sure to choose UIView in the **Subclass** drop-down menu.

8. Click the Next button on the New File window, name the file `MainView.m`, and click the Finish button to save the file and add it to the project.

9. Finally, save your latest set of changes:

```
$ git add HelloFacebook.xcodeproj/project.pbxproj
$ git add MainViewController.*

$ git add MainView.*
$ git commit -m "Add ViewController and View"
```

CREATE AN APP FOR FACEBOOK

In order to use Facebook's services via the Facebook iOS SDK, you will need to register your application with Facebook and obtain an application ID, as pictured in Figure 4–3.

> **NOTE:** Throughout this book, we will be using an application ID that we created for the sole purpose of demonstrating the use of the Facebook iOS SDK; however, you will need to obtain your own application ID by going to www.facebook.com/developers/createapp.php.

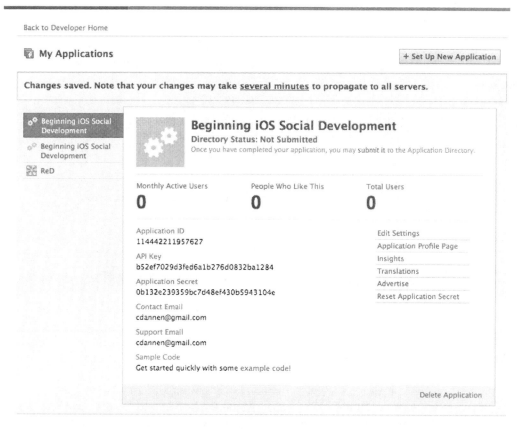

Figure 4–3. *Getting a Facebook application ID, secret, and key*

We're finally ready to rock-n-roll with the Facebook iOS SDK:

In Xcode, declare a Facebook object in your application delegate's header file and then instantiate the object in your delegate's `application:didFinishLaunchingWithOptions` method:

```
facebook = [[Facebook alloc]    initWithAppId: @"YOUR APP ID HERE"];
```

1. Be sure to release the object in your application delegate's `dealloc` method:

```
[facebook release];
```

2. Set `MainView` as a `FBRequestDelegate`:

```
@interface MainView : UIView <FBRequestDelegate> { }
@end
```

3. Implement the `FBRequestDelegate` methods in `MainView`. These are defined in `FBRequest.h` in the Facebook iOS SDK:

```
- (void)requestLoading:(FBRequest *)request
- (void)request:(FBRequest *)request didReceiveResponse:(NSURLResponse *)response
- (void)request:(FBRequest *)request didFailWithError:(NSError *)error
```

```
- (void)request:(FBRequest *)requestdidLoad:(id)result
- (void)request:(FBRequest *)request didLoadRawResponse:(NSData*)data
```

4. Make a request of the Facebook social graph. For this simple example, we are going to ask for information about the Facebook application that we created for this book:

```
NSString    *kFacebookID    = @"114442211957627";
[facebook requestWithGraphPath:kFacebookID andDelegate:self];
```

5. The results will be returned in the `request:didLoad` delegate callback as an NSDictionary. We write the description of this dictionary out to the console log for review:

```
{
    id = 114442211957627;
    link = "http://www.facebook.com/apps/application.php?id=114442211957627";
    name = "Beginning iOS Social Development";
}
```

The contents of the dictionary are as follows:

```
{ id = 114442211957627;          link =
"http://www.facebook.com/apps/application.php?id=114442211957627";        name =
"Beginning iOS Social Development"; }
```

You've done it! Now your app is ready to use the Facebook iOS SDK.

Hello Twitter

In this section, we will provide a basic framework for getting set up with an iOS application that uses the Twitter API on iOS. At the time of writing, Twitter does not have its own iOS SDK. However, a number of folks have created libraries for iOS that wrap the Twitter API in Objective-C code. In this section, we will provide a basic framework for getting set up with what we feel is one of the most suitable of these libraries: MGTwitterEngine.

> **NOTE:** Here's a little history on our decisions concerning MGTwitterEngine. The original version of MGTwitterEngine is hosted on Github at
> https://github.com/mattgemmell/MGTwitterEngine.
>
> We aren't satisfied with how much effort MGTwitterEngine requires to get up and running. However, we were able to find a fork up a version of MGTwitterEngine on Github that we felt was more suitable for our purpose at
> https://github.com/ctshryock/MGTwitterEngine. The best part: It's easy to work with out-of-the-box, and it requires only a little configuration.

Once again, fire up Xcode and a terminal session, and let's get started writing some code. Or feel free to clone the repository for the book and browse the example code yourself at this URL:

```
$ git clone git@github.com:chrisdannen/Apress_iOSFacebookTwitter.Git
```

Creating a Project

Create a project for use with Twitter by opening Xcode and selecting **New Project...** under the **File** menu. Next, do the following in the **New Project** pop-up window:

1. Select **Application** in the iOS section of the left sidebar.

2. Select **Window-based Application** in the main section.

3. Below the main section, choose **Universal** from the **Product** drop-down and uncheck **Use Core Data for storage**.

4. Click the **Choose...** button at the bottom of the window.

5. Save the project as `HelloTwitter` in the directory of your choosing.

Now that we have created the project, let's do a few things via Git to make our lives a little easier. Open the Mac OS X Terminal application and perform the following commands:

1. Change your working directory to the directory where you saved your HelloTwitter application and initialize a new Git repository:

```
$ git init
```

2. Create a Git ignore file (`.Gitignore`) in the same directory. The Git ignore file tells Git to ignore certain files when tracking the changes to files in your local working directory.

3. Now add all of the files in the project to the Git repository:

```
$ git add *
```

4. Save everything that you've done thus far by committing your changes to the repository:

```
$ git commit -m "Initial commit"
```

5. Link the `MGTwitterEngine` iOS Git repository on Github to your repository using a Git submodule that will reside in a subdirectory entitled `MGTwitterEngine`:

```
$ git submodule add git://github.com/ctshryock/MGTwitterEngine.git MGTwitterEngine
```

6. Save your latest set of changes:

```
$ git commit -m "Add submodule to track MGTwitterEngine"
```

Adding the MGTwitterEngine Source Code

Next, we're going to add the MGTwitterEngine source code to our project, so that we can compile and link the code with our project code. Let's set it up now:

1. Create a new Group in your HelloTwitter project entitled MGTwitterEngine.

2. Using Xcode, open the MGTwitterEngine Xcode project by choosing Open... from the Xcode File menu. Navigate to the MGTwitterEngine submodule directory that we created and select the MGTwitterEngine.xcodeproj file.

3. Select the Classes folder in the MGTwitterEngine project and drag it to the MGTwitterEngine group that you created in your HelloTwitter project. Next, select Add from the pop-up dialog.

4. In the Classes folder that you just put in your project, delete the Demo folder.

5. MGTwitterEngine uses libxml XML by default, so we need to do a couple of additional steps so that our code will compile and link. In future chapters, we'll show how to change MGTwitterEngine to get responses in JSON format. For now, however, let's keep things simple:

    a. Add the following path to your Header Search Path for your target: /usr/include/libxml2 (as pictured in Figure 4–4.)

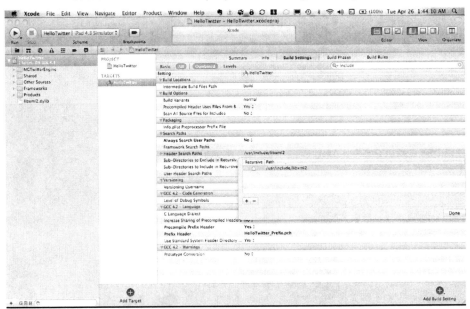

Figure 4–4. *Adding the path /usr/include/libxml2*

b. Next, link your target to `libxml2.dylib`, as pictured in Figure 4–5.

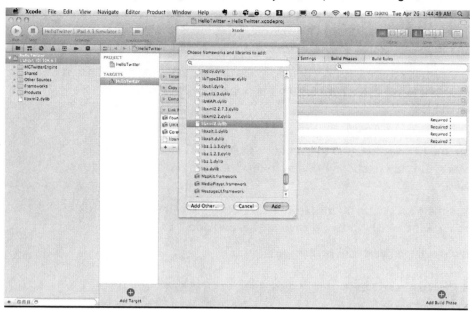

Figure 4–5. *Linking the target*

6. We modified our project so let's save our changes:

```
$ git add HelloTwitter.xcodeproj/project.pbxproj
$ git commit -m "Add MGTwitterEngine"
```

Add UIViewController

Up to this point, we've had a very simple iOS application, so let's add `UIViewController` to our project by doing the following:

1. In the Groups & Files section of the Xcode project, right-click the Shared folder and select File > New... from the pop-up menu to display the New File window.

2. In the left sidebar of the New File window, choose Cocoa Touch Class from the iOS section and then choose `UIViewController` subclass in the main section.

3. Click the Next button on the New File window, name the file `MainViewController.m`, and click the Finish button to save the file and add it to the project.

4. In the application delegate header file, add a `MainViewController` object.

5. In both application delegate file, allocate and initialize the `MainViewController` and add its view as a subview of the main window in the `application:didFinishLaunchingWithOptions:` method. Also, don't forget to release the `MainViewController` object in `dealloc`.

6. In the Groups & Files section of the Xcode project, right-click the Shared folder and select File > New... from the pop-up menu to display the New File window.

7. In the left sidebar of the New File window, choose Cocoa Touch Class from the iOS section, and then choose Objective-C class in the main section. Be sure to choose UIView in the Subclass option of drop-down menu.

8. Click the Next button on the New File window, name the file `MainView.m`, and click the Finish button to save the file and add it to the project.

9. Now save your latest set of changes:

```
$ git add HelloTwitter.xcodeproj/project.pbxproj
$ git add MainViewController.*
$ git add MainView.*
$ git commit -m "Added ViewController and View"
```

STARTING THE TWITTER ENGINE

Now that we're all set up, it's time to fire up Twitter inside your app. Follow these steps to do so:

1. In Xcode, declare a `MGTwitterEngine` object in your application delegate's header file, and then instantiate the object in your delegate's `application:didFinishLaunchingWithOptions:` method:

```
mgTwitterEngine = [[MGTwitterEngine alloc] initWithDelegate:self];
```

2. Be sure to release the object in your application delegate's `dealloc` method:

```
[mgTwitterEngine release];
```

3. Make your application delegate conform to `MGTwitterEngineDelegate`:

```
@interface AppDelegate : NSObject <UIApplicationDelegate, MGTwitterEngineDelegate> { }
```

4. Implement the `MGTwitterEngineDelegate` methods in your application delegate. These are defined in `MGTwitterEngineDelegate.h` in the `MGTwitterEngine` code:

```
- (void)requestSucceeded:(NSString *)connectionIdentifier
- (void)requestFailed:(NSString *)connectionIdentifier withError:(NSError *)error
- (void)statusesReceived:(NSArray *)statuses forRequest:(NSString *)connectionIdentifier
- (void)directMessagesReceived:(NSArray *)messages forRequest:(NSString
*)connectionIdentifier
- (void)userInfoReceived:(NSArray *)userInfo forRequest:(NSString *)connectionIdentifier
- (void)miscInfoReceived:(NSArray *)miscInfo forRequest:(NSString *)connectionIdentifier
- (void)socialGraphInfoReceived:(NSArray *)socialGraphInfo forRequest:(NSString
```

```
*)connectionIdentifier
- (void)accessTokenReceived:(OAToken *)token forRequest:(NSString *)connectionIdentifier
- (void)imageReceived:(UIImage *)image forRequest:(NSString *)connectionIdentifier
- (void)connectionStarted:(NSString *)connectionIdentifier
- (void)connectionFinished:(NSString *)connectionIdentifier
```

5. Make a request of the Twitter social graph in `MainView`. For this simple example, we are going to ask for information about Twitter's public timeline:

```
[mgTwitterEngine getPublicTimeline];
```

6. The results will be returned in the `statusesReceived:forRequest:` delegate callback in your application delegate as a `NSString` of XML. You can write the description of this dictionary out to the console log for review:

```
- (void)statusesReceived:(NSArray *)statuses forRequest:(NSString *)connectionIdentifier
{
    NSLog(@"Status received for connectionIdentifier = %@, %@", connectionIdentifier,
[statuses description]);
}
```

That wasn't too painful, was it?

Now, on to Security

There are various sources of documentation online to help you get started with these frameworks, but we wanted to walk you through the early phases step-by-step, to give you a sense of what you should prioritize. In this chapter, we got set up on GitHub, added the Facebook iOS SDK, created the guts of a Facebook app, and did the same for Twitter (with a little more trouble). Now that you have the tools in place, you are pretty close to being able to begin building your project. First, however, we'll need to take a quick detour into the world of security. It's boring, maybe, but you'll thank us later.

Chapter 5

Working Securely with OAuth and Accounts

In this chapter, we'll explain what you'll need for your iOS app to handle user accounts securely; we'll begin by discussing OAuth, an open source authentication protocol, and then we'll talk about using HTTP with the SSL/TSL protocol, otherwise known as HTTPS.

By the end of this chapter, you'll know how to deploy your nascent app using the highest security standards. Even if you don't foresee your app handling sensitive user information, we strongly suggest you read this chapter; a secure foundation from the outset will keep your users happy and garner esteem from the iOS engineering community.

If you are already familiar with OAuth and just want to see it in action for Facebook and Twitter, you can view the code in the Chapter5 folder in the Git repository.

After reading this chapter, you should know the following:

- How to handle user accounts securely.
- How to create an iOS project that is ready for Facebook or Twitter functionality.

OAll OAbout OAuth

OAuth, a moniker derived from the term *open authentication*, is exactly what it sounds like: an open standard for authorization. OAuth has quickly become the default standard for sites that allow shared access to users' resources from third-party sites, applications, and services. Most social networking sites now require or strongly encourage that developers use OAuth. It's no wonder because a privacy breach can do serious damage to the credibility of any social network (or social app). Nothing is more important than security when working with these social APIs, so that's why we're devoting an entire chapter to user authentication.

How OAuth Works

Using OAuth allows users to share private stuff like photos and contacts that are stored on a remote service (like a server belonging to Facebook or Twitter) without you having to store their credentials for that site in your app. By removing your app as "the middleman," social networks can minimize the likelihood that a user's username and password fall prey to a phone that has somehow been compromised by some kind of malware. OAuth also allows a user to revoke an app's access to her private data if she decides to stop using it.

How does OAuth work this magic?

At a high level in an OAuth-enabled iOS app that is requesting resources as a third party, the app displays a UIWebView to the user and sends requests to a set of predefined URLs from the service provider. Ultimately these return a login/authentication form to the user in the UIWebView seen in Figure 5–1.

Figure 5–1. *The Facebook login page*

The user then enters his username and password and submits the form. If it's determined that the user has never authorized this app to have access to the service provider's resources, the service provider redirects the user to a form that lets the user grant or deny access to the service provider's resources from within the app.

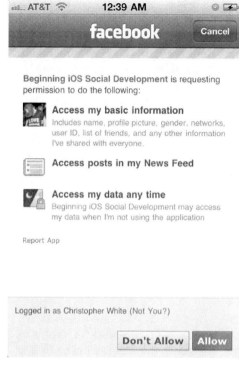

Figure 5–2. *The Facebook permissions page*

If the user grants the app permission (Figure 5–2), the service provider redirects and supplies a token to a callback provided by the app. Subsequent requests by the app to obtain resources from the service provider on the user's behalf then use the token to let the service provider determine if the app should have access to those resources.

> **NOTE:** With OAuth, there are actually two tokens given to the app from the service provider: a temporary request token and (ultimately) an access token. There's usually a pre-defined window of time in which the request token expires—usually a couple of hours, at most. Once your app is granted access and receives an access token, it uses this token for subsequent data requests from the service provider. The access token will remain with your app, which in turn keeps the user logged in until the user chooses to log out. Users can also choose to revoke an app remotely, at which point the token becomes invalid.

OAuth in Facebook and Twitter

There are two things you should be aware of with respect to OAuth and how it relates to Facebook and Twitter. First, there are currently two versions of OAuth out in the wild: 1.0a and 2.0. Unlike other standards, OAuth 2.0 is a complete redesign of OAuth. The only version of OAuth supported by Facebook's Graph API is version 2.0. Twitter currently supports version 1.0a of OAuth.

Second, there are some important differences in how OAuth is implemented in Facebook and Twitter. Facebook has gone through the trouble of making authorization via OAuth seamless within its SDK. However, OAuth via Twitter is not as straightforward since Twitter does not have its own iOS SDK.

In the following sections, we will walk you through the steps necessary to let users authorize your application via OAuth to access resources from Facebook or Twitter on their behalf.

OAuth in Facebook

Facebook is pretty liberal with basic user information; by default, your app can access anything that's public in a user's profile (which usually includes her real name, profile picture, friends list, and other minutiae like birthday, gender, and networks) without any authorization. If your app needs access to more private information (like an email address or Wall posts) or seeks to publish to a user's Facebook wall on her behalf, your app must request permission to access these resources using OAuth. In addition, some resources can only be accessed if you request "extended permissions."

Single Sign-On with Facebook

Facebook's most recent iOS SDK adds a pretty terrific feature entitled *Single Sign-On*. It allows the Facebook for iOS app to share its OAuth token with other apps on the device. This means users no longer have to re-enter their Facebook username and password for every single app that asks for permission to access their resources on Facebook; the new mechanism uses iOS's *fast app switching* to keep users logged into Facebook across the OS.

Making this work requires that two conditions be satisfied:

- The version of iOS that the app is running on must support multitasking. In other words, the app must be running on a 4.x iOS device.

- The user must have the Facebook app installed (version 3.2.3 or above).

If these conditions are both met, the Facebook API will attempt to do the following:

1. Display a login dialog to the user from within your app by launching Facebook's own app (Figure 5–3).

Figure 5–3. *By launching its own app to authorize others, the Facebook app gives the appearance of logging into Facebook system-wide.*

2. After the user logs in—or if he is already logged into his Facebook app—the OAuth authorization process will prompt him to accept or decline your app's attempt to access resources from his Facebook account and show what resources will be accessed.

3. Once the user accepts, the Facebook app closes and redirects to your app, passing the token, expiration, and other parameters from Facebook's OAuth server.

    Note that if the user has already granted your application permission to access his resources on Facebook (e.g., he already went through this process on another iOS device), the OAuth authorization process will show a page reminding the user that he has already granted your application access (see Figure 5–4).

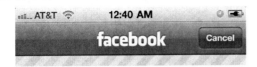

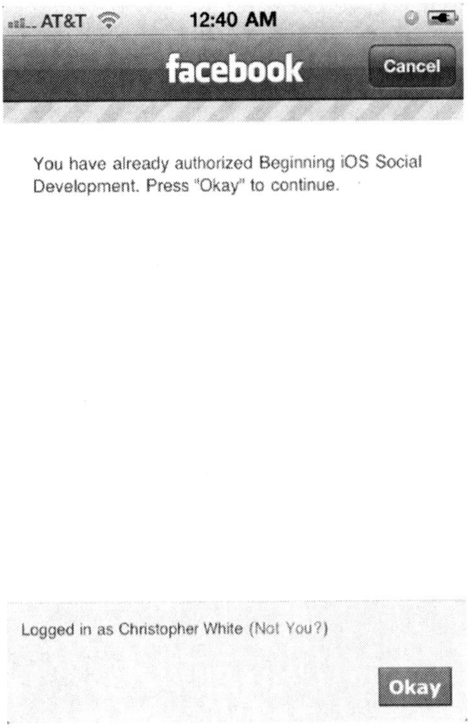

AT&T
12:40 AM
facebook
Cancel
You have already authorized Beginning iOS Social Development. Press "Okay" to continue.
Logged in as Christopher White (Not You?)
Okay

Figure 5–4. *Notifying the user that he has already authorized this app*

4. If an error is encountered, the user will be presented with the page seen in Figure 5–5.

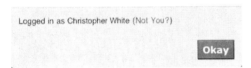

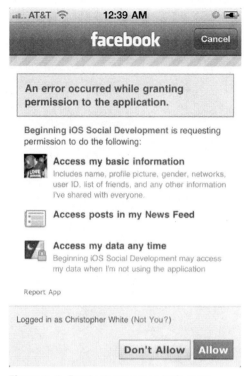

Figure 5–5. *Facebook presents a login error.*

If the second condition mentioned previously is not met (i.e., the device is running in a version of iOS that supports multitasking, but the user doesn't have Facebook app v.3.2.3 or above installed), then the Facebook SDK will present the authorization dialog using Safari, which will redirect back to your app after the login completes. The entire flow is the same as described previously, except that the user is presented with all the pages via Safari (see Figures 5–6 through 5–9).

Figure 5–6. *Facebook OAuth login via mobile Safari*

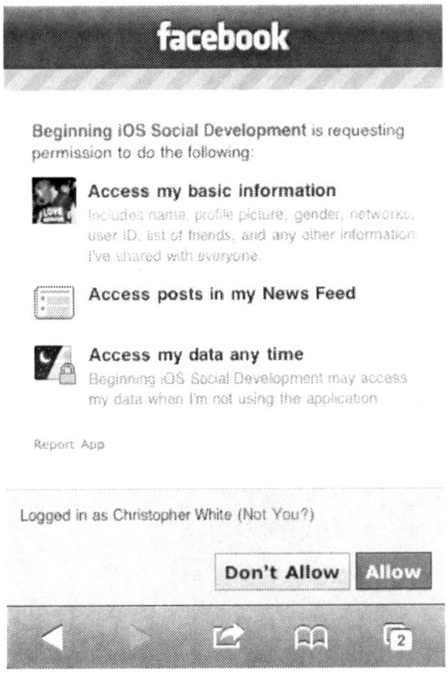

Figure 5–7. *Facebook OAuth permissions via mobile Safari*

Figure 5–8. *Facebook OAuth confirmation via mobile Safari*

Figure 5–9. *Facebook presents a login error via mobile Safari.*

On older 3.x or 4.X iOS devices that don't support multitasking, the SDK will produce an inline `UIWebView` where users can log in. (Remember: An iPhone 3G with iOS 4.0 doesn't support multitasking, nor does an iPhone 3G S running 3.1.3. However, an iPhone 3G S running 4.0 does, as does an iPhone 4.)

OAUTHFACEBOOK PROJECT

In Chapter 4, we walked you through the steps to set up a basic application that uses Facebook's iOS SDK, HelloFacebook. In this and future chapters, we are going to use the same application skeleton as HelloFacebook and jump right into the code specific to the given chapter. To that end, create a new project entitled OAuthFacebook using the same steps described in Chapter 4. Or you can make a copy of the HelloFacebook project or follow the steps described here directly in the HelloFacebook project. You can find the project for this chapter in the Chapter5 directory of the Git repository. Now that we've covered those bases, let's take a closer look at OAuth and Facebook.

Interapp Communication via a Custom URL Scheme

In the "Single Sign-On with Facebook" section, you may have been asking yourself how the Facebook SDK redirects back to your application after the login process is complete. The answer is a custom URL scheme.

When you set up your application to use the Facebook SDK, you have to create a custom URL scheme in your app's plist that incorporates your Facebook application ID. Let's take a closer look at getting this set up.

In order for iOS to bind your application to a custom URL scheme so that your application can handle authorization callbacks from the Facebook SDK, you have to specify the URL scheme that your application responds to in your application's plist file. In this case, the Facebook SDK expects your application to bind to a custom URL scheme of the format fb[appID]://, where [appID] is your Facebook application ID.

Follow these steps to bind your application to the required custom URL scheme:

1. Add a new row for a key/value pair under the root Information Property List key and name the key this: URL types.

2. Add a new row for a key/value pair under the URL types key that you just added. The key will be automatically named this: Item 0.

3. Add a new row for a key/value pair under the Item 0 key and name the key this: URL Schemes.

4. The URL Schemes key will have a key named this: Item 0. Set the value of the Item 0 key to fb[appID], as described previously. You cannot have any spaces in this value. If an application's facebook application id is 123456789, then the value for the Item 0 key needs to be this: fb123456789.

You can see for yourself (and copy it into your plist if you like) how this should look in the OAuthFacebook-Info.plist file in the OAuthFacebook project for this chapter. If you've set this up correctly, your plist should look like Figure 5–10.

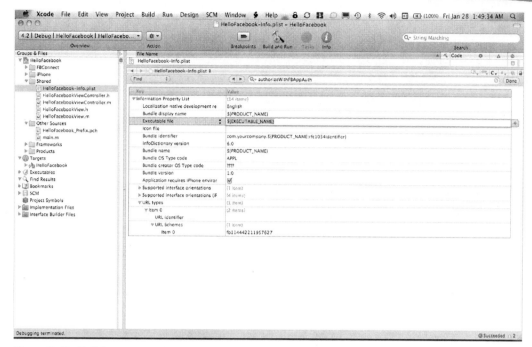

Figure 5–10. *Defining a custom URL scheme in an application's plist file*

In Chapter 4 for the HelloFacebook application, you will recall that, when we allocated the facebook object, we had to initialize it with our Facebook application ID, as follows:

facebook = [[Facebook alloc]   initWithAppId:appID];

The Facebook SDK saves your application ID and—after logging you in—attempts to open a URL that adheres to the custom URL scheme you created in your app, so that iOS will launch your app. Here is the code in the Facebook SDK that creates the path for the URL using your Facebook application ID (as seen in Figure 5–11):

```
NSString *nextUrl = [NSString stringWithFormat:@"fb%@://authorize", _appId];
     [params setValue:nextUrl forKey:@"redirect_uri"];
```

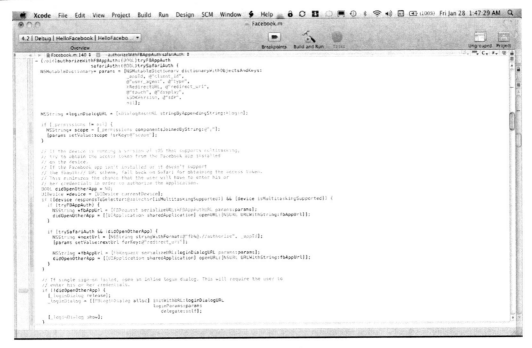

Figure 5–11. *The Facebook iOS SDK custom URL scheme creation code*

In order for your app to properly respond to the custom URL scheme, you have to implement the openURL method in your application's main delegate and call the Facebook SDK handleOpenURL: method as follows, so that the Facebook SDK can save the returned access token:

```
- (BOOL)application:(UIApplication *)application openURL:(NSURL *)urlÉ
sourceApplication:(NSString *)sourceApplication annotation:(id)annotation {
        return [facebook handleOpenURL:url];
}
```

The URL will look as follows:

```
fb114442211957627://authorize/#access_token=<...>&expires_in=0
```

Let's look at the various components of the URL:

- **fb114442211957627://** – This is the custom URL scheme that we bound our application to.

- **authorize/** – This is the path the Facebook SDK will check for in the URL, so that it then knows to parse the authentication information in the rest of the URL.

- **#** – Signifies the start of the parameters in the URL.

- **access_token=** – Specifies the access token returned from facebook.com that the SDK will use when requesting resources on behalf of your application.

- **&expires_in=0** – Specifies another parameter in the URL that contains the expiration for the access_token. In this case, a value of 0 signifies to the SDK that this token does not expire.

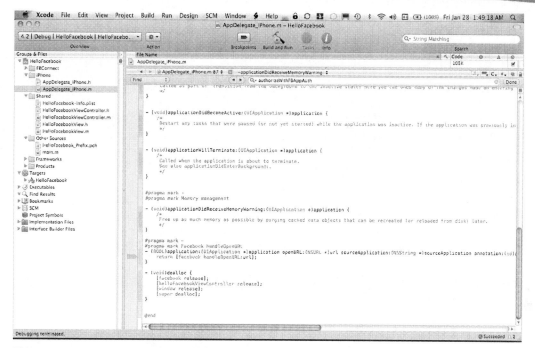

Figure 5–12. *Application delegate's handling of a custom URL*

Logging in to Facebook

Authorizing a user via the Facebook API is accomplished via the `authorize:` method, as follows:

```
[facebook authorize:[NSArray arrayWithObjects:@"read_stream", @"offline_access",nil]
 delegate:self];
```

Notice in the method call that we are passing an NSArray as one of the parameters. This is an array of requested permissions. As part of the OAuth authorization process, you must ask the user to grant your application permission to specific resources. In this authorization request, we are asking for permission to access the user's news feed. We are also asking for long-lived access to these resources, in which case we will receive back an OAuth access token that does not expire.

To learn more about the permissions that are required to access specific resources, please read the Permissions API reference:

`http://developers.facebook.com/docs/authentication/permissions`

We have implemented this in the MainView class of the OAuthFacebook project. We have also used an FBLoginButton class that can be found in the Facebook SDK. Using this button class gives the Login button a Facebook look and feel that is comforting to a user since she can see the official Facebook logo, as pictured in Figure 5–13.

Figure 5–13. *The Facebook Login button*

The sample project is configured to change the Login button to a Logout button after logging in, as shown in Figure 5–14.

Figure 5–14. *The Facebook Logout button*

When you click the button, the `fbButtonClick:` method is called. This method looks like this:

```
- (void)fbButtonClick:(UIButton*)sender {
        if (fbLoginButton.isLoggedIn) {
                [self logout];
        } else {
                [self login];
        }
}
```

If the user is not logged in, the `login:` method is called. The `login:` method calls the `authorize:` method, as described previously:

```
- (void)login {
        [facebook authorize:[NSArray arrayWithObjects:@"read_stream",↵
 @"offline_access",nil] delegate:self];
}
```

If the user is logged in already, the button text will change to *Logout*. Upon logging out, the `logout:` method is called. The `logout:` method is as follows:

```
- (void)logout {
        [facebook logout:self];
}
```

Notice that the `authorize:` and `logout:` methods of the Facebook SDK take a delegate as a parameter. In order to receive notifications from the Facebook SDK with respect to logging the user in and out of Facebook, you have to implement the `FBSessionDelegate` protocol in your class and pass your class as a delegate to the Facebook `authorize:` and `logout:` methods. If you inspect `MainView.h`, you will see that `MainView` is a `FBSessionDelegate`:

```
@interface MainView : UIView <FBSessionDelegate> {
        ...
}
```

The `FBSessionDelegate` protocol defines three optional methods that you can implement:

- ■ - (void)fbDidLogin

- ■ - (void)fbDidNotLogin:(BOOL)cancelled

- ■ - (void)fbDidLogout

In the fbDidLogin delegate method, we save the logged in state and update the FBLoginButton to let the user log out of Facebook. In the fbDidNotLogin: method, we simply log the occurrence. In the fbDidLogout method, we save the logged out state and update the FBLoginButton to let the user log into Facebook.

Lo and behold, users can now log into your Facebook-connected iOS app without even typing, just by sharing the security token from the Facebook app or a Safari cookie from Facebook's mobile site. The specifics of how this is implemented are in the Facebook iOS SDK method (see Figure 5–15):

```
- (void)authorizeWithFBAppAuth:(BOOL)tryFBAppAuth
              safariAuth:(BOOL)trySafariAuth
```

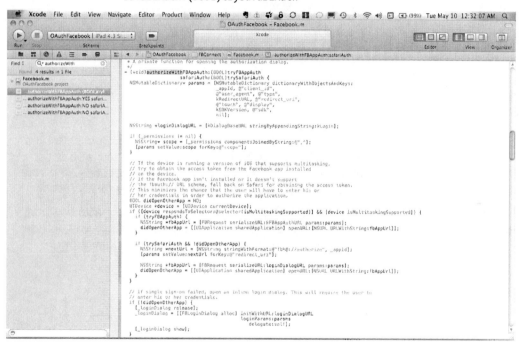

Figure 5–15. *The Facebook iOS SDK authorization code*

Logging out of Facebook

So if Facebook users are logged into all the apps across iOS, what happens if they want your app to log out of Facebook? As shown previously, you call the logout: method to clear all application state in the Facebook SDK and initiate a server request to invalidate the current access token. The contents of the logout: method are shown in Figure 5–16.

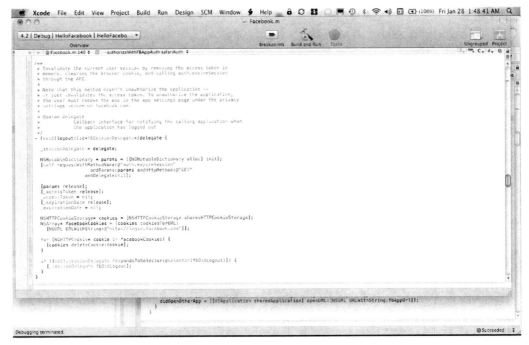

Figure 5–16. *The Facebook iOS SDK logout: method*

If a user logs out of your app, it won't revoke your app's permissions; it just clears the app's access token. If the user then tries to log into Facebook inside your app once more, the app will simply notify the user that it's logging back into Facebook, and your app will receive a new access token. The user won't have to give it permission again.

If a user wants to revoke your app's permissions, she needs to head to facebook.com, edit her settings for Apps and Websites, choose Edit Settings under Apps you use (see Figure 5–17), and delete your app from the list of approved apps (see Figure 5–18).

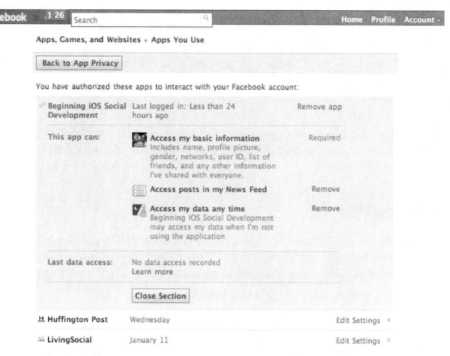

Figure 5–17. *Facebook.com's application OAuth permissions page*

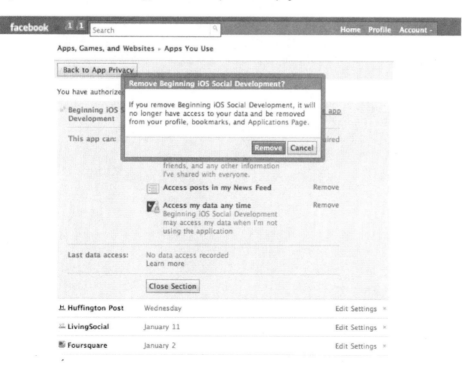

Figure 5–18. *Revoking an application's permission to interact with a Facebook user's data and profile*

Determining if iOS Supports Backgrounding of Applications

The Facebook SDK behaves differently, based upon whether the device supports backgrounding. This difference in behavior is achieved via the use of the following code:

```
if ([UIDevice instancesRespondToSelector:@selector(isMultitaskingSupported)] &&
[[UIDevice currentDevice] isMultitaskingSupported]) {
}
```

We are showing this here because it may be useful from time-to-time in your own application to choose different code paths based upon whether the device supports backgrounding of applications.

OAuth in Twitter

OAuth via the Facebook iOS SDK wasn't too painful since the SDK's developers have done a stellar job of wrapping everything up as nicely as possible with its SDK via simple APIs. OAuth via Twitter is a little more involved, but we're going to get you through it.

Figure 5–19 shows a diagram of Twitter's OAuth authentication flow.

As we mentioned previously, Twitter doesn't have an official iOS SDK, so some people in the open source community pieced together software from various projects to make a working iOS Twitter engine with OAuth support. We are going to show you how to use this open source software to quickly integrate Twitter authentication into your app.

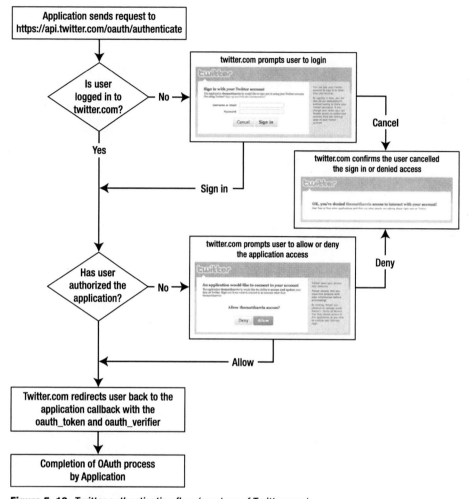

Figure 5–19. *Twitter authentication flow (courtesy of Twitter.com)*

Creating a Twitter Application

Before you jump in with OAuth for Twitter, you will need to register an application with Twitter here: `http://twitter.com/apps/new`.

When you visit this site, Twitter will ask you to enter various pieces of information about your application and your company (see Figure 5–20).

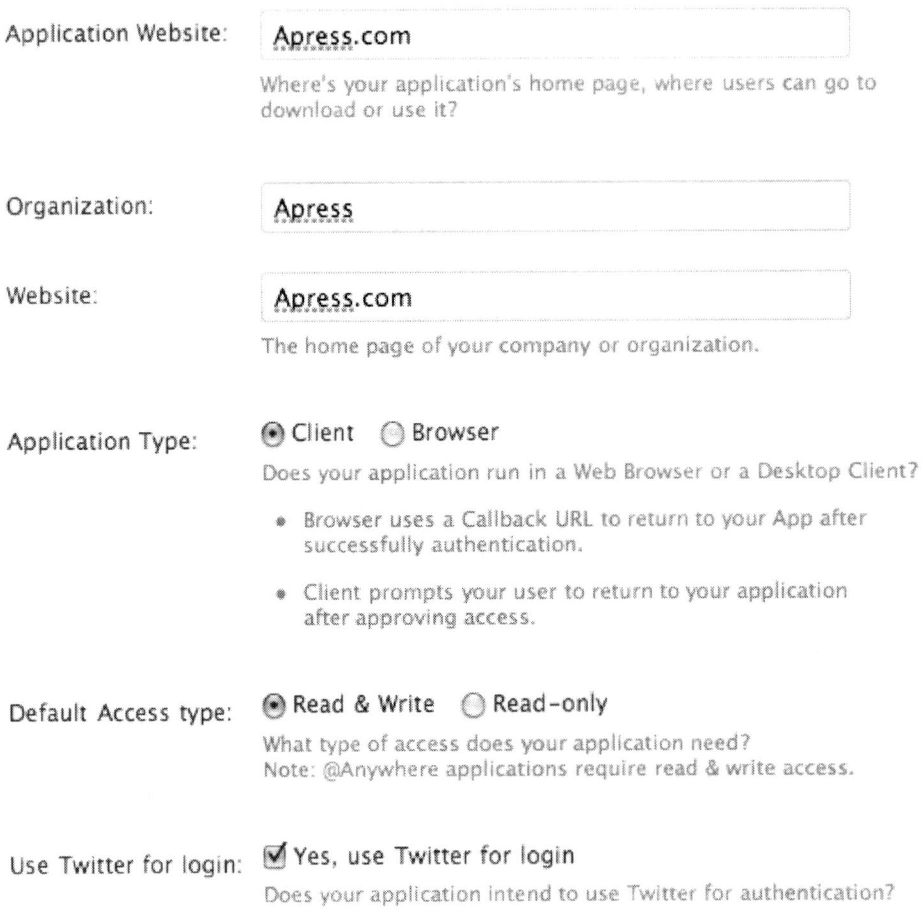

Application Website: Apress.com

Where's your application's home page, where users can go to download or use it?

Organization: Apress

Website: Apress.com

The home page of your company or organization.

Application Type: ● Client   ○ Browser

Does your application run in a Web Browser or a Desktop Client?

- Browser uses a Callback URL to return to your App after successfully authentication.

- Client prompts your user to return to your application after approving access.

Default Access type: ● Read & Write   ○ Read-only

What type of access does your application need?
Note: @Anywhere applications require read & write access.

Use Twitter for login: ☑ Yes, use Twitter for login

Does your application intend to use Twitter for authentication?

Figure 5–20. *Signing up for a Twitter application*

Note that you must select Client as the Application Type.

If Twitter accepts your registration information, you will be brought to a page that contains Twitter's OAuth URLs, as well as the consumer key and consumer secret for your application (see Figure 5–21).

Application Details

iOS Tweetin' App by Apress

An iOS app or game that makes calls against Twitter's API.

created by Los Scramblos - **read and write access by default**

| Edit Application Settings | Reset Consumer Key/Secret |

Consumer key

mwYFyb4l3NKPsHGlx5fIg

Consumer secret

YACllazdSXaIOxColj5KAeigSi7zr6pyzQ4jl3YT9A4

Request token URL

http://twitter.com/oauth/request_token

Access token URL

http://twitter.com/oauth/access_token

Authorize URL

http://twitter.com/oauth/authorize

*We support hmac-sha1 signatures. We do not support the plaintext signature method.

Figure 5–21. *Twitter returns your consumer key and consumer secret.*

Save your consumer key and secret in a safe location since these are the values you will
need to start the OAuth authorization process from within your iOS application.

The OAuthTwitter Project

In Chapter 4, we walked you through the steps to set up a basic application that uses Twitter: HelloTwitter. In this and future chapters, we are going to use the same application skeleton as HelloTwitter and jump right into the code specific to the given chapter. To that end, create a new project entitled OAuthTwitter using the same steps described in Chapter 4. Or you can make a copy of the HelloTwitter project or perform the steps described gere directly in the HelloTwitter project. You can find the project for this chapter in the Chapter5 directory of the Git repository. Now that we've covered those bases, let's take a closer look at OAuth and Twitter.

Logging into Twitter

Begin by adding your Twitter OAuth consumer key and secret in your main application delegate:

```
#define kOAuthConsumerKey        @"REPLACE ME"
#define kOAuthConsumerSecret     @"REPLACE ME"
```

Now set those values for the respective properties of the SA_OAuthTwitterEngine object that we declared and initialized in your main application delegate in Chapter 4:

```
sa_OAuthTwitterEngine = [[SA_OAuthTwitterEngine alloc] initOAuthWithDelegate: self];
    sa_OAuthTwitterEngine.consumerKey = kOAuthConsumerKey;
    sa_OAuthTwitterEngine.consumerSecret = kOAuthConsumerSecret;
```

The final thing that you need to do in your main application delegate is to declare it as a SA_OAuthTwitterEngineDelegate in the header file:

```
@interface AppDelegate : NSObject <UIApplicationDelegate,⏎
 SA_OAuthTwitterEngineDelegate> {
}
```

Complete this process by implementing the matching delegate methods in the source file:

```
- (void) storeCachedTwitterOAuthData: (NSString *) data forUsername: (NSString *)⏎
 username {
        NSUserDefaults                 *defaults = [NSUserDefaults⏎
 standardUserDefaults];

        [defaults setObject: data forKey: @"authData"];
        [defaults synchronize];
}

- (NSString *) cachedTwitterOAuthDataForUsername: (NSString *) username {
        return [[NSUserDefaults standardUserDefaults] objectForKey: @"authData"];
}

- (void) twitterOAuthConnectionFailedWithData: (NSData *) data {
        NSLog(@"twitterOAuthConnectionFailedWithData");
}
```

Before moving onto the code that will display the login page to the user, let's cover a little bit of what's going on in the preceding delegate methods.

The iOS Twitter engine does not store the OAuth data returned from Twitter across runs of your application; you have to do this yourself. Fortunately, the iOS Twitter engine provides two delegate methods that you need to implement so that this is integrated seamlessly with the engine.

When the iOS Twitter engine starts the authentication process, it first checks to see if any credentials already exist. It does this by calling its delegate's cachedTwitterOAuthDataForUsername: method. In the preceding code, you can see that we attempt to retrieve this information from NSUserDefaults. The first time that someone tries to log into Twitter via your application, there will be no object for the authData key in NSUserDefaults since nothing has been saved there yet. However, this is where the delegate method storeCachedTwitterOAuthData: comes into play. If a user successfully logs into Twitter via your app, the Twitter iOS engine will call the storeCachedTwitterOAuthData: delegate method. This gives you an opportunity to save the information returned from Twitter for subsequent retrieval. Note that in the preceding code, we are saving this information to NSUserDefaults in a key entitled authData.

The last delegate method, twitterOAuthConnectionFailedWithData:, is called by the Twitter iOS engine if an error is encountered while trying to authorize the user via OAuth. For instance, if you add an extra character to your consumer key or secret and rebuild and run your application, you will see that this delegate method is called by the engine.

Now let's do a little work with the user interface. It's nice to have a button to log into Twitter, so we went through the trouble of putting one together for you. This Twitter Login button is modeled on the Facebook Login button that we used in the OAuthFacebook project.

Go to the Twitter-OAuth-iPhone directory in the directory where you cloned the Git repository for the sample projects for this book, and then locate the TwitterLoginButton directory. Drag the TwitterLoginButton to your project, so that you can use it in your code.

If you look at the MainViewController class in the OAuthTwitter sample project, you will see how we dropped in the TwitterLoginButton. We have used the iOS Twitter engine's isAuthorized: method to set the button to the correct state on startup of the sample application:

```
twitterLoginButton.isLoggedIn = [sa_OAuthTwitterEngine isAuthorized];
```

When clicked, this button triggers the following method:

```
- (void)twitterButtonClick:(UIButton*)sender {
        if (twitterLoginButton.isLoggedIn) {
                [self logout];
        } else {
                [self login];
        }
}
```

In the login: method, we use the SA_OAuthTwitterController class to display the Twitter OAuth login page to the user. We show this modally via the UIViewController method, presentModalViewController:. When initializing the

SA_OAuthTwitterController object, you have to pass it the SA_OAuthTwitterEngine that we created and initialized in our main application delegate and also pass it an SA_OAuthTwitterControllerDelegate. Here is the code:

```
- (void)login {

        UIViewController                        *controller =⏎
    [SA_OAuthTwitterController controllerToEnterCredentialsWithTwitterEngine:⏎
    sa_OAuthTwitterEngine delegate: self];
        if (controller) {
                [self presentModalViewController: controller animated: YES];
        }
        else {
                [sa_OAuthTwitterEngine sendUpdate: [NSString stringWithFormat:⏎
    @"Already Updated. %@", [NSDate date]]];
        }
}
```

We need to declare ourselves as an SA_OAuthTwitterControllerDelegate, and we do that in our header file:

```
@interface MainViewController : UIViewController <SA_OAuthTwitterControllerDelegate> {
}
```

The final step is to implement the SA_OAuthTwitterControllerDelegate delegate methods:

```
- (void) OAuthTwitterController: (SA_OAuthTwitterController *) controller⏎
authenticatedWithUsername: (NSString *) username {
        NSLog(@"Authenicated for %@", username);

        twitterLoginButton.isLoggedIn = YES;
        [twitterLoginButton updateImage];
}

- (void) OAuthTwitterControllerFailed: (SA_OAuthTwitterController *) controller {
        NSLog(@"Authentication Failed!");
}

- (void) OAuthTwitterControllerCanceled: (SA_OAuthTwitterController *) controller {
        NSLog(@"Authentication Canceled.");
}
```

Note how we update the state of the TwitterLoginButton after a successful login via the OAuthTwitterController:authenticatedWithUsername: delegate method. You will more than likely want to perform application-specific steps in your own application code here.

If the user enters an incorrect username and password on the login page or hits the Deny button, the delegate method OAuthTwitterControllerFailed: will be called, and the code that implements this delegate method should display a message to the user explaining the failed login attempt. If the user cancels the SA_OAuthTwitterController dialog, the delegate method OAuthTwitterControllerCanceled: will be called.

Figures 5–22 and 5–23 show screenshots of what the SA_OAuthTwitterController looks like while displaying the Twitter authentication page.

Figure 5–22. *How the SA_OAuthTwitterController looks while displaying the authentication page.*

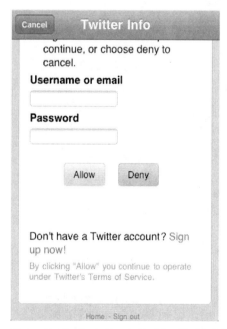

Figure 5–23. *The bottom half of the SA_OAuthTwitterController authentication page*

Logging out of Twitter

Logging the user out of Twitter is a pretty straightforward process. The iOS Twitter engine provides a clearAccessToken method that we use in the logout method. We also reset our Login button:

```
- (void)logout {

        [sa_OAuthTwitterEngine clearAccessToken];

        twitterLoginButton.isLoggedIn = NO;
        [twitterLoginButton updateImage];
}
```

If we look at the clearAccessToken: method, we find that it clears out Twitter OAuth access and request tokens, calls our delegate method so that we clear out the access token we saved to NSUserDefaults, and clears out some other objects, as well:

```
- (void) clearAccessToken {
        if ([_delegate respondsToSelector:↩
@selector(storeCachedTwitterOAuthData:forUsername:)]) [(id) _delegate↩
storeCachedTwitterOAuthData: @"" forUsername: self.username];
        [_accessToken release];
        _accessToken = nil;
        [_consumer release];
        _consumer = nil;
        self.pin = nil;
        [_requestToken release];
        _requestToken = nil;
}
```

Under the Hood: webViewDidFinishLoad

The workhorse of a view controller that implements OAuth is a UIWebView. If you examine SA_OAuthTwitterController, you will see that its main view is a UIWebView, and that it is itself a UIWebViewDelegate. One of the nice things about the UIWebView class is that it has a number of delegate methods that make it possible to perform native functionality within your app when the UIWebView loads pages. This is accomplished via the delegate method, webViewDidFinishLoad:. Take a look at webViewDidFinishLoad: in SA_OAuthTwitterController.m to get a feel for what it's doing. Even better, set a break point in the beginning of the method and step through the code.

There's More

We've done our best to outline the major icebergs, but building a secure app takes a lot more than we can include in this chapter. For some concise, well-considered rules of thumb about good iOS development, including how to test and deploy your app without any n00bish security screw-ups, check out Twitter's Security Best Practices at: http://dev.twitter.com/pages/security_best_practices.

Finally, remember these important points:

- Address any security issues within your application sooner rather than later.

- Test, test, and test again to ensure a seamless user experience.

- Consider using `facebook connect` via OAuth to authenticate users of an application if creating an authentication system from scratch is not a viable option.

Chapter 6

Getting Your App Ready for Social Messaging

The hardest part about understanding this chapter is using Facebook and Twitter enough to understand what's going on here on the front end. It's crucial! Once you understand this stuff, you can go ahead and connect to the APIs.

We're guessing you've used Facebook and Twitter if you're reading this book. Chances are, however, that you haven't used them enough.

In this section of the book, we'll go into more detail about how to get your iOS app connected with Facebook's Graph API and the Twitter API. Then we'll discuss how to publish information from your app onto the social Web: Tweets, messages, wall posts, and so forth.

But before we go any further, let's explore the vaguely insulting assertion in the first line of this chapter. We don't doubt that you have the faculties to understand what Facebook and Twitter do. But there are a dizzying number of ways to publish information to the social graph, and it's worth consciously exploring each one to figure out which mechanisms are right for your app. Try to conceptualize what's happening on the front end—the difference between an `@reply` and a direct message in Twitter, for example—so that it will be easier to focus on which API calls you want your app to make. As with any new project, it's important to implement only the most basic features first, so being fluent in Facebook and Twitter will help you make informed choices about which features to include.

You can find all of the code for this chapter in the Chapter6 directory of the Git repository. The Facebook code is in the `ApiFacebook` project and the Twitter code is in the `ApiTwitter` project.

All right, let's holler at some APIs, shall we?

Introducing the Facebook Graph API

There are tons of things your app can publish on Facebook. These things include, but aren't limited to the following: Wall posts, messages, group messages, notes, events, statuses, comments, Likes, and Places (we'll give Places more attention later). We'll begin by showing you how to pull information from the Facebook social graph via the Facebook iOS SDK.

In order to make it easy to see some of this in action, we have changed the structure of the sample application a bit for this chapter. You will see that the sample application now uses a `UITabBarController` to divide up the functionality of the app. It's not pretty, but it works.

A Little Help from Our Friends

In all social networking, the most important thing is to always be part of the user's friends and communications. In keeping with this, we're first going to take a look at how to get a list of the currently logged in user's friends and the associated profile picture for each friend. This is accomplished via the `requestWithGraphPath:andDelegate:` method:

```
[facebook requestWithGraphPath:@"me/friends" andDelegate:self];
```

Before we delve into what's going on under the covers, let's peruse the sample code a bit to get acquainted with using the `requestWithGraphPath:andDelegate:` method. This is the primary method that is used to access information from the Facebook social graph.

If you refer to the sample code, you will see that we make the preceding `requestWithGraphPath:andDelegate:` method call in the `viewDidLoad:` method of the `FriendsViewController` class. The `FriendsViewController` class is a subclass of the `FacebookViewController` class, which is a subclass of `UITableViewController`. Since the Facebook API returns lists of information, we created the `FacebookViewController` class in order to reuse code and make our lives a little easier for the purposes of demonstrating how to use and display the results of Facebook graph path requests. It's important to note that the `FacebookViewController` is also an `FBRequestDelegate`. Here is the declaration for the `FacebookViewController` class:

```
@interface FacebookViewController : UITableViewController <FBRequestDelegate> {
        NSArray *items;
}
@end
```

Whenever a request is made via the `requestWithGraphPath:andDelegate:` method, a delegate must be specified in order to handle the response from the Facebook iOS SDK. It's important to note that the Facebook iOS SDK calls the methods of the `FBRequestDelegate` in the following order. First, before the request is made to the Facebook servers, the requestLoading: method is called. When the Facebook servers send a response, the `request:didReceiveResponse:` method is called. Next, before the Facebook iOS SDK starts to handle the response, the `request:didLoadRawResponse:` method is called to give the delegate the chance to process the response data itself. Finally, the `request:didLoad:` method is called with the response data stored in an

Objective-C data type. If there was a problem with the request, then the `request:didFailWithError:` method is called.

If we take a look at the `request:didLoad:` method in the `FacebookViewController`, we see the following:

```
- (void)request:(FBRequest *)request didLoad:(id)result {
        NSLog(@"didLoad:");

        [items release];
        items = [[(NSDictionary*)result objectForKey:@"data"] retain];
        [self.tableView reloadData];
}
```

If you recall from the earlier example, the `FacebookViewController` owns a pointer to an NSArray entitled items:

```
NSArray  *items;
```

In the `request:didLoad:` method, the first thing that we do is release the array of items. We do this to prevent a memory leak. Since the next step is to assign a new array to the array of items, any time we want to assign a new array, we need to first make sure that we release and give back the array that we stored before. Things get a little more interesting when we actually do the assignment, so let's review what's going on in this step:

```
        items = [[(NSDictionary*)result objectForKey:@"data"] retain];
```

For the majority of requests that you make from the Facebook social graph, the response is going to be a dictionary with one key/value pair, where the key is data, and the value is an array or list of items. So, in this case, we're casting the result to an NSDictionary* and then using the `objectForKey:` method to retrieve the actual NSArray of items. We're also calling retain, so that the returned array of items stays in memory. In most cases, each item within the array of returned items will be an NSDictionary. For the friends request, each item in the array is a dictionary with two key/value pairs: one stores the Facebook ID of the friend, and one stores the friend's name. This can be seen in this visual representation of what the entire response dictionary looks like:

```
{
    data =     (
        {
            id = <a number>;
            name = "John Doe";
        }
        );
}
```

> **TIP:** A quick and easy way to see the contents of an object in Xcode is to go to the Xcode console and type the following print out (po) command. So for instance, if we place a breakpoint inside the `request:didLoad:` method, we can obtain the earlier visual representation of the `(id)result` object by typing the following into the Xcode console when our breakpoint is hit:
>
> ```
> (gdb) po result
> ```

Finally, we ask the UITableView that is owned by our UITableViewController to reload its data, so that the user interface is updated. When the UITableView reloads, it will need to know how many total rows it contains, so we return the count for the items array:

```
- (NSInteger)tableView:(UITableView *)tableView numberOfRowsInSection:(NSInteger)section
{
        // Return the number of rows in the section.
        if (nil == items) {
                return 0;
        }
        return [items count];
}
```

When the UITableView needs a specific row, we retrieve the dictionary that represents the friend for that row from our array of friends (i.e., the items array) in FriendsViewController's tableView:cellForRowAtIndexPath: method:

```
NSDictionary *friendDictionary = [items objectAtIndex:[indexPath row]];
```

For this sample, we're using our own UITableViewCell class entitled FriendTableViewCell. This enables us to encapsulate the retrieval of a friend's profile picture. The FriendTableViewCell uses the style UITableViewCellStyleDefault, which displays a text label and an optional image. The FriendTableViewCell class is itself an FBRequestDelegate, and it owns a pointer to a dictionary, which in this case will be the dictionary for the friend that is associated with the cell. Here is the declaration for the FriedTableViewCell:

```
@interface FriendTableViewCell : UITableViewCell <FBRequestDelegate> {
        NSDictionary *data;
}

@property(nonatomic, retain) NSDictionary *data;

@end
```

We assign the FriendTableViewCell's data dictionary in FriendsViewController's tableView:cellForRowAtIndexPath: method:

```
cell.data = friendDictionary;
```

When we do the preceding assignment, FriendTableViewCell's setData method is called. Therefore, we have overridden this method to perform our own custom actions:

```
- (void)setData:(NSDictionary *)dictionary {
    [data release];
```

```
    data = [dictionary retain];

    self.textLabel.text = [data objectForKey:@"name"];

        self.imageView.image = nil;
        [self setNeedsLayout];

        [[NSNotificationCenter defaultCenter] removeObserver:self];

        self.requestPath = [NSString stringWithFormat:@"%@/picture", [data
objectForKey:@"id"]];
        [[FacebookRequestController sharedRequestController]
enqueueRequestWithGraphPath:self.requestPath];

        //listen for a notification with the name of the identifier
        [[NSNotificationCenter defaultCenter] addObserver:self
selector:@selector(facebookRequestDidComplete:) name:kRequestCompletedNotification
object:nil];
}
```

First, we set the text for the textLabel of the cell to the value associated with the name key in the data dictionary. Second, we initiate a request for this particular friend's profile picture from the Facebook social graph via the requestWithGraph: method. To obtain the profile picture of a user from the Facebook graph, we make the request using this format:

```
<user ID>/picture
```

In this case, we are constructing this for each friend by using NSString's stringWithFormat: and passing it the value associated with the id key in the data dictionary. The Facebook iOS SDK returns the image as bytes within an NSData object. Next, we create an image from this object, as shown here in FriendTableViewCell's facebookRequestDidComplete: method:

```
- (void)facebookRequestDidComplete:(NSNotification*)notification {

    if (YES == [self.requestPath isEqualToString:[notification.userInfo
objectForKey:@"path"]]) {

        UIImage *image = [UIImage imageWithData:(NSData*)[notification.userInfo
objectForKey:@"result"]];
        self.imageView.image = image;
        [self setNeedsLayout];
    }
}
```

If you run the sample application, log in via your Facebook user account, and tap the Friends tab, then you will see it download and display your list of friends. It will also download each of their profile pictures (see Figure 6–1). Note that this sample has not been optimized; it's intended solely to show you how to get up and running with these APIs.

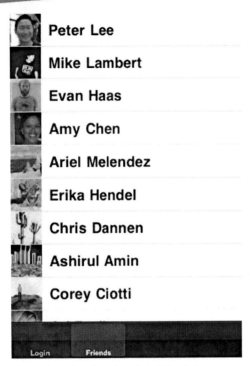

Figure 6–1. *A rudimentary list of friends*

Paging Graph Responses

One interesting thing that we'd like to point out is that you can limit the number of items you get in a response from the Facebook graph when making a request. This is accomplished by adding the `limit` parameter to the request. You can do this via the `requestWithGraphPath:andDelegate:` method:

```
[facebook requestWithGraphPath:@"me/friends?limit=3" andDelegate:self];
```

You can also do this via `requestWithGraphPath:andParams:andDelegate:` by creating a dictionary of parameters. For each object in the dictionary, the key is the name of the parameter—`limit`, in this case—and the value is a string representation of the value. Here is what the code looks like:

```
NSMutableDictionary *params = [NSMutableDictionary dictionary];
[params setObject:@"3" forKey:@"limit"];
[facebook requestWithGraphPath:@"me/feed" andParams:params andDelegate:self];
```

You can also specify that you would like to retrieve items from a given starting point or offset by using the `offset` parameter:

```
[facebook requestWithGraphPath:@"me/friends?limit=3&offset=5" andDelegate:self];
```

Alternatively, you can also accomplish this same task by passing in a dictionary of parameters:

```
NSMutableDictionary *params = [NSMutableDictionary dictionary];
[params setObject:@"3" forKey:@"limit"];
[params setObject:@"5" forKey:@"offset"];
[facebook requestWithGraphPath:@"me/feed" andParams:params andDelegate:self];
```

Under the Hood: The FBRequest Class

The actual Facebook Graph API is an HTTP-based API, where HTTP requests are formatted and sent to Facebook's servers, and responses are sent back in JSON format. The Facebook iOS SDK provides us with a set of clean and simple-to-use Objective-C wrapper classes that we can use within our iOS apps to request information via the Facebook Graph API.

The Facebook iOS SDK class that actually makes the requests and handles the responses is FBRequest. The Facebook iOS SDK takes advantage of the fact that the underlying base URL that it needs to use to make requests never changes: https://graph.facebook.com. The SDK also knows that certain parameters for a request never change. This means that you only need to provide the request methods with those parts of the Graph Path that change based on the context of your application.

So, if we were to construct the full URL to request the current user's friends from the Facebook graph, it would look as follows:

```
https://graph.facebook.com/me/friends?sdk=ios&sdk_version=2&access_token=<your
token>&format=json
```

We are using the Facebook iOS SDK, so we only need to give the SDK the Graph Path "me/friends" (along with any other parameters to control the request) since the underlying SDK classes construct the full URL for us.

The final request is constructed in FBRequest's connect method, so it is worth studying. This is where the actual request is made, and the JSON response is handled. The JSON response is handled in the method handleResponseData:(NSData *)data. In the case of a request for a user's friends, this is what the JSON response looks like:

```
{"data":[{"name":"John Dor","id":"<some ID>"}]}
```

It is also worth studying FBRequest's getRequestWithParams:httpMethod:delegate:requestURL: method and Facebook's openUrl:params:httpMethod:delegate:.

A General Note on Error Handling

There is no right or wrong way to handle errors from the Facebook iOS SDK. It all depends on you and your application. We encourage you to implement any delegate methods that notify you of errors, so that you can take the appropriate action and notify the user or update your application's user interface. With respect to what we have covered for Facebook in this chapter, be sure to implement FBRequestDelegate's request:didFailWithError: method.

Introducing the Twitter APIs

There are tons of things your app can publish on Twitter. These things include, but aren't limited to the following: Tweets, direct messages (although note that this is fading out), @replies, #hashtags, and so on. We'll begin by showing you how to pull information from Twitter via MGTwitterEngine.

As with the Facebook sample app for this chapter, we have changed the structure of the Twitter sample application a bit for this chapter in order to make it easy to see some of this in action. You will see that the sample application now uses a UITabBarController to divide up the functionality of the app. Again, it's not pretty, but it works.

Welcome to the Timeline

If you're wondering what a Twitter *timeline* is, it's Twitter's own term for any stream of Tweets. Twitter treats all your own Tweets as one timeline, the stream of Tweets you see from people you follow as another timeline, and any stream of Tweets coming from a curated list that you've made as still another timeline.

It Always Feels Like Somebody's Following Me

The most coveted thing for a Twitter user is to have a lot of followers. To that end, we're going to take a look at how to get a list of the currently logged in user's followers and the associated profile picture for each follower. This is accomplished via MGTwitterEngine's getFollowersIncludingCurrentStatus: method:

```
[sa_OAuthTwitterEngine getFollowersIncludingCurrentStatus:YES];
```

Unlike the Facebook iOS SDK, where every request is issued via the requestWithGraphPath: method, MGTwitterEngine uses different methods to accomplish different requests. There is also no formal request object, so some different coding mechanisms are required since we can't specify a different delegate per request. Unfortunately, this makes coding against MGTwitterEngine slightly more difficult; however, all of the MGTwitterEngine request methods return a unique request connection identifier string, and we will use this to our advantage in our sample app for this chapter.

Looking at the sample code, we make the previously mentioned getFollowersIncludingCurrentStatus: method call in the viewDidLoad: method of the FollowersViewController class. The FollowersViewController class is a UITableViewController. Since the Twitter API returns lists of information, a UITableViewController is an ideal class to use to demonstrate how to use the API to retrieve someone's list of followers. Here is the declaration for the FollowersViewController class:

```
@interface FollowersViewController : UITableViewController {
        NSArray *followers;
}
@end
```

Recall that when we created the MGTwitterEngine, we had to set an MGTwitterEngineDelegate, which in this case is our AppDelegate class. Whenever a request is made of Twitter via MGTwitterEngine, the methods of the MGTwitterEngineDelegate will be called. It's important to note that MGTwitterEngine calls the methods of its delegate in the following order:

1. After a successful request is made to Twitter's servers, the requestSucceeded: method is called.

2. Next, depending on what was requested, one of the *Received:forRequest: methods is called (in this case, when requesting followers, the userInfoReceived:forRequest: method is called), and the response data is stored in an Objective-C data type.

3. Finally, the connectionFinished: method is called. If there was a problem with the request, then the requestFailed:withError: method is called.

If we take a look at the userInfoReceived:forRequest: method in the AppDelegate, we see the following:

```
- (void)userInfoReceived:(NSArray *)userInfo forRequest:(NSString *)⏎
connectionIdentifier
  {
        NSLog(@"User info for connectionIdentifier = %@", connectionIdentifier);

        //tell the UI to update itself

        NSDictionary *userInfoDictionary = [NSDictionary dictionaryWithObjects:⏎
[NSArray arrayWithObjects:userInfo, nil] forKeys:[NSArray arrayWithObjects:⏎
@"followers", nil]];
        [[NSNotificationCenter defaultCenter] postNotificationName:connectionIdentifier

object:self

userInfo:userInfoDictionary];
  }
```

At this point, you might be wondering what we're doing with the NSNotificationCenter. Well, as it turns out, the NSNotificationCenter is a great mechanism for allowing a class within an app to notify other classes that something has happened and pass along information without having to use delegates. In this case, we want tell the FollowersViewController that the information for its request is available. But before we talk more about what's going on within FollowersViewController, let's finish taking a look at the preceding code.

The userInfo parameter is an NSArray of NSDictionary objects. Each NSDictionary contains information about an individual follower. When you post a notification, you can specify a dictionary of objects that the receiver of the notification can access. We want the FollowersViewController to receive the array of followers, so we create a dictionary with one key, followers, and assign the array of followers to that key. When we finally post the notification, we have to give it a unique name, and what better name to use than the connection identifier?

You probably recall that the `FollowersViewController` owns a pointer to an `NSArray` entitled `followers`:

```
NSArray *followers;
```

In order to assign the array that we got back in the `userInfoReceived:forRequest:` delegate method, we have to do a couple of things in `FollowersViewController`. We begin by telling the `NSNotificationCenter` that we want to receive notifications that match the name of the unique connection identifier for our request. Recall that this will be the same connection identifier that is given to the `userInfoReceived:forRequest:` delegate method. We also tell `NSNotificationCenter` that we want the method `twitterFollowersRequestDidComplete:` to be executed if a notification that matches our unique connection identifier is fired. Here is the code that does this:

```
- (void)viewDidLoad {
        [super viewDidLoad];
        // Uncomment the following line to display an Edit button in the navigation
bar
  for this view controller.
        // self.navigationItem.rightBarButtonItem = self.editButtonItem;

        NSString *identifier = [sa_OAuthTwitterEngine
getFollowersIncludingCurrentStatus:YES]; // statuses/followers

        //listen for a notification with the name of the identifier
        [[NSNotificationCenter defaultCenter] addObserver:self
                selector:@selector(twitterFollowersRequestDidComplete:)
                name:identifier
                object:nil];
}
```

Now let's examine what's going on in our method that handles the notification:

```
- (void)twitterFollowersRequestDidComplete:(NSNotification*)notification {

        [followers release];
        followers = [[notification.userInfo objectForKey:@"followers"] retain];

        [[NSNotificationCenter defaultCenter] removeObserver:self];

        [self.tableView reloadData];
}
```

In this method, the first thing that we do is release the array of followers. We do this to prevent a memory leak. Since the next step is to assign a new array to the array of followers, any time we want to assign a new array, we need to first make sure that we release and give back the array that we stored before. Things get a little more interesting when we actually do the assignment, so let's review what's going on in this step:

```
        followers = [[notification.userInfo objectForKey:@"followers"] retain];
```

Remember that, when we posted the notification from `AppDelegate`, we sent a dictionary that contained one key/object pair with the key `followers` in the dictionary. Thus, all we're doing is assigning the value for this key from the notifications userInfo dictionary to our followers array. We finish off this method by removing ourselves as an observer of notifications, and then telling our table to reload itself since we have new data.

> **NOTE:** It's always a good practice to remove yourself as an observer of notifications as soon as you feel the class in question no longer needs to receive the notifications. If you fail to do this before setting your class to receive notifications again, your class will receive multiple notifications for the same event, which is probably not the behavior you want.

When the table reloads, we return the number of followers as the number of rows in the table:

```
- (NSInteger)tableView:(UITableView *)tableView numberOfRowsInSection:↩
(NSInteger)section {
        // Return the number of rows in the section.
        if (nil == followers) {
                return 0;
        }

        return [followers count];
}
```

When the UITableView needs a specific row, we retrieve the dictionary that represents the follower for that row from our array of followers in FollowersViewController's tableView:cellForRowAtIndexPath: method:

```
NSDictionary *dictionary = [followers objectAtIndex:[indexPath row]];
```

For this sample, we're using our own UITableViewCell class entitled FollowersTableViewCell. This lets us encapsulate the retrieval of a follower's profile picture. The FollowersTableViewCell uses the style UITableViewCellStyleDefault, which displays a text label and an optional image. The FollowersTableViewCell class owns a pointer to a dictionary, which in this case will be the dictionary for the follower that is associated with the cell. Here is the declaration for the FriendTableViewCell:

```
@interface FollowersTableViewCell : UITableViewCell {
        NSDictionary *data;
}

@property(nonatomic, retain) NSDictionary *data;

@end
```

We assign the FollowersTableViewCell's data dictionary in FollowersViewController's tableView:cellForRowAtIndexPath: method:

```
cell.data = dictionary;
```

When we do the preceding assignment, FollowersTableViewCell's setData method is called, so we have overridden this method to perform our own custom actions:

```
- (void)setData:(NSDictionary *)dictionary {
        [data release];
```

```
        data = [dictionary retain];

        self.textLabel.text = [data objectForKey:@"screen_name"];

        self.imageView.image = nil;
        [self setNeedsLayout];

        [[NSNotificationCenter defaultCenter] removeObserver:self];

        NSString *identifier = [sa_OAuthTwitterEngine getImageAtURL:[dictionary⏎
objectForKey:@"profile_image_url"]];

        //listen for a notification with the name of the identifier
        [[NSNotificationCenter defaultCenter] addObserver:self
            selector:@selector(twitterProfileImageRequestDidComplete:)
            name:identifier
            object:nil];
}
```

First, we set the text for the `textLabel` of the cell to the value associated with the screen_name key in the data dictionary. Second, we initiate a request for this particular follower's profile picture from Twitter via MGTwitterEngine's `getImageAtURL:` method. We pass to this method the URL of the follower's profile image that was returned to us from Twitter and is the value associated with the profile_image_url key in the data dictionary. Note that the `getImageAtURL:` method can be used to retrieve an image from any URL, not just a Twitter URL.

When we make the request for the image, MGTwitterEngine returns the connection identifier and, just like in `FollowersViewController`, we tell `NSNotificationCenter` that we want to receive notifications matching the value of the connection identifier.

MGTwitterEngine notifies our application that the image is available and passes it to us via the `imageReceived:forRequest:` `MGTwitterEngineDelegate` method. We then issue a notification for the returned connection identifier that contains the image:

```
- (void)imageReceived:(UIImage *)image forRequest:(NSString *)connectionIdentifier {
        NSLog(@"Image receieved for connectionIdentifier = %@", connectionIdentifier);

        NSDictionary *userInfoDictionary = [NSDictionary dictionaryWithObjects:⏎
[NSArray arrayWithObjects:image, nil] forKeys:[NSArray⏎
 arrayWithObjects:@"profile_image", nil]];
        [[NSNotificationCenter defaultCenter] postNotificationName:connectionIdentifier
            object:self
            userInfo:userInfoDictionary];
}
```

Back in FollowersViewController, in the notification handler, we get the image object out of the notification, set it as the cell's image, and then update the cell's layout:

```
- (void)twitterProfileImageRequestDidComplete:(NSNotification*)notification {

        [[NSNotificationCenter defaultCenter] removeObserver:self];

        self.imageView.image = [notification.userInfo objectForKey:@"profile_image"];
        [self setNeedsLayout];
}
```

If you run the sample application, log in via your Twitter user account, and tap the Followers tab, then you will see it download and display your list of followers. It will also download each of their profile pictures (see Figure 6–2). Note that this sample has not been optimized; it's intended solely to show you how to get up and running with these APIs.

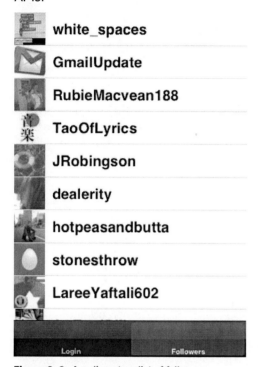

Figure 6–2. *A rudimentary list of followers*

Under the Hood: MGTwitter HTTP Connections and XML Parsing

The actual Twitter API is an HTTP-based API, where HTTP requests are formatted and sent to Twitter's servers, and responses are sent back in XML format. MGTwitterEngine provides us with a set of clean and simple to use Objective-C wrapper classes that we can use within our iOS apps to request information from Twitter.

The class in MGTwitterEngine that actually makes the requests and handles the responses is the MGTwitterEngine class itself. If you refer to the header file for MGTwitterEngine, you will notice that it owns a dictionary of connections:

```
NSMutableDictionary *_connections;
```

Each time a request is made, MGTwitterEngine creates a new MGTwitterHTTPURLConnection, which is an NSURLConnection. Each MGTwitterHTTPURLConnection creates a unique identifier (UUID) for itself. This is

accomplished via an NSString category class in MGTwitterEngine entitled
NSString+UUID that has one method:

```
+ (NSString*)stringWithNewUUID
{
    // Create a new UUID
    CFUUIDRef uuidObj = CFUUIDCreate(kCFAllocatorDefault);

    // Get the string representation of the UUID
    NSString *newUUID = (NSString*)CFUUIDCreateString(kCFAllocatorDefault, uidObj);
    CFRelease(uuidObj);
    return [newUUID autorelease];
}
```

When MGTwitterEngine creates a connection, it saves the object for that connection in
its connections dictionary, where the key is the connection identifier returned by the
connection. We'll get to why this is important in a second, but let's first look at the URL
to request someone's followers from Twitter:

```
https://twitter.com/statuses/followers.xml
```

When MGTwitterEngine creates an MGTwitterHTTPURLConnection object, it assigns it a
request type and a response type. Why is that? Well, when the response is received
from Twitter, MGTwitterEngine uses this information to decide how to parse the returned
XML data. Note that MGTwitterEngine has a number of XML parsers that all derive
themselves from MGTwitterXMLParser. If you examine MGTwitterEngine's
_parseDataForConnection: method, you will see that it performs a switch on the
response type of the connection. In the case of requesting followers, a
MGTwitterUsersParser is created to parse the response. The XML is parsed and
returned to us via MGTwitterEngineDelegate's userInfoRecieved:forRequest: method
as an array of dictionaries. Here is what one of these dictionaries looks like:

```
(
{
    "contributors_enabled" = false;
    "created_at" = "Thu Mar 25 16:29:19 +0000 2010";
    description = "Phone Numbers Are Dead. Go800 is the new way of placing phone calls↵
by giving a voice to the names in your social world. Public launch March 1st.";
    "favourites_count" = 0;
    "follow_request_sent" = false;
    "followers_count" = 675;
    following = 1;
    "friends_count" = 939;
    "geo_enabled" = false;
    id = 126361254;
    "is_translator" = false;
    lang = en;
    "listed_count" = 9;
    location = "New York, NY";
    name = Go800;
    notifications = false;
    "profile_background_color" = ffffff;
    "profile_background_image_url" = "http://a3.twimg.com/profile_background_images↵
/207991705/bkg_go800_850_v_full_v9.png";
    "profile_background_tile" = true;
```

```
    "profile_image_url" = "http://a2.twimg.com/profile_images↵
/1235044022/go800_logo_twitter_logo_normal.png";
    "profile_link_color" = 3f90b3;
    "profile_sidebar_border_color" = 333333;
    "profile_sidebar_fill_color" = ffffff;
    "profile_text_color" = 333333;
    "profile_use_background_image" = true;
    protected = 0;
    "screen_name" = Go800;
    "show_all_inline_media" = false;
    "source_api_request_type" = 11;
    status =       {
        contributors = "";
        coordinates = "";
        "created_at" = "Tue Feb 22 21:49:40 +0000 2011";
        favorited = false;
        geo = "";
        id = 40166359300050944;
        "in_reply_to_screen_name" = "";
        "in_reply_to_status_id" = "";
        "in_reply_to_user_id" = "";
        place = "";
        "retweet_count" = 6;
        retweeted = false;
        source = web;
        "source_api_request_type" = 11;
        text = "Phone Numbers Are Dead. Teach twitter a new trick on March 1st.↵
 Follow @Go800 for preview invite.";
        truncated = 0;
    };
    "statuses_count" = 83;
    "time_zone" = "Eastern Time (US & Canada)";
    url = "http://www.go800corp.com";
    "utc_offset" = "-18000";
    verified = false;
}
)
```

Conclusion

We covered a lot of interesting areas within this chapter related to using the Facebook iOS SDK to obtain a user's list of friends and MGTwitterEngine to obtain a user's list of followers. Along the way, we took a closer look at what's going on under the covers in each of these SDKs. We also went into some generally useful programming techniques for programming iOS apps in Objective-C.

In the next chapter, we will build on this knowledge base to delve deeper into what's going on under the covers and expand this chapter's sample projects to show you how to use these SDKs to post information for users, as well as how to get more of their information.

Chapter 7

Accessing People, Places, Objects, and Relationships

In this chapter, we'll cover the nuts and bolts of Facebook methods, objects, properties, and connections—and how to get at them. We'll also introduce JSON, or JavaScript Object Notifications, which are ancillary to the use of the Graph API. Finally, we'll talk about retrieving basic data from Twitter's REST (Representational State Transfer)[1] API.

You can find all of the code for this chapter in the Chapter7 directory of the Git repository. The Facebook code is in the ApiFacebook project, and the Twitter code is in the ApiTwitter project. These projects build off the same application structure that was introduced in the Chapter 6's sample projects; and once again, the projects aren't pretty, but they get the job done.

More Fun with the Facebook Graph API

In the last chapter, we showed you how to pull information from Facebook's social graph. As you did this, you were probably left wondering how to go about adding or posting information from your own app to Facebook's social graph. Well, since we're such nice guys, we've gone through the trouble of dedicating an entire section of this chapter to posting to the Facebook social graph. We've also added a thorough review of additional information that you can pull from the social graph, including how that information relates to authorization and extended permissions. Read on for the gory details.

---

[1] See, for example, http://en.wikipedia.org/wiki/Representational_State_Transfer

Facebook Dialogs

One of the great ways to spice up your iOS application and make it a hit with users is to let them post to their Facebook page directly from within your app. Even though iOS supports copy and paste and fast switching between apps, users won't find your app appealing if they have to switch to the iOS Facebook app itself to, for instance, post a link to an interesting article from within your application to their Facebook wall.

Fortunately for us, the Facebook SDK has made it as simple as possible to get up and running with this functionality. This brings us to the dialog: methods in the Facebook class that we have yet to discuss:

```
- (void)dialog:(NSString *)action
  andDelegate:(id<FBDialogDelegate>)delegate;

- (void)dialog:(NSString *)action
    andParams:(NSMutableDictionary *)params
  andDelegate:(id <FBDialogDelegate>)delegate;
```

Both of these methods are in Facebook.h; and while there are two methods available to us, we will focus on using the second one, which lets us pass in additional parameters. The first method without parameters is usable, but more often than not you will need to pass parameters to the dialog: method. Moreover, if you look in Facebook.m, you will see that the first method calls the second method with an empty dictionary for the parameters:

```
- (void)dialog:(NSString *)action
  andDelegate:(id<FBDialogDelegate>)delegate {
  NSMutableDictionary * params = [NSMutableDictionary dictionary];
  [self dialog:action andParams:params andDelegate:delegate];
}
```

Both of these methods also take an *action* parameter and a *delegate* parameter. We will look at these now in our sample application. In the sample application for this chapter, we have a new class entitled DialogViewController. This class will look awfully similar to the LoginViewController class because, lo and behold, it's modeled directly after it. That said, we want to focus our attention on a few things within the DialogViewController class.

Since we are going to be displaying dialogs to the user from the DialogViewController class, we need to declare that it is an FBDialogDelegate in our header file, DialogViewController.h:

```
@interface DialogViewController : UIViewController <FBDialogDelegate> {
}
@end
```

In DialogViewController.m, it's up to us to define each of the following delegate callback methods:

```
- (void)dialogDidComplete:(FBDialog *)dialog;
- (void)dialogCompleteWithUrl:(NSURL *)url;
- (void)dialogDidNotCompleteWithUrl:(NSURL *)url;
- (void)dialogDidNotComplete:(FBDialog *)dialog;
```

```
- (void)dialog:(FBDialog*)dialog didFailWithError:(NSError *)error;
- (BOOL)dialog:(FBDialog*)dialog shouldOpenURLInExternalBrowser:(NSURL *)url;
```

Before we discuss these delegate callbacks a bit further, it's high time we use the dialog: method to do some work for us. The Facebook SDK will display content within a pop-up dialog according to what you pass in as the action parameter to the dialog: method. In the case of posting information to a user's Facebook wall, the appropriate action is feed. Therefore, in the most simple case, if we want to display a dialog that lets a user enter any freeform text and post it to his wall, we would call the dialog: method as follows and ensure that we pass the appropriate class (in this case, DialogViewController) as the delegate:

```
NSMutableDictionary * params = [NSMutableDictionary dictionary];
[facebook dialog:@"feed" andParams:params andDelegate:self];
```

Calling the dialog: method this way displays this dialog to the user (see Figure 7–1):

Figure 7–1. *Calling the dialog: method presents this dialog to the user.*

As you can see, this is really bare bones and not what you are used to seeing from within web apps that let you post content to your Facebook wall. So let's spice things up a bit via some additional parameters. Additional parameters can be specified for the feed dialog, and each parameter has a specific name and purpose. Posting YouTube videos is incredibly popular on Facebook, so let's assume you want to post a link to a YouTube video to a user's wall from within your application. To accomplish this, add a key/value pair to the parameters dictionary where the key is link and the value is the URL for the YouTube video (or whatever other web content you want to share):

```
NSDictionary* params = [NSDictionary dictionaryWithObject:
    @http://www.youtube.com/watch?v=nqMc9B7uDV8 forKey:@"link"];

[facebook dialog:@"feed" andParams:params andDelegate:self];
```

Since the underlying guts of the Facebook SDK's dialog is a web view (more on this later), this code is formatted nicely into something you would expect and shows an image preview of what's in the YouTube video with the post (see Figure 7–2).

Figure 7–2. *Since Facebook dialogs are Web views, you can embed previews of content there.*

Now that was easy, wasn't it? Let's take it a step further, though, and see how we can customize the display of the feed dialog even more. The code that follows creates a sample dialog that Facebook likes to use:

```
NSDictionary* params = [NSDictionary dictionaryWithObjectsAndKeys:

    @"http://developers.facebook.com/docs/reference/dialogs/", @"link",
    @"http://fbrell.com/f8.jpg", @"picture",
    @"Facebook Dialogs", @"name",
    @"Reference Documentation", @"caption",
    @"Dialogs provide a simple interface for apps to interact with users.",
@"description",
    @"Facebook Dialogs are so easy!", @"message", nil];
        [facebook dialog:@"feed" andParams:params andDelegate:self];
```

In this example, we're setting a bunch of values for different keys that Facebook makes available, so that you can really spice up the look and feel of the dialog. Setting a URL to an image as the value for the picture key lets you control what image is displayed with the post on the user's Facebook wall. The value for the name key controls what will be displayed in the classic Facebook font as the main title of the wall post. The `caption` and `description` values let you provide preset text with the wall post. Last but not least, the `message` key lets you preset the text in the editable text field in the dialog. All this information is displayed in the dialog, as shown in Figure 7–3.

Figure 7–3. *Anatomy of a Facebook dialog*

Before we jump ahead to discuss some of the inner workings of the Facebook SDKs dialogs, we should take a short detour and go over the `FBDialogDelegate` methods. We've found through our own personal experience that how you use the `FBDialogDelegate` methods depends upon the context you use them in. For instance, you might want to implement these methods if you like to track some analytics within your application.

Whenever the user takes an action with the dialog by pressing one of the Skip or Publish action buttons on the dialog, the SDK first calls the `dialogCompleteWithUrl:` method, and then the `dialogDidComplete:` method. If the user presses the Skip button, this URL will be passed to the `dialogCompleteWithUrl:` method:

`"fbconnect://success"`

If the user presses the Publish button instead, this URL will be passed to the `dialogCompleteWithUrl:` method:

`"fbconnect://success/?post_id=623441509_10150094754996510"`

We'll be the first to admit that we didn't actually know what to make of this response at first; however, we did a little digging, so you're in luck. It turns out that the `post_id` parameter in the URL contains two separate pieces of identifying information that are concatenated together with an underscore. Here is the definition of the post_id parameter:

```
post_id=<userIdentifier>_<postIdentifier>
```

In this case, userIdentifier indicates the Facebook Graph path for the logged in user who made the post via our application. Similarly, postIdentifier indicates the Facebook Graph path identifier for that post. If you parse those two pieces of information out of the post_id parameter, you can put them into the following URL scheme to see the actual result:

```
www.facebook.com/<userIdentifier>/posts/<postIdentifier>
```

Armed with this knowledge, you could show the user her actual post on Facebook's mobile site by directing her to the properly constructed URL, which is shown here:

```
www.facebook.com/623441509/posts/10150094754996510
```

On a final note, if the user chooses to close the dialog via the X button in the upper-right corner, the dialogDidNotCompleteWithUrl: delegate method is called with a nil NSURL object as its parameter, and then dialogDidNotComplete: is called.

Under the Hood: The FBDialog Class

If you're thinking that last section was too easy, you're right. We tip our hat to the Facebook engineers for making this as painless as possible. A good SDK has well thought out, easy-to-use methods that make things as painless as possible.

Given our discussion in the last chapter about the workings of the FBRequest class, it should come as no surprise that posting information to Facebook is also done ultimately via an HTTP-based API. Once again though, the engineers at Facebook were good sports and provided us with the FBDialog class in their SDK to do all of the heavy lifting.

The code for the FBDialog class is found in the FBDialog.m and FBDialog.h files in the FBConnect folder in all of the sample projects. There are a lot of interesting things to be learned by just examining the declaration of the FBDialog class:

```
@interface FBDialog : UIView <UIWebViewDelegate> {
  id<FBDialogDelegate> _delegate;
  NSMutableDictionary *_params;
  NSString * _serverURL;
  NSURL* _loadingURL;
  UIWebView* _webView;
  UIActivityIndicatorView* _spinner;
  UIImageView* _iconView;
  UILabel* _titleLabel;
  UIButton* _closeButton;
  UIDeviceOrientation _orientation;
  BOOL _showingKeyboard;

  // Ensures that UI elements behind the dialog are disabled.
  UIView* _modalBackgroundView;
}
@end
```

The first two points of interest are that FBDialog is just a UIView and that it owns a modal background view:

```
// Ensures that UI elements behind the dialog are disabled.
UIView* _modalBackgroundView;
```

Why would the FBDialog class be just a normal UIView? Also, why would a dialog class have something like a modal background view within it? Doesn't the iOS SDK already have a class for showing a modal pop-up dialog?

Although this would be nice to have, it turns out that the iOS SDK doesn't provide an out-of-the-box solution for showing a modal pop-up dialog. This means it's up to developers to home grow their own. The most trusted way to accomplish this is to create a view that is the size of the entire application frame, so that users cannot interact with anything "behind" the modal pop-up dialog. The code for this sits in FBDialog's show: method, and it is useful if you ever need to accomplish something like this for your own application (note that we already created the _modalBackgroundView object in FBDialog's init: method):

```
UIWindow* window = [UIApplication sharedApplication].keyWindow;
if (!window) {
    window = [[UIApplication sharedApplication].windows objectAtIndex:0];
}

_modalBackgroundView.frame = window.frame;
[_modalBackgroundView addSubview:self];
[window addSubview:_modalBackgroundView];

[window addSubview:self];
```

Another important piece to the FBDialog puzzle is that it owns a UIWebView and is a UIWebViewDelegate:

```
UIWebView* _webView;
```

It turns out that this UIWebView is what handles all of the rendering magic of the majority of the content in an FBDialog. The main content of the FBDialog is actually fetched over the web from Facebook via its dialog URL, and it is displayed in the UIWebView in FBDialog. In particular, it has a mobile version of its dialog URL, which is defined in Facebook.m:

```
static NSString* kDialogBaseURL = @"https://m.facebook.com/dialog/";
```

When you use the Facebook SDK's dialog: method to create a dialog and pass it an action, this action gets added to the dialog URL, and the SDK also adds required parameters such as the version of the Facebook SDK, the display style, and a redirect URI. For a bare bones feed dialog, the final request looks like this:

```
https://m.facebook.com/dialog/feed?sdk=2&redirect_uri=fbconnect%3A%2F%2Fsuccess&app_id=1
14442211957627&display=touch
```

We've included the actual dialog: method here, so that you can see how it presets some of the parameters for the dialog URL, creates the dialog, and then shows it. Note that the final dialog URL is constructed in FBDialog's generateURL: method:

```
- (void)dialog:(NSString *)action
```

```
        andParams:(NSMutableDictionary *)params
    andDelegate:(id <FBDialogDelegate>)delegate {

  [_fbDialog release];

  NSString *dialogURL = [kDialogBaseURL stringByAppendingString:action];
  [params setObject:@"touch" forKey:@"display"];
  [params setObject:kSDKVersion forKey:@"sdk"];
  [params setObject:kRedirectURL forKey:@"redirect_uri"];

  if (action == kLogin) {
    [params setObject:@"user_agent" forKey:@"type"];
    _fbDialog = [[FBLoginDialog alloc] initWithURL:dialogURL
                loginParams:params delegate:self];
  } else {
    [params setObject:_appId forKey:@"app_id"];
    if ([self isSessionValid]) {
      [params setValue:[self.accessToken
      stringByReplacingPercentEscapesUsingEncoding:NSUTF8StringEncoding]
                                          forKey:@"access_token"];
    }
    _fbDialog = [[FBDialog alloc] initWithURL:dialogURL
                                       params:params
                                     delegate:delegate];
  }

  [_fbDialog show];
}
```

Posting to Facebook and Authorization

Before we move onto other feats of magic and wonder, we'd like to mention that, if your main goal is to let users share information from your app or the web to their Facebook page, it really is as simple as integrating with the Facebook iOS SDK in general—as we've shown here when using the dialog: method. In fact, you don't even have to worry about doing any separate authorization calls since Facebook will handle this for you via various web redirects when you request a dialog without authorization. When you request a dialog without authorization, the dialog will *automagically* bring the user to the Facebook mobile OAuth authorization page (see Figure 7–4). Once the user logs in, he will be redirected back to the original dialog that you requested. It really doesn't get any easier than that, does it?

Figure 7–4. *The Facebook OAuth login view*

We would also like to point out that posting to Facebook does not require extended permissions, so you get this feature for free. What this means in practical terms is that you don't have to pass in any extra permissions to the authorize: call that we covered in Chapter 5 if you are using that method of authorization.

Getting More Goodies from the Facebook Graph

As you can see, we're going to great lengths in this book to not only give you a solid understanding of how to use the Facebook iOS SDK in your application, but also to explain what it's doing under the covers. In Chapter 6, we showed you the technical details of how to retrieve your list of Facebook friends, covered how the nuts and bolts of how Facebook Graph paths are structured, and explained how the FBRequest class works. If you haven't already read that chapter, it might be a good idea to skim it over now because we're going to run through some new examples of how to retrieve additional information from the Facebook Social Graph. This time, however, we will leave out the technical details unless there is something new to discuss.

Remember that fetching information from the Facebook graph is accomplished via the requestWithGraphPath: method of the Facebook class in the Facebook iOS SDK.

This example illustrates how to accomplish that basic task:

```
NSMutableDictionary *params = [NSMutableDictionary dictionary];
//does not require extended permissions
```

```
[facebook requestWithGraphPath:@"me/friends"
                  andParams:params
                  andDelegate:self];
```
The string that you pass to this method uses the following format:

```
<facebook_id>/<requested graph path>
```

In this case, it will retrieve the list of friends for the currently logged in user:

```
me/friends
```

Notice our code comment. Requesting friends does not require any extended permissions when you authorize the user via OAuth, as described in Chapter 5.

> **NOTE:** You can find the code for these examples in the `viewDidLoad:` method in the `FriendsViewController` class in the sample app.

If you want to fetch someone's news feed, then change the graph path to home:

```
NSMutableDictionary *params = [NSMutableDictionary dictionary];
[facebook requestWithGraphPath:@"me/home"
                  andParams:params
                  andDelegate:self];
```

This returns an array of dictionaries. Each dictionary contains information about one item in the news feed. The dictionary for each item will contain keys for the creation time, the post id, the content of the message, the type (e.g., status), actions for commenting or liking, and comments:

```
{
    actions =      (
            {
            link = "http://www.facebook.com/<facebook id>/posts/<post id>";
            name = Comment;
        },
            {
            link = "http://www.facebook.com/<facebook id>/posts/<post id>";
            name = Like;
        }
    );
    "created_time" = "2011-02-28T02:23:08+0000";
    from =       {
        id = <facebook id>;
        name = "<facebook "name>;
    };
    id = "<post id>";
    message = "....";
    type = status;
    "updated_time" = "2011-02-28T02:23:08+0000";
}
```

Fetching notes requires the extended permission user_notes, and the graph path is notes(see Figure 7–5):

Beginning iOS Social Development is requesting
permission to do the following:

Access my profile information
Groups

Report App

Logged in as Christopher White (Not You?)

Don't Allow   Allow

Figure 7–5. *Requesting permission*

```
NSMutableDictionary *params = [NSMutableDictionary dictionary];
// requires 'user_notes' extended permissions
[facebook requestWithGraphPath:@"me/notes" andParams:params andDelegate:self];
```

This returns an array of dictionaries. Each dictionary contains information about one of
the user's notes. The dictionary for each note will contain keys for the creation time, the
note id, the content of the note/message, and comments:

```
{
    comments =      {
        data =          (
            {
                "created_time" = "2009-08-02T13:41:44+0000";
                from =     {
                    Id = <facebook id>;
                    name = "<facebook name>";
                };
                id = "<post id>";
                message = "<comment>";
            },
            {
                "created_time" = "2009-08-02T13:43:01+0000";
                from =     {
                    id = <facebook id>;
                    name = "<facebook name>";
                };
                id = "<post id>";
                message = "<comment>";
```

```
        }
      );
  };
  "created_time" = "2009-08-02T13:23:35+0000";
  from =     {
      id = <facebook id>;
        name = "<facebook name>";
  };
  icon = "http://static.ak.fbcdn.net/rsrc.php/v1/yY/r/1gBp2bDGEuh.gif";
  id = <note id>;
  message = "<note contents>";
  subject = quotes;
  "updated_time" = "2010-05-14T01:35:42+0000";
}
```

Fetching events requires the extended permission user_events, and the graph path is events (see Figure 7–5):

```
NSMutableDictionary *params = [NSMutableDictionary dictionary];
// requires 'user_events' extended permissions
[facebook requestWithGraphPath:@"me/events" andParams:params andDelegate:self];
```

This returns an array of dictionaries. Each dictionary contains information about one of the user's events. The dictionary for each event will contain keys for the start and end time, the event id, the name of the event, the location, and the user's RSVP status:

```
{
    "end_time" = "2011-03-10T13:00:00+0000";
    id = 106092242803326;
    location = "Electric Pickle";
    name = "WMC :: GODFATHER *James Brown Tribute* meets CHAMPION SOUND";
    "rsvp_status" = unsure;
    "start_time" = "2011-03-10T06:00:00+0000";
}
```

Fetching groups requires the extended permission user_groups, and the graph path is groups (see Figure 7–5):

```
NSMutableDictionary *params = [NSMutableDictionary dictionary];
//requires 'user_groups' extended permissions
[facebook requestWithGraphPath:"@me/groups" andParams:params andDelegate:self];
```

This returns an array of dictionaries. Each dictionary contains information about one of the user's groups. The dictionary for each group will contain keys for the id of the group, the group name, and the group version:

```
{
    id = 166023750105785;
    name = "SkateSide Events";
    version = 1;
}
```

Fetching likes, movies, music, and books requires the extended permission user_likes, and the graph path is likes, movies, music, or books, respectively (see Figure 7–5).

Each request returns an array of dictionaries. Each dictionary contains information about one of the user's likes, movies, music, or books. The dictionary for each item will contain keys for the category, creation time, Facebook id, and name. For example, this code returns information about the user's likes:

```
NSMutableDictionary *params = [NSMutableDictionary dictionary];
// requires 'user_likes' extended permissions
[facebook requestWithGraphPath:@"me/likes"
                andParams:params
                andDelegate:self];
```

```
{
    category = "Product/service";
    "created_time" = "2011-02-23T00:09:34+0000";
    id = 186242738068007;
    name = AAdvantage;
}
```

Similarly, this code returns information about the user's movies:

```
[facebook requestWithGraphPath:@"me/movies"
                andParams:params
                andDelegate:self];
```

```
{
    category = Movie;
    "created_time" = "2010-12-28T18:50:40+0000";
    id = 104167709618686;
    name = "Ferris Bueller's Day Off";
}
```

This code returns information about the uers's music:

```
[facebook requestWithGraphPath:@"me/music"
                andParams:params
                andDelegate:self];
```

```
{
    category = "Musician/band";
    "created_time" = "2011-01-16T02:11:26+0000";
    id = 47167209984;
    name = "New York Night Train";
}
```

And this code returns information about the user's books:

```
[facebook requestWithGraphPath:@"me/books"
                andParams:params
                andDelegate:self];
```

Fetching a user's wall posts requires the extended permission read_stream, and the graph path is feed:

```
NSMutableDictionary *params = [NSMutableDictionary dictionary];
// requires 'read_stream' extended permissions
[facebook requestWithGraphPath:@"me/feed"
                andParams:params
                andDelegate:self];
```

The preceding snippet returns an array of dictionaries. Each dictionary contains information about one item on the user's wall. The dictionary for each item will contain keys for the creation time, the post id, the content of the message, the type (e.g., status), actions for commenting or liking, and comments:

```
{
    actions =     (
        {
            link = "http://www.facebook.com/<facebook id>/posts/<post id>";
            name = Comment;
        },
        {
            link = "http://www.facebook.com/<facebook id>/posts/<post id>";
            name = Like;
        }
    );
    application = "<null>";
    caption = "www.youtube.com";
    comments =     {
        count = 4;
        data = (
            {
                "created_time" = "2011-02-24T15:30:59+0000";
                from ={
                        id = <facebook id>;
                        name = "<facebook name>";
                    };
                id = "<post id>";
                message = "…";
            },
            {
                "created_time" = "2011-02-26T00:28:32+0000";
                from = {
                        id = <facebook id>;
                        name = "<facebook name>";
                    };
                id = "<post id>";
                message = "i like the abe lincoln one as well :)";
            }
        );
    };
    "created_time" = "2011-02-24T04:12:30+0000";
    description = "Description here…";
    from =     {
        id = <facebook id>;
        name = "<facebook name>";
    };
    icon = "http://static.ak.fbcdn.net/rsrc.php/v1/yj/r/v2OnaTyTQZE.gif";
    id = "<post id>";
    likes =     {
        count = 2;
        data = (
            {
                id = <facebook id>;
                name = "<facebook name>";
            },
            {
                id = <facebook id>;
                name = "<facebook name>";
```

```
                }
        );
    };
    link = "http://www.youtube.com/watch?v=jL68NyCSi8o";
    message = "hahaha!";
    name = "Drunk History Vol. 5";
    picture = "<URL>";
    privacy =      {
        deny = 389937081509;
        description = "Friends Only; Except: restricted";
        friends = "ALL_FRIENDS";
        value = CUSTOM;
    };
    source = "http://www.youtube.com/v/jL68NyCSi8o&autoplay=1";
    type = video;
    "updated_time" = "2011-02-26T00:28:32+0000";
}
```

Of course, you can also fetch a user's tagged photos, albums, and videos. Doing so requires the extended permission user_photos, and the graph path is photos, albums, or videos, respectively (see Figure 7–5). This snippet fetches a user's tagged photos:

```
NSMutableDictionary *params = [NSMutableDictionary dictionary];
// requires 'user_photos' extended permissions
[facebook requestWithGraphPath:@"me/photos"
                andParams:params
                andDelegate:self]; //tagged photos
```

Similarly, this snippet fetches a user's tagged albums:

```
[facebook requestWithGraphPath:@"me/albums"
                andParams:params
                andDelegate:self];
```

Finally, this snippet fetches a user's tagged videos:

```
[facebook requestWithGraphPath:@"me/videos"
                andParams:params
                andDelegate:self];
```

Note that if the correct user permissions are not included when authorizing the user, then the request:didFailWithError delegate method is called.

Limiting Results

One nice thing you can do is limit the number of fields that Facebook returns in the dictionary for each item in the preceding examples. The method is the same, regardless of what you are requesting. This is accomplished via the fields parameter. For example, when requesting friends, you might want only the Facebook id, name, and picture of each friend. You can accomplish this by using the requestWithGraphPath:andParams:andDelegate method:

```
NSMutableDictionary *params = [NSMutableDictionary dictionary];
[params setObject:@"id,name,picture" forKey:@"fields"];
[facebook requestWithGraphPath:@"me/friends"
                andParams:params
                andDelegate:self];
```

Date Formatting

You'll notice that a lot of the returned information in the preceding examples contained timestamps for things like creation time. By default, all of the date fields returned by Facebook are an ISO-8601 formatted string. If you'd rather have these strings in a different format, you can specify an additional date_format parameter with your requests:

```
NSMutableDictionary *params = [NSMutableDictionary dictionary];
[params setObject:@"U" forKey:@"date_format"];
[facebook requestWithGraphPath:@"me/feed"
                andParams:params
                andDelegate:self];
```

The immediately preceding example requests all date strings in unixtime-format by specifying U as the date_format value. You can see more date formatting options available to you at this link:

```
http://php.net/manual/en/function.date.php
```

More Fun with the Twitter API

We ended the last chapter by showing you how to retrieve and display who a user follows on Twitter. Twitter gives you access to a bunch of other goodies as well, so let's see how we go about doing some more. These other goodies include getting someone's favorite Tweets, tweeting something, sending someone a direct message, and a host of other things. As usual, we've hacked up our sample app a bit to give you an idea of how to use the APIs in MGTwitterEngine to access everything. If you run the Twitter sample app for this chapter, you will see another tab entitled, "Tweetin" with a "Twitter" button. Change the code in TimelineViewController's twitterButtonClick: method to experiment with the different requests that we discuss here. And on with the show!

A Tweetin' We Will Go

You're probably itching to Tweet something directly from an iOS app, right? Well, beginning with iOS 5, Apple has made it easy for deveopers to include Twitter posting functionality in their apps. Users can login to Twitter from inside iOS, and new Tweet posting buttons can be found in several preloaded apps including Camera, Photos, Safari, YouTube and Maps. However, Apple's support for Twitter functions stop at POSTing, so we're going to show you how to roll your own Twitter integration in case your app needs to do something a little more powerful. To Tweet something for the currently logged in user, use the following MGTwitterEngine method:

```
- (NSString *)sendUpdate:(NSString *)status;
```

It's as easy as pie. Tweets can be at most 140 UCS-2 characters long. If this length is exceeded, the Tweet is truncated. For the status parameter, just pass in what you want to Tweet and you're done:

```
[sa_OAuthTwitterEngine sendUpdate:@"this is a test tweet! tweet tweet!"];
```

We won't go over the `MGTwitterEngineDelegate` again in too much detail; however, recall that we set up our main application delegate as a `MGTwitterEngineDelegate`, so you can see what happens when you make each of these calls by going to that class. We will refer to the methods here and assume that you can find them in `AppDelegate.m`. Remember that if the request is successful, the first thing that happens is `requestSucceeded:` is called; next, a follow-up delegate method is called, depending on the request.

Ultimately, when you Tweet something, the `statusesReceived:` delegate method is called with the actual details of the Tweet returned from Twitter. We've modified the `statusesReceived:` method to show you some more information. The main parameter that you receive in this method is an array of items from Twitter. Each element in this array is a dictionary that represents one item. The set of key value pairs that represent an item changes, depending on what you originally requested from Twitter. In our new implementation of `statusesReceived:`, we take the first item in the array and, if it exists, get the Twitter ID for the Tweet and print it out to the console log. Check out how in this example:

```
-   (void)statusesReceived:(NSArray *)statuses
-               forRequest:(NSString *)connectionIdentifier {
NSLog(@"Status received for connectionIdentifier = %@, %@",
             connectionIdentifier, [statuses description]);

NSDictionary *dictionary = [statuses objectAtIndex:0];
if (dictionary) {
    NSString *twitterID = [dictionary objectForKey:@"id"];
    NSLog(@"TwitterID = %@", twitterID);
}
}
```

> **NOTE:** Here's something to keep in mind about Twitter IDs: like the Facebook graph, everything in Twitter has a unique ID. These IDs are used through a number of Twitter's APIs, so we just wanted to make a quick mention of them.

The ID for an item from Twitter is always stored in the id key in the dictionary of the item. The `MGTwitterEngine` code was originally written to accept unsigned longs for these IDs; however, the Twitter IDs have since grown and can no longer be held in an unsigned long variable. To make our lives (and hopefully yours) easier, we modified the version of `MGTwitterEngine` that is used for this book to take a string whenever a method needs a Twitter ID.

The entire dictionary for a Tweet contains a ton of useful information. For example, we would see this if we were to print out the entire dictionary in the `statusesReceived:` method:

```
{
    contributors = "";
    coordinates = "";
    "created_at" = "Fri Mar 04 04:18:55 +0000 2011";
    favorited = false;
```

```
        geo = "";
        id = 43525805485199360;
        "in_reply_to_screen_name" = "";
        "in_reply_to_status_id" = "";
        "in_reply_to_user_id" = "";
        place = "";
        "retweet_count" = 0;
        retweeted = false;
        source = "<a href=\"http://www.apress.com\"
                        rel=\"nofollow\">Tweetin' iOS OAuth</a>";
        "source_api_request_type" = 5;
        text = "this is a test tweet! tweet tweet!";
        truncated = 0;
        user =     {
            "contributors_enabled" = false;
            "created_at" = "Sat Jan 09 21:25:41 +0000 2010";
            description = "";
            "favourites_count" = 4;
            "follow_request_sent" = false;
            "followers_count" = 24;
            following = 0;
            "friends_count" = 186;
            "geo_enabled" = false;
            id = <twitter user id>;
            "is_translator" = false;
            lang = en;
            "listed_count" = 0;
            location = "";
            name = Christopher;
            notifications = false;
            "profile_background_color" = CODEED;
            "profile_background_image_url" = "URL";
            "profile_background_tile" = false;
            "profile_image_url" = "URL";
            "profile_link_color" = 0084B4;
            "profile_sidebar_border_color" = CODEED;
            "profile_sidebar_fill_color" = DDEEF6;
            "profile_text_color" = 333333;
            "profile_use_background_image" = true;
            protected = 1;
            "screen_name" = christhepiss;
            "show_all_inline_media" = false;
            "statuses_count" = 451;
            "time_zone" = "Eastern Time (US & Canada)";
            url = "http://christhepiss.tumblr.com";
            "utc_offset" = "-18000";
            verified = false;
        };
    }
```

Take note of the id that we mentioned before. Also take note of the text and the source
of the Tweet. Since we're using the app identifier for this book when authorizing users,
the source is listed as "Tweetin' iOS OAuth." On Twitter, this would look like what you
see in Figure 7–6.

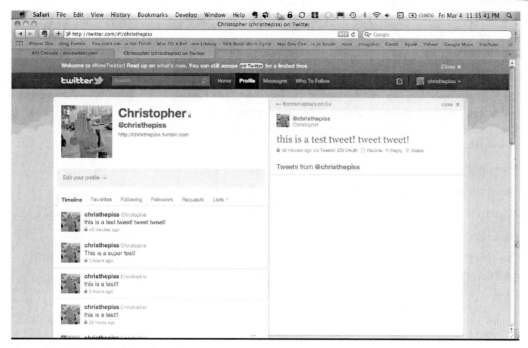

Figure 7–6. *A test Tweet. And it works!*

So now that you've tweeted, you must be feeling pretty good. We know we feel good. However, let's say you want to see all of your Tweets. Doing so is simple:

```
[sa_OAuthTwitterEngine getUserTimeline];
```

In the world of Twitter, tweets exist along a timeline since each Tweet occurs at a specific point in time. So you can get a user's timeline of tweets (as we did earlier), or you can get the timeline of the user and all of her followers:

```
[sa_OAuthTwitterEngine getHomeTimeline];
```

You can even get the entire public timeline on Twitter of all Twitter users who have public Tweets:

```
[sa_OAuthTwitterEngine getPublicTimeline];
```

Similarly, you can get the favorite Tweets of the currently logged in user:

```
[sa_OAuthTwitterEngine getFavoriteUpdatesFor:nil startingAtPage:0];
```

For each of these cases (and others), Twitter returns an array of dictionaries (via statusesReceived:), where each dictionary is the same as the preceding one, contains all of the relevant info and stats for the given Tweet, and indicates where it originated from.

With the Twitter API, you can also delete Tweets. If we wanted to delete the preceding Tweet, we would do the following, where we pass in the ID of the Tweet:

```
[sa_OAuthTwitterEngine deleteUpdate:@"43525805485199360"];
```

In Chapter 6, we showed you how to get someone's followers; however, you can also request information about a specific Twitter user at any time using his Twitter name or his Twitter ID:

```
[sa_OAuthTwitterEngine getUserInformationFor:@"TWITTER USERNAME HERE"];
```

This will return the same dictionary of information we showed in Chapter 6, so we won't show it again here. Please refer to Chapter 6 to see what is contained in this response. Next, set a breakpoint in XCode in `userInfoReceived:` in the main application delegate to see this in action.

If you wanted to follow someone, you could use this code do that, too:

```
[sa_OAuthTwitterEngine enableNotificationsFor:@"christhepiss"];
```

When you want to send a direct message, do the following:

```
[sa_OAuthTwitterEngine sendDirectMessage:@"how goes it?" to:@"christhepiss"];
```

The response from Twitter will be received via the `directMessagesReceived:` delegate method; the dictionary for a direct message looks like this:

```
{
    "created_at" = "Fri Mar 04 06:33:49 +0000 2011";
    id = 2542673717;
    recipient =     {
        "contributors_enabled" = false;
        "created_at" = "Sat Jan 09 21:25:41 +0000 2010";
        description = "";
        "favourites_count" = 4;
        "follow_request_sent" = false;
        "followers_count" = 24;
        following = 0;
        "friends_count" = 187;
        "geo_enabled" = false;
        id = 103384600;
        "is_translator" = false;
        lang = en;
        "listed_count" = 0;
        location = "";
        name = Christopher;
        notifications = false;
        "profile_background_color" = CODEED;
        "profile_background_image_url" = "URL";
        "profile_background_tile" = false;
        "profile_image_url" = "URL";
        "profile_link_color" = 0084B4;
        "profile_sidebar_border_color" = CODEED;
        "profile_sidebar_fill_color" = DDEEF6;
        "profile_text_color" = 333333;
        "profile_use_background_image" = true;
        protected = 1;
        "screen_name" = christhepiss;
        "show_all_inline_media" = false;
        "statuses_count" = 451;
        "time_zone" = "Eastern Time (US & Canada)";
        url = "http://christhepiss.tumblr.com";
        "utc_offset" = "-18000";
```

```
            verified = false;
    };
    "recipient_id" = 103384600;
    "recipient_screen_name" = christhepiss;
    sender =        {
        "contributors_enabled" = false;
        "created_at" = "Sat Jan 09 21:25:41 +0000 2010";
        description = "";
        "favourites_count" = 4;
        "follow_request_sent" = false;
        "followers_count" = 24;
        following = 0;
        "friends_count" = 187;
        "geo_enabled" = false;
        id = 103384600;
        "is_translator" = false;
        lang = en;
        "listed_count" = 0;
        location = "";
        name = Christopher;
        notifications = false;
        "profile_background_color" = CODEED;
        "profile_background_image_url" = "URL";
        "profile_background_tile" = false;
        "profile_image_url" = "URL";
        "profile_link_color" = 0084B4;
        "profile_sidebar_border_color" = CODEED;
        "profile_sidebar_fill_color" = DDEEF6;
        "profile_text_color" = 333333;
        "profile_use_background_image" = true;
        protected = 1;
        "screen_name" = christhepiss;
        "show_all_inline_media" = false;
        "statuses_count" = 451;
        "time_zone" = "Eastern Time (US & Canada)";
        url = "http://christhepiss.tumblr.com";
        "utc_offset" = "-18000";
        verified = false;
    };
    "sender_id" = 103384600;
    "sender_screen_name" = christhepiss;
    "source_api_request_type" = 15;
    text = "hey jerky!";
}
```

The one thing that is missing from the MGTwitterEngine SDK is a dialog class that makes it easy to construct Tweets or Direct Messages, so this is something that you will have to build on your own. :(Don't forget to look in `MGTwitterEngine.h` for more methods that you can use since we didn't cover them all here.

Under the Hood: Twitter URLs

One nice thing about all of the preceding operations is that they share a common URL scheme from the underlying Twitter HTTP API:

```
http://twitter.com/
```

The rest of the path of the URL is then constructed based on what you want to do. For status-related operations, the path is:

```
http://twitter.com/statuses
```

For user-related operations, the path is:

```
http://twitter.com/users
```

And for direct messages, the path is:

```
http://twitter.com/direct_messages
```

The final part of the path is the specific operation you want to perform. This is followed by the extension (which will match what you want the response to be formatted in), and then the parameters. So, if we were going to get the public timeline in XML (MGTwitterEngine requests XML responses by default), it would look like this:

```
http://twitter.com/statuses/public_timeline.xml
```

Review the code in SA_OAuthTwitterEngine's _sendRequestWithMethod: if you want a more detailed understanding of how the final URL is constructed for each request.

The Twitter Dev Console

If you'd rather get used to using some of the Twitter APIs from your web browser, Twitter has a great online tool for doing so that we highly recommend. The tool can be found at this URL:

```
http://dev.twitter.com/console
```

The Twitter dev console lets you construct different requests or make different types of posts and see what the response is from Twitter. Figure 7–7 shows what the main part of the page looks like.

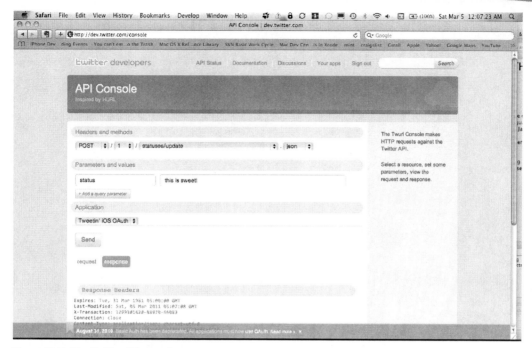

Figure 7–7. *The Twitter API console*

Another great resource is the documentation for each Twitter HTTP API, where you can get exact details on using each API:

`http://dev.twitter.com/doc`

Conclusion

You are now officially armed and dangerous. We've now covered enough APIs for Facebook and Twitter and shown you how to use them with the respective iOS SDKs. In theory, you could start building your own Facebook or Twitter application at this point. It's a pretty daunting task, but you've now got the tools to do it. However, keep reading to gain more insight into working with real-time data and location, as well as to see different ways to mesh these two APIs together.

Chapter 8

POSTing, Data Modeling, and Going Offline

This chapter covers the nuts and bolts of posting photos to Facebook and Twitter. We'll also discuss offline storage; and finally, we'll talk about a popular cross-posting library and how to use it on your own.

Up to this point, we've covered a lot of different topics on programming for Facebook and Twitter on iOS. In order to show these topics as clearly as possible, however, we broke some good programming practices. So in this chapter, we are going to mend our ways and show better techniques for integrating these services into your application. We are also going to cover offline scenarios and storage. But before we go there, we need to add one more essential skill to our toolbelt: posting photos to Facebook and Twitter.

Strike a Pose

For most applications that use images on an iOS device, the images are either downloaded from the web or created by the app and stored as part of the application's data. It's also possible to retrieve images from the device's Photo Library. Fortunately for us, Apple has made it easy to grab images from the Photo Library, so we're going to take this path for our sample applications. The photo upload example applications for this chapter are in the ApiFacebook and ApiTwitter folders, respectively, in the Chapter8 folder of the Git repository.

Saving a Picture to the iOS Simulator's Photo Library

Getting pictures into an iOS simulator's Photo Library is tricky since the simulators do not emulate camera hardware; however, there's a nice, quick way to do it by saving an image from a web page. Begin by firing up the Safari browser on the simulator and going to www.google.com. Hold your mouse down for a second or two on the Google image above the search bar, and then let your mouse go. You will see the pop-up dialog in Figure 8–1 that lets you save or copy the image. Select Save Image to store it in the simulator's Photo Library.

Figure 8–1. *Tap and hold an image on a web page in Mobile Safari to save or copy the image.*

NOTE: It has been our experience that sometimes you have to carry out the just described step a couple of times before the image shows up in the Photo Library.

Working with UIImagePickerController

Now that we have an image saved in the simulator's Photo Library, we need to access the image from within our code. This is where the UIImagePickerController class comes into play. The engineers at Apple crafted a very easy-to-use class to grab images from the Photo Library and use the data for the image within your application as a UIImage object. The following code fragment can be dropped into any UIViewController class that you may have in order to display the UIImagePickerController. In the next section, we will go over how we incorporated this fragment into the sample applications for this chapter.

We begin by checking to see if the Photo Library is an accessible source of images. Next, we create a UIImagePickerController and tell it that we want it to use the Photo Library as its source. Finally, we set ourselves as its delegate and use UIViewController's presentModalViewController method to display it:

```
if ([UIImagePickerController isSourceTypeAvailable:

UIImagePickerControllerSourceTypePhotoLibrary]) {
        UIImagePickerController *uiImagePickerController =
                                        [[UIImagePickerController alloc] init];
        uiImagePickerController.sourceType =

UIImagePickerControllerSourceTypePhotoLibrary;
        uiImagePickerController.delegate = self;
        [self presentModalViewController:uiImagePickerController animated:YES];
        [uiImagePickerController release];
}
```

When working with `UIImagePickerController`, we must set our view controller to be a `UIImagePickerControllerDelegate` and implement the following method:

```
- (void)imagePickerController:(UIImagePickerController *)picker⏎
 didFinishPickingMediaWithInfo:(NSDictionary *)info;

- (void)imagePickerControllerDidCancel:(UIImagePickerController *)picker;
```

When an image is chosen, `UIImagePickerControllerDelegate`'s `imagePickerController: didFinishPickingMediaWithInfo:` method is called. The data for the `UIImage` object is stored in the `NSDictionary` that is passed to this method in the key, `UIImagePickerControllerOriginalImage`. Here's the code to accomplish all this (note that `savedImage` is declared elsewhere):

```
- (void)imagePickerController:(UIImagePickerController *)picker⏎
 didFinishPickingMediaWithInfo:(NSDictionary *)info
{
    [savedImage release];
    savedImage = [info objectForKey:@"UIImagePickerControllerOriginalImage"];
    [self dismissModalViewControllerAnimated:YES];
}
```

It's worth noting that you are responsible for closing the `UIImagePickerController` via `UIViewController`'s `dismissModalViewControllerAnimated` method:

```
- (void)imagePickerControllerDidCancel:(UIImagePickerController *)picker
{
    [self dismissModalViewControllerAnimated:YES];
}
```

At runtime, the `UIImagePickerController` displays a table of the Photo albums on the device, as shown in Figure 8–2.

Figure 8–2. *A table of saved photos presented by UIImagePickerController*

Once you select an album, you can then select a photo, as seen in Figure 8–3.

Figure 8–3. *Tap an image in UIImagePickerController.*

ImagePostController

In the ApiFacebook and ApiTwitter sample projects for this chapter, you will find a new UIViewController entitled ImagePostController. It contains a button that displays the UIImagePickerController when clicked. ImagePostController is a UIImagePickerControllerDelegate; thus, when an image is selected, it saves the image to the UIImage object, savedImage, which is declared in ImagePostController.h. ImagePostController then posts the image to the currently logged in user's Facebook photos or Twitter feed.

Facebook Photo Upload

We covered how to retrieve the UIImage via the delegate callback in the previous section, so now we're going to focus on posting the picture to the user's Facebook photos. The code discussed next is in ImagePostController.m/.h in the ApiFacebook sample application for this chapter.

To do this, we are going to use our old trusted friend, requestWithGraphPath:andParams:andHttpMethod:andDelegate:. We set the graph path to "me/photos" in order to specify that we are targeting the current user's photos. We then pass in a dictionary of arguments. This dictionary is where the data for the picture is stored. The image itself is stored as an object for the key image in the dictionary. If you would like to put a caption with the image, you can also add caption text for the key message. Next, we set the HTTP method to POST since we are posting data. Finally, we assign ourselves as an FBRequestDelegate:

```
- (void)imagePickerController:(UIImagePickerController *)picker

didFinishPickingMediaWithInfo:(NSDictionary *)info
{
    [savedImage release];
    savedImage = [info objectForKey:@"UIImagePickerControllerOriginalImage"];
    [self dismissModalViewControllerAnimated:YES];

    NSMutableDictionary *args = [[NSMutableDictionary alloc] init];
    [args setObject:@"This is a test image" forKey:@"message"];
    [args setObject:savedImage forKey:@"image"];
    [facebook requestWithGraphPath:@"me/photos"
                                 andParams:args
                             andHttpMethod:@"POST"
                                andDelegate:self];
    [args release];
}
```

If successfully posted, FBRequestDelegate's request:didLoad: method will be called. If you log into your Facebook account, you should see a new Photo album with the image contained in it. The name of the Photo album will match the application name you used when you registered your application with Facebook. In the case of this book, the Photo album is entitled, "Beginning iOS Social Development" (see Figure 8–4).

Figure 8–4. *Facebook groups together photos posted from third-party applications.*

Twitter Photo Upload

As is usually the case, the Facebook iOS SDK spoils us rotten. As you can tell from the previous section, it takes a minimal amount of effort to incorporate posting images to a user's Facebook photos. Unfortunately, it's not so simple to accomplish the same task via Twitter, although as of this writing, Twitter is forging a partnership with Photobucket to make posting photo-Tweets less of a hassle for developers. In this chapter we will show you how to post your image to an image-hosting service such as TwitPic (www.twitpic.com/), and then post the URL for the image on twitpic.com to the user's Twitter timeline. The following example code uses TwitPic, but there are a number of other services available, such as twitgoo (www.twitgoo.com/) and yfrog (www.yfrog.com/).

In order to post images to twitpic.com, we must first register on the service's site for a TwitPic API Key. Go to http://dev.twitpic.com/apps/new and log in with your Twitter credentials (see Figures 8–5 and 8–6).

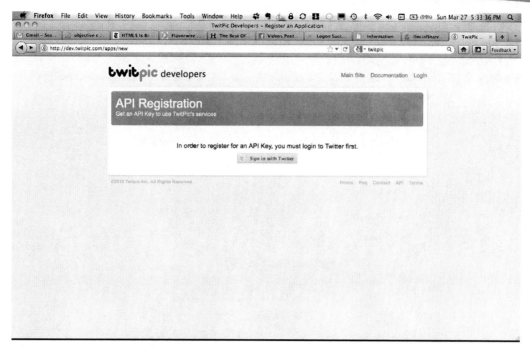

Figure 8–5. *Register for a TwitPic API Key to use the company's service from within an iOS application.*

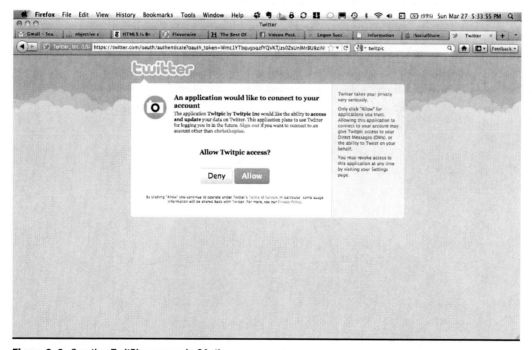

Figure 8–6. *Granting TwitPic access via OAuth*

Next, enter the required information about your application (see Figure 8–7).

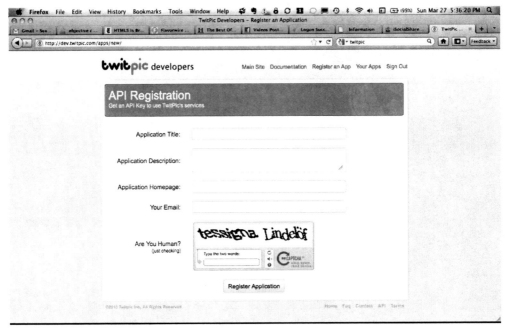

Figure 8–7. *Providing TwitPic with basic application information*

Finally, store the returned TwitPic API Key for use later (see Figure 8–8).

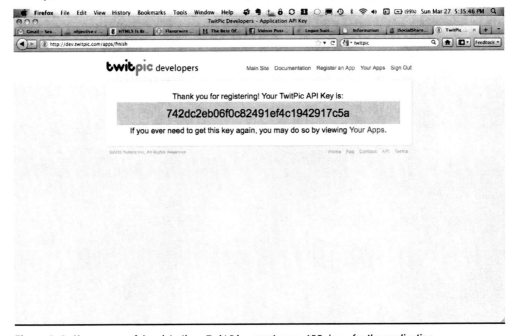

Figure 8–8. *Upon successful registration,* `TwitPic` *creates an* `API key` *for the application.*

As is the norm for such services, TwitPic offers an HTTP-based API to post photos to its site. The API documentation is located at `http://dev.twitpic.com/docs/`. Also, as fate would have it, someone was nice enough to build an iOS Objective-C wrapper around this API and host it on Github (GSTwitPicEngine) at `https://github.com/Gurpartap/GSTwitPicEngine`. GSTwitPicEngine is designed to work with MGTwitterEngine, so it fits nicely (with a few adjustments—more on this to follow) into the setup that we already have. Unfortunately, GSTwitPicEngine depends on a few other pieces of software, and not everything works correctly out-of-the-box. The good news: We were nice enough to smooth out all of the rough edges for you.

So, before we look at how to use GSTwitPicEngine, we have to get some code for other libraries from Github, set up Git submodules, and then add the files to our project. All of the project changes and code are in the `ApiTwitter` project for this chapter and its `ImagePostController.m/.h` files.

GSTwitPicEngine

You can link the GSTwitPicEngine iOS Git repository on Github to your repository using a Git submodule that will reside in a subdirectory entitled `GSTwitPicEngine`:

```
$ git submodule add git://github.com/chrisdannen/GSTwitPicEngine.git GSTwitPicEngine
```

Create a new group in your project entitled `GSTwitPicEngine` and drag `GSTwitPicEngine.m/.h` to it:

Finally, set the following values in `GSTwitPicEngine.h`:

```
-#define TWITTER_OAUTH_CONSUMER_KEY @"<>"
-#define TWITTER_OAUTH_CONSUMER_SECRET @"<>"
-#define TWITPIC_API_KEY @"<>"
```

ASIHTTPRequest

ASIHTTPRequest is an open source library that makes the work of implementing HTTP requests a snap. GSTwitPicEngine uses this library to do its heavy lifting.

Link the `ASIHTTPRequest` Objective-C Git repository on Github to your repository using a Git submodule that will reside in a subdirectory entitled `asi-http-request`:

```
$ git submodule add git://github.com/pokeb/asi-http-request.git asi-http-request
```

Now create a new group in your project entitled `ASIHttpRequest` and drag the necessary files from `./asi-http-request/Classes` to your project. Review the `ApiTwitter` sample project for this chapter for the specific subset of files that you will need.

Next, link your target in your Xcode project against `CFNetwork`, `SystemConfiguration`, `MobileCoreServices`, and `zlib.1.2.3.dylib`. (see Figure 8–9).

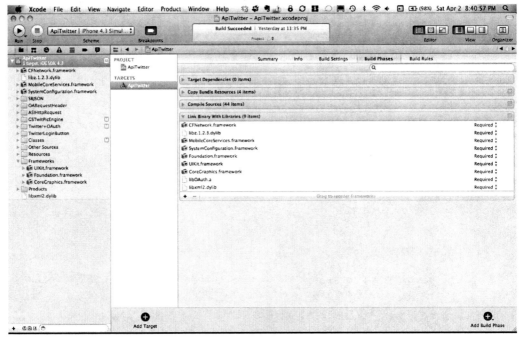

Figure 8–9. *Update linker settings after adding ASIHTTPRequest to the Xcode project.*

SBJSON

SBJSON is one of a few open source JSON parsing Objective-C frameworks. In
./GSTwitPicEngine/GSTwitPicEngine.h, we specify SBJSON as our JSON framework of
choice, so we need to have the files in our project:

```
#define TWITPIC_USE_SBJSON 1
```

Link the SBJSON Objective-C Git repository on Github to your repository using a Git
submodule that will reside in a subdirectory entitled json-framework:

```
$ git submodule add git://github.com/stig/json-framework.git json-framework
```

Next, create a new group in your project entitled SBJSON and drag all of the files from
./json-framework/Classes to your project.

OARequestHeader

Link the OARequestHeader Objective-C Git repository on Github to your repository using
a Git submodule that will reside in a subdirectory entitled OARequestHeader:

```
$ git submodule add git://github.com/chrisdannen/OARequestHeader.git OARequestHeader
```

Create a new group in your project entitled OARequestHeader and drag the files
./OARequestHeader.m/.h to your project.

Now add any updated files to your Git commit (your Xcode project file, for instance), and then commit and push your changes to Github.

Post a Photo

We're finally set up to throw some code in our sample project that will post a link to a photo to a user's Twitter feed. Most of the relevant changes are in `ImagePostController.m/.h`; you can also find a couple of small changes in `AppDelegate.m`. In this section, we will focus on the changes in `ImagePostController.m/h`.

We begin by declaring a number of objects that we will need in `ImagePostController.h`:

```
#import <UIKit/UIKit.h>
#import "GSTwitPicEngine.h"

@interface ImagePostController : UIViewController <UINavigationControllerDelegate,
                                        UIImagePickerControllerDelegate,
GSTwitPicEngineDelegate> {
    UIButton *twitterButton;
    UIImage *savedImage;
    GSTwitPicEngine *twitpicEngine;
}

@end
```

We need an instance of GSTwitPicEngine to post a photo to twitpic.com. We also need to save the returned image, and we need to declare ourselves as a GSTwitPicEngineDelegate in order to be notified when GSTwitPicEngine has completed posting the photo to twitpic.com.

Figure 8–10. *An image uploaded to TwitPic from an iOS application*

When the `ImagePostController`'s view is loaded, we need to create and initialize the `GSTwitPicEngine` instance:

```
- (void)loadView
{
    [super loadView];

    twitterButton = [UIButton buttonWithType:UIButtonTypeRoundedRect];
    twitterButton.frame = CGRectMake(127.0f, 68.0f, 72.0f, 37.0f);
    [twitterButton setTitle:@"Twitter" forState:UIControlStateNormal];
    [twitterButton addTarget:self
                                action:@selector(twitterButtonClick:)
                forControlEvents:UIControlEventTouchUpInside];
    [self.view addSubview:twitterButton];

    twitpicEngine = [GSTwitPicEngine twitpicEngineWithDelegate:self] retain];
    [twitpicEngine setAccessToken:[sa_OAuthTwitterEngine accessToken]];
}
```

Note that we set ourselves as the `GSTwitPicEngine`'s delegate and that we pass our accessToken from our main Twitter engine to GSTwitPicEngine, so that it has the necessary OAuth params. Note that you will first have to log in to Twitter from the Login tab when running the sample application.

When an image is chosen via the `UIImagePickerController`, we can then use `GSTwitPicEngine`'s `uploadPicture:withMessage:` method to post the image to twitpic.com:

```
- (void)imagePickerController:(UIImagePickerController *)picker↵
  didFinishPickingMediaWithInfo:(NSDictionary *)info
{
    [savedImage release];
    savedImage = [info objectForKey:@"UIImagePickerControllerOriginalImage"];
    [self dismissModalViewControllerAnimated:YES];

    // This message is supplied back in success delegate call in request's userInfo.
    [twitpicEngine uploadPicture:savedImage  withMessage:@"Hello world!"];
}
```

If the photo is uploaded successfully to twitpic.com, `GSTwitPicEngineDelegate`'s `twitpicDidFinishUpload:` method will be called with an `NSDictionary` of response information:

```
- (void)twitpicDidFinishUpload:(NSDictionary *)response
{
    NSLog(@"TwitPic finished uploading: %@", response);

    // [response objectForKey:@"parsedResponse"] gives an NSDictionary of the
    // response one of the parsing libraries was available.
    // Otherwise, use [[response objectForKey:@"request"]
    // objectForKey:@"responseString"] to parse yourself.

    if ([[[response objectForKey:@"request"] userInfo] objectForKey:@"message"] > 0 &&
                                [[response objectForKey:@"parsedResponse"]
count] > 0) {
        NSString *update = [NSString stringWithFormat:@"%@ %@",
                [[response objectForKey:@"parsedResponse"] objectForKey:@"text"],
```

```
            [[response objectForKey:@"parsedResponse"] objectForKey:@"url"]];
        [sa_OAuthTwitterEngine sendUpdate:update];
    }
}
```

The returned response dictionary contains another dictionary for the key `parsedResponse` that contains the information we need to make a post to twitter.com:

```
TwitPic finished uploading: {
    parsedResponse =        {
        height = 128;
        id = 4ga09b;
        size = 15551;
        text = "Hello world!";
        timestamp = "Sun, 03 Apr 2011 01:04:55 +0000";
        type = jpg;
        url = "http://twitpic.com/4ga09b";
        user =         {
            id = 103384600;
            "screen_name" = christhepiss;
        };
        width = 366;
    };
    request = "<ASIFormDataRequest: 0x50a4c00>";
}
```

We grab the values for the `text` and `url` keys from the `parsedResponse` dictionary, and we call our Twitter engine's `sendUpdate:` method with the values to make the final post to Twitter, as seen in Figure 8–11.

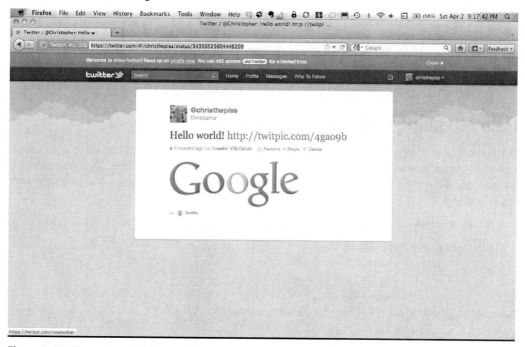

Figure 8–11. *The end result: A Tweet with a link to an image hosted on TwitPic*

Offline Paradigm and Background Processing

For an iOS app, working with data that is retrieved or synchronized from a server can make your app vulnerable to broken connections. To enable offline operation, store the data on the local device, so that the app can still present the data, even if 3G or WiFi is unavailable. If you are interested in hacking together a fully-capable Twitter or Facebook iOS app—or you just want to learn some additional techniques—then this section is required reading.

In this section, we will build a simple Twitter application that can retrieve Twitter status updates and store them on the device. This way, there is always data to display, even if the device is offline. The sample application is entitled OfflineTwitter, and it can be found in the Chapter8/OfflineTwitter directory of the Git repository.

If you are familiar with the Model-View-Controller (MVC) programming paradigm, then you will notice that what we are actually doing is building the Model portion of this paradigm. The user interface (or View) always retrieves its data from the Model. When new data is received from the server, the data is stored in the Model. Next, the View is refreshed, and it grabs the latest data from the Model.

One nice facility for storing data that is available to iOS applications is *Core Data*. Although we don't recommend it for large data sets (we recommend SQLite for those), Core Data can be useful for doing proof-of-concept work and helping to design the API for your Model. We will go through all of the steps for setting up the API for the Model using Core Data; however, if you've never worked with Core Data on iOS, we also recommend reading the following or keeping this link available as a good quick reference:

```
http://developer.apple.com/library/ios/#DOCUMENTATION/DataManagement/
Conceptual/iPhoneCoreData01/Introduction/Introduction.html#//apple_ref/doc/uid/
TP40008305-CH1-SW1
```

Data Modeling with TwitterDataStore

One of the best things to do when working on a data model for an application is to think about the high level operations that the data model will have to perform. To keep things simple, we would like our Twitter data model for our sample application to support three main actions:

- Return the current set of stored Tweets.

- Delete all of the stored Tweets.

- Store Tweets.

For our sample application, we have defined the class, TwitterDataStore. Go to the sample project and click TwitterDataStore.h in the Model folder:

```
@interface TwitterDataStore : NSObject {
}
```

```
- (NSArray*)tweets;
- (void)deleteTweets;
- (void)synchronizeTweets:(NSArray*)tweets;

@end
```

Now that we have the basic interfaces in place, we need them to perform their required actions. This is where Core Data comes into play. What follows are the steps necessary to get your application to use Core Data.

First, we have to add a Core Data model file to our project. The Core Data model is where we create the different entities that we want to represent and store for our application. From Xcode's main menu, go to File ➤ New ➤ New File...

Choose Core Data in the iOS section, and then choose the Data Model file type and give the file an appropriate name (see Figure 8–12).

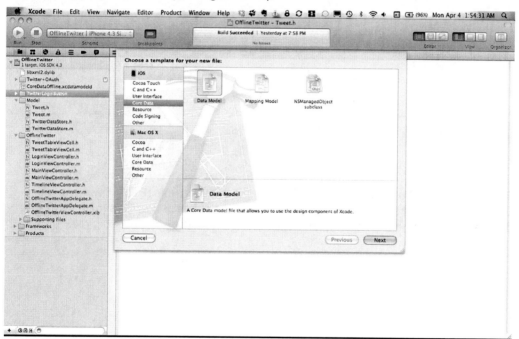

Figure 8–12. *Add a Core Data object model to the application's Xcode project.*

Next, link your project against the Core Data framework (see Figure 8–13).

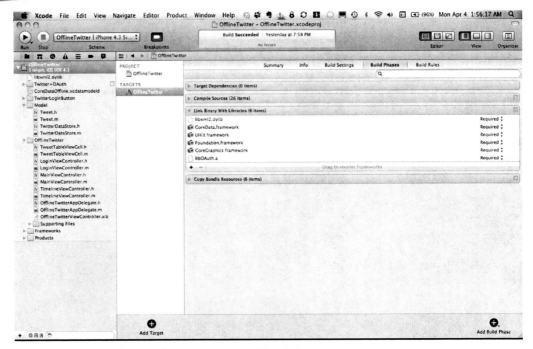

Figure 8–13. *Updated linker settings to support use of Core Data*

Now that we have our Core Data model in place, we need to add an entity to it. Since our application is supposed to store Tweets offline, let's add a Tweet entity. Select the Core Data model file in your Xcode project (in the sample project, this file is entitled CoreDataOffline.xcdatamodeld) in order to show the model in Xcode's main window. At the bottom of the model window, click the Add Entity button—it has a big plus sign on it (see Figure 8–14).

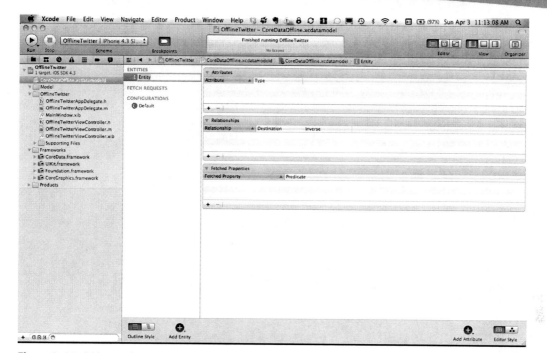

Figure 8–14. *Add an entity to the data model.*

Next, rename this entity to Tweet (see Figure 8–15).

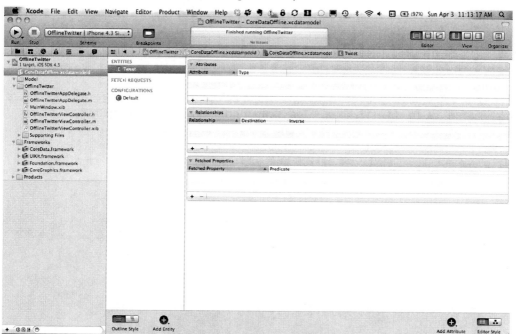

Figure 8–15. *The Tweet entity in the data model*

Actual Tweets from Twitter have a lot of information associated with them; however, this is a simple application, so we are only going to store the id and the actual text content of each Tweet. The goal here is just to show the overall concept of setting up a model. Make sure that the Tweet entity is selected, and then click the + sign in the Attributes section to add a new attribute (see Figure 8–16). Name this attribute id and set its type to Integer 64. Next, add another attribute entitled text and set its type to String.

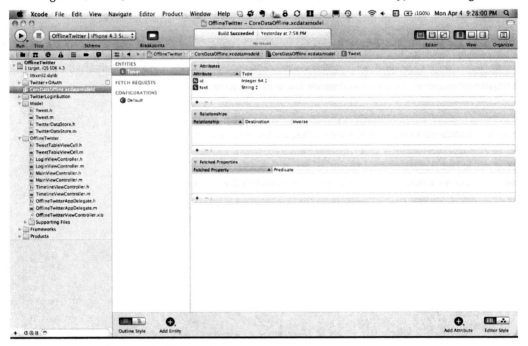

Figure 8–16. *Add attributes to the Tweet entity.*

The final step to setting up our data model is to create actual Tweet Objective-C classes that map to our Tweet entity in our Core Data model, so that we can instantiate actual Tweet objects in our application code and keep them in memory (see Figure 8–17). Add a new file to your project of the NSManagedObject type subclass (in Xcode's New File dialog, select Core Data under the iOS section to get to this option) and click Next.

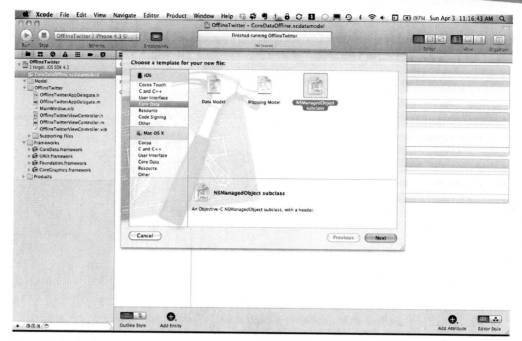

Figure 8–17. *Add a class to the Xcode project to associate with the Tweet object in the data model.*

In the following dialog, check the box next to the Tweet entity to associate it with the Tweet class that we created (see Figure 8–18).

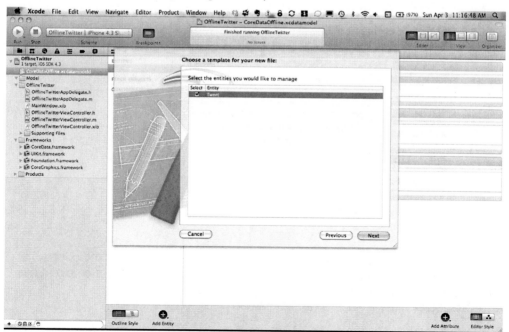

Figure 8–18. *Choose the Tweet entity to associate with the new class.*

When we examine the contents of the Tweet.h and Tweet.m files, we find that they are very sparse. They simply offer the ability to get and set values on the attributes for a Tweet entity in our Core Data model:

Tweet.h

```
@interface Tweet : NSManagedObject {
@private
}
@property (nonatomic, retain) NSNumber * id;
@property (nonatomic, retain) NSString * text;

@end
```

Tweet.m

```
@implementation Tweet
@dynamic id;
@dynamic text;

@end
```

Now that we've gotten some additional setup out of the way, recall that TwitterDataStore is a class that provides a high level interface for obtaining stored information on the device. The actual storing of the data (in this case, the Tweet entities) within TwitterDataStore is performed using Core Data APIs. Core Data consists of a number of classes that work together to provide a convenient way to store and retrieve information, so we have to add these classes to TwitterDataStore.h:

```
@class NSManagedObjectContext;
@class NSManagedObjectModel;
@class NSPersistentStoreCoordinator;
@interface TwitterDataStore : NSObject {
}

@property (nonatomic, retain, readonly) NSManagedObjectContext *managedObjectContext;
@property (nonatomic, retain, readonly) NSManagedObjectModel *managedObjectModel;
@property (nonatomic, retain, readonly) NSPersistentStoreCoordinator↵
 *persistentStoreCoordinator;

- (void)saveContext;
- (NSURL *)applicationDocumentsDirectory;

- (NSArray*)tweets;
- (void)deleteTweets;
- (void)synchronizeTweets:(NSArray*)tweets;

@end
```

The most important of these classes is NSManagedObjectContext. Under the covers via Core Data magic, the NSManagedObjectContext class manages the collection of entities in the model. The creation of the NSManagedObjectContext owned by our TwitterDataStore class is handled in the method managedObjectContext:

```
/**
 Returns the managed object context for the application.
```

```
If the context doesn't already exist, it is created and bound to the persistent store
coordinator for the application.
*/
- (NSManagedObjectContext *)managedObjectContext
{
    if (__managedObjectContext != nil)
    {
        return __managedObjectContext;
    }

    NSPersistentStoreCoordinator *coordinator = [self persistentStoreCoordinator];
    if (coordinator != nil)
    {
        __managedObjectContext = [[NSManagedObjectContext alloc] init];
        [__managedObjectContext setPersistentStoreCoordinator:coordinator];
    }
    return __managedObjectContext;
}
```

The NSManagedObjectContext class is given an NSPersistentStoreCoordinator object that is responsible for managing the lifecycle of the context and creates a managed object model:

```
/**
 Returns the persistent store coordinator for the application.
 If the coordinator doesn't already exist, it is created and the application's store
 added to it.
 */
- (NSPersistentStoreCoordinator *)persistentStoreCoordinator
{
    if (__persistentStoreCoordinator != nil)
    {
        return __persistentStoreCoordinator;
    }

    NSURL *storeURL = [[self applicationDocumentsDirectory]↩
URLByAppendingPathComponent:@"CoreDataOffline.sqlite"];

    NSError *error = nil;
    __persistentStoreCoordinator = [[NSPersistentStoreCoordinator alloc]
        initWithManagedObjectModel:[self managedObjectModel]];
    if (![__persistentStoreCoordinator addPersistentStoreWithType:NSSQLiteStoreType
            configuration:nil
            URL:storeURL
            options:nil
            error:&error])
    {
        /*
        */
        NSLog(@"Unresolved error %@, %@", error, [error userInfo]);
        abort();
    }

    return __persistentStoreCoordinator;
}
```

You need to replace the preceding implementation with your own code to handle the error appropriately.

> **NOTE:** Using abort() causes the application to generate a crash log and terminate. You should not use this function in a shipping application, although it may be useful during development. If it is not possible to recover from the error, display an alert panel that instructs the user to quit the application by pressing the Home button.

Typical reasons for an error here include the following:

- The persistent store is not accessible.
- The schema for the persistent store is incompatible with the current managed object model.

Check the error message to determine what the actual problem was.

If the persistent store is not accessible, there is typically something wrong with the file path. Often, a file URL is pointing into the application's resources directory instead of a writeable directory.

If you encounter schema incompatibility errors during development, you can reduce their frequency by doing the following:

- Simply deleting the existing store:

  ```
  [[NSFileManager defaultManager] removeItemAtURL:storeURL error:nil]
  ```

- Performing automatic lightweight migration by passing the following dictionary as the options parameter:

  ```
  [NSDictionary dictionaryWithObjectsAndKeys:
      [NSNumber numberWithBool:YES],
      NSMigratePersistentStoresAutomaticallyOption,
      [NSNumber numberWithBool:YES],
      NSInferMappingModelAutomaticallyOption, nil];
  ```

Lightweight migration will only work for a limited set of schema changes; consult "Core Data Model Versioning and Data Migration Programming Guide" for details:

This is how the managed object model is created:

```
/**
 Returns the managed object model for the application.
 If the model doesn't already exist, it is created from the application's model.
 */
- (NSManagedObjectModel *)managedObjectModel
{
    if (__managedObjectModel != nil) {
        return __managedObjectModel;
    }
    NSURL *modelURL = [[NSBundle mainBundle] URLForResource:@"CoreDataOffline"
        withExtension:@"momd"];
```

```
    __managedObjectModel = [[NSManagedObjectModel alloc]
initWithContentsOfURL:modelURL];
    return __managedObjectModel;
}
```

We also have a helper method for getting the location of the application's Documents directory:

```
/**
 Returns the URL to the application's Documents directory.
 */
- (NSURL *)applicationDocumentsDirectory
{
    return [[[NSFileManager defaultManager] URLsForDirectory:NSDocumentDirectory

inDomains:NSUserDomainMask] lastObject];
}
```

We encourage you to read up on some of these Core Data APIs. We hope that you've found this information useful, but delving deeper into this subject is beyond the scope of this book, and it's time to get on with the show!

Updating the View from the Model

Before we finish going over the final details of the implementation of TwitterDataStore, it is beneficial to see how it will be used and accessed from the user interface of the application. The user interface for displaying the Tweets from TwitterDataStore is a UITableViewController class entitled TimelineViewController. This class simply shows the main text for each Tweet in its UITableViewCells, as shown in Figure 8–19.

The grass always seems gre...

"@JonOliverMusic: #TheMai...

I hear new orleans in every...

From Search Engines To Lu...

RT @SnareForce: @atrak I...

Love u Toronto.....

Male Fertility Determined by...

RT @JacinaLoveDTF: Talib...

The A in A-Trak stands for...

| Login | Tweets |

Figure 8–19. *Stored Tweets displayed in a basic user interface*

Before we show the technical details of how it's implemented, let's list what `TimelineViewController` does:

- When loaded, it asks the `TwitterDataStore` for any Tweets that it contains, saves the results in an `NSArray`, and submits a request to Twitter.com via MGTwitterEngine for the latest set of Tweets from the currently logged in user's Twitter timeline.

- If any Tweets are received from Twitter.com via MGTwitterEngine's delegate methods, then the new Tweets are saved in the `TwitterDataStore` on a background thread.

- Once the Tweets are saved in the `TwitterDataStore`, the table is refreshed on the main thread.

- When the table is refreshed, for each item in the `NSArray` of Tweets, it creates a `TweetTableViewCell` and sets the text of the cell to the text of the associated Tweet.

If we examine the definition of `TimelineViewController` in `TimelineViewController.h`, we see that it owns an `NSArray` of Tweets and a `TwitterDataStore`:

```
#import <UIKit/UIKit.h>

@class TwitterDataStore;
@interface TimelineViewController : UITableViewController {
```

```
        NSArray            *tweets;
        TwitterDataStore   *twitterDataStore;
}

@end
```

In `TimelineViewController.m`, we create the `TwitterDataStore`, retrieve any Tweets from the `TwitterDataStore`, make a request for new Tweets, and set ourselves up to be notified when the request completes in the `viewDidLoad` method:

```
- (void)viewDidLoad {
    [super viewDidLoad];

    twitterDataStore = [[TwitterDataStore alloc] init];
    tweets = [[twitterDataStore tweets] retain];

    NSString *identifier = [sa_OAuthTwitterEngine getHomeTimeline];

    //listen for a notification with the name of the identifier
    [[NSNotificationCenter defaultCenter]
                            addObserver:self

selector:@selector(twitterTimelineRequestDidComplete:)
                                    name:identifier
                                  object:nil];
}
```

We need to notify other parts of our application when our request for new Tweets has completed. To do this, we update `statusesReceived:forRequest:` in our delegate to store the returned array of Tweets as the value for the key Tweets in an `NSDictionary` that we set as the `userInfo` of a notification:

```
(void)statusesReceived:(NSArray *)statuses
        -     forRequest:(NSString *)connectionIdentifier {
        NSLog(@"Status received = %@, %@", connectionIdentifier, [statuses
description]);

        NSArray *objects = :[NSArray arrayWithObjects:statuses, nil];
        NSArray *keys = [NSArray arrayWithObjects:@"tweets", nil];
        NSDictionary *userInfoDictionary = [NSDictionary dictionaryWithObjects:objects

forKeys:keys];
        [[NSNotificationCenter defaultCenter]
                postNotificationName:connectionIdentifier
                        object:self
                          userInfo:userInfoDictionary];

        NSDictionary *dictionary = [statuses objectAtIndex:0];
        if (dictionary) {
                NSString *twitterID = [dictionary objectForKey:@"id"];
                NSLog(@"TwitterID = %@", twitterID);
        }
}
```

When the preceding method posts a notification that the request for Tweets has completed, `TimelineViewController`'s `twitterTimelineRequestDidComplete:` method is called via `NSNotificationCenter`. Using `NSObject`'s performSelectorInBackground:withObject: method, TimelineViewController's synchronizeTweets: method is executed on a background thread and is passed the Tweets array from the NSDictionary in the notification:

```
- (void)twitterTimelineRequestDidComplete:(NSNotification*)notification {

    [[NSNotificationCenter defaultCenter] removeObserver:self];

    [self performSelectorInBackground:@selector(synchronizeTweets:)
                           withObject:[notification.userInfo
                          objectForKey:@"tweets"]];
}
```

TwitterDataStore's synchronizeTweets: method is designed to emit a notification when it has completed the synchronization process (more on this to follow). Therefore, in TimelineViewController's synchronizeTweets: method, we set ourselves up to receive a notification when TwitterDataStore has completed its task. Once that happens, we start the synchronization process:

```
- (void)synchronizeTweets:(NSArray*)newTweets
{
        //listen for a notification with the name of the identifier
        [[NSNotificationCenter defaultCenter] addObserver:self

selector:@selector(tweetsDidSynchronize:)

name:@"tweetsDidSynchronize"

object:nil];

        [twitterDataStore synchronizeTweets:newTweets];
}
```

When TwitterDataStore completes the synchronization process, it will emit a notification via NSNotificationCenter, and TimelineViewController's tweetsDidSynchronize: method will be executed, calling refreshUI on the main thread to get the latest Tweets from the TwitterDataStore and updating the table in the user interface. A note on threading: We always recommend processing or synchronizing data on a background thread, so that the user interface remains responsive. However, if you emit a notification or execute a delegate callback method from the background thread, the execution will still be in the background thread. If your user interface needs to be updated, we recommend using NSObject's performSelectorOnMainThread: withObject:waitUntilDone: method to refresh the user interface on the main thread of execution:

```
- (void)tweetsDidSynchronize:(NSNotification*)notification
{
    [[NSNotificationCenter defaultCenter] removeObserver:self];

    //update the UI on the main thread
    [self performSelectorOnMainThread:@selector(refreshUI)
                          withObject:nil
                       waitUntilDone:YES];

}
```

Here is the code that actually refreshes the user interface and associates the information for a given Tweet with its associated UITableViewCell:

```
- (void)refreshUI
{
    [tweets release];
    tweets = [[twitterDataStore tweets] retain];

    [self.tableView reloadData];
}

// Customize the appearance of table view cells.
- (UITableViewCell *)tableView:(UITableView *)tableView
        cellForRowAtIndexPath:(NSIndexPath *)indexPath {

    static NSString *CellIdentifier = @"Cell";

    TweetTableViewCell *cell =
        (TweetTableViewCell*)[tableView
dequeueReusableCellWithIdentifier:CellIdentifier];
    if (cell == nil) {
        cell = [[[TweetTableViewCell alloc] initWithStyle:UITableViewCellStyleDefault

reuseIdentifier:CellIdentifier] autorelease];
    }

    // Configure the cell...
    Tweet *tweet = [tweets objectAtIndex:[indexPath row]];
    cell.tweet = tweet;

    return cell;
}
```

TimelineViewController uses TwitterDataStore to obtain and store the data that it displays, so let's take a look at how TwitterDataStore uses Core Data to store and retrieve Tweets. Before TwitterDataStore can give us back Tweets, we have to give it some Tweets to store. TwitterDataStore stores Tweets in its synchronizeTweets: method, which takes an array of Tweets as its only argument.

This synchronization method is a bit barbaric. The first thing that it does is delete any stored Tweets via TwitterDataStore's deleteTweets method. It then loops through the Tweets that were passed in, creates a new Tweet for each one, initializes the Tweet's data, and saves it to the Core Data model.

Let's look at this in more detail. Remember that MGTwitterEngine returns an array of Tweets and that each Tweet in the array is represented by an NSDictionary object of key/value pairs with all of the information about the Tweet. When we loop through the array of Tweets, we use a nice for-loop mechanism available in Objective-C:

```
for (NSDictionary *tweetDictionary in tweets) {
}
```

In short, this for-loop says that we will execute the body of the for-loop for each of the elements in the tweets array. Each time the body of the for-loop is executed, the next element in the tweets array is stored in an NSDictionary object (since each element is an

NSDictionary) entitled tweetDictionary. We can reference this element within the body of the for-loop.

For each of the Tweets in the array, we create a new Tweet object via NSEntityDescription's insertNewObjectForEntityForName:inManagedObjectContext: method. Passing Tweet as the entity name has Core Data create a new unpopulated instance of the Tweet class stored in the managed object context. We also supply our managed object context. Next, we set the value of the text attribute of the Tweet and the id value of the Tweet (note the use of NSNumberFormatter to convert an NSString object to an NSNumber object). As the final step, we tell the managed object context to save its state to disk. Failing to call save on the managed object context would result in no data being permanently stored in our Core Data model. Before exiting the method, we post a notification, so that other parts of our application can perform any necessary actions when all of the new Tweets are stored in the model (i.e., we update the user interface):

```
- (void)synchronizeTweets:(NSArray*)tweets
{
    NSAutoreleasePool *autoReleasePool = [[NSAutoreleasePool alloc] init];

    @synchronized(self) {
        [self deleteTweets];

        for (NSDictionary *tweetDictionary in tweets) {
            Tweet *tweet = (Tweet *)[NSEntityDescription↵
    insertNewObjectForEntityForName:@"Tweet"↵
    inManagedObjectContext:self.managedObjectContext];

            NSNumberFormatter * f = [[NSNumberFormatter alloc] init];
            NSNumber * tweetId = [f numberFromString:[tweetDictionary
    objectForKey:@"id"]];
            [tweet setId:tweetId];
            [f release];

            NSString *text = [tweetDictionary objectForKey:@"text"];
            [tweet setText:text];
        }

        NSError *error = nil;
        if (![self.managedObjectContext save:&error]) {
            // Handle the error.
        }
    }

    // post a notification that the tweets are available
    // have responder update itself on the main thread
    [[NSNotificationCenter defaultCenter]
        postNotificationName:@"tweetsDidSynchronize"
                          object:self
                        userInfo:nil];

    [autoReleasePool release];
}
```

When it comes time to fetch the Tweets from our Core Data model, we use the Core Data class, NSFetchRequest. NSFetchRequest takes an entity description (Tweet, in this case) and a managed object context. Next, we retrieve the Tweets from our Core Data model by calling the managed object context's executeFetchRequest: method and passing it the NSFetchRequest object that we initialized. The array of Tweets is then returned from the method. Note that, if you want to sort the results of the fetch request from the managed object context, you need to create and set an NSSortDescriptor for the NSFetchRequest. In this example, we initialize an NSSortDescriptor that will sort the returned array of Tweets in descending order, based on the value of the id attribute of the Tweets:

```objc
- (NSArray*)tweets
{
    NSMutableArray *tweets = nil;

    @synchronized(self) {
        NSFetchRequest *request = [[NSFetchRequest alloc] init];
        NSEntityDescription *entity =
                                    [NSEntityDescription entityForName:@"Tweet"
inManagedObjectContext:self.managedObjectContext];
        [request setEntity:entity];

        NSSortDescriptor *sortDescriptor = [[NSSortDescriptor alloc] initWithKey:@"id"
ascending:NO];
        NSArray *sortDescriptors = [[NSArray alloc] initWithObjects:sortDescriptor,
nil];
        [request setSortDescriptors:sortDescriptors];
        [sortDescriptors release];
        [sortDescriptor release];

        NSError *error = nil;
        NSMutableArray *mutableFetchResults =
                [[self.managedObjectContext executeFetchRequest:request error:&error]
mutableCopy];
        if (mutableFetchResults == nil) {
            // Handle the error.
        }

        tweets = [mutableFetchResults retain];
        [mutableFetchResults release];
        [request release];
    }

    return tweets;
}
```

To delete all of the Tweets in our Core Data model, we fetch all of the Tweets that are currently stored in our model, loop through them one-by-one, tell the managed object context to delete the given Tweet, and then save the managed object context to commit the results to disk:

```objc
- (void)deleteTweets
{
```

```
@synchronized(self) {
    NSArray *tweets = [self tweets];
    for (Tweet *tweet in tweets) {
        [self.managedObjectContext deleteObject:tweet];
    }

    // Commit the change.

    NSError *error = nil;

    if (![self.managedObjectContext save:&error]) {
        // Handle the error.
    }
}
}
```

Conclusion

We covered some really interesting new ground in this chapter with respect to uploading photos and building a simple data model for our application using Core Data. There are other options available for building a data model—such as SQLite—so we recommend you explore other ways of storing data for offline or quick retrieval within your application. Be aware that you may want to build some smarts into your model that limit the amount of storage that your application uses. For instance, you may want to store only a certain number of recent Tweets or perhaps only Tweets within the last 12 hours.

In the next chapter, we will go over different location-based scenarios; explain how to integrate location information into your app, as well as with social networking data for Facebook and Twitter; and also continue to refine how we integrate these services into our application by setting up a stand alone controller that we can use anywhere within our app.

Chapter 9

Working with Location Awareness and Streaming Data

This chapter covers the nuts and bolts of using location on iOS with Facebook and Twitter. We'll also discuss working with streaming APIs.

One of the main trends to have emerged within social applications is adding a location context to user experiences. In the worlds of Facebook and Twitter, this involves letting users *check in* to places on Facebook or search for nearby Tweets on Twitter, as well as a host of other scenarios. We're going to walk you through the ins and outs of using iOS's CoreLocation and MapKit libraries to incorporate location and maps into your application, and then use the location information from these libraries to show some location-based features of Facebook and Twitter.

Here, There, and Everywhere

At first glance, incorporating location information into your application seems like a trivial task; however, there are a number of considerations to make with respect to privacy for your users, power/battery conservation on a device, and the CoreLocation and MapKit APIs. The sample applications for this chapter incorporate all of the techniques that follow. Since CoreLocation and Map Kit are themselves extensive APIs, it's necessary to run through the core features that these APIs provide and highlight some new features that debuted iOS 4.0. After that, this chapter will delve into the Facebook and Twitter APIs for location.

Location Privacy, Disclosure, and Opt-Out

As much as we all love sharing information on social networking sites such as Twitter and Facebook, there are times when we don't always want to share certain things about ourselves. One of these things is location. We are all pretty easy going with sharing a photo on a website; however, it's an entirely different thing to share a photo if it also includes information about where the photo was taken. Similarly, it's one thing to use a feature of a site that lets you tell your friends where you are, but something else entirely if the site automatically tells your friends where you are—without letting you turn off the automatic updates. In the latter case, you will probably not be a big fan of that site.

So why is this? Why do we guard our location so closely and want to have so much control over whom we share it with and when? Ultimately, it's about protecting ourselves from some of the unpleasant aspects of human nature, such as jealousy, stalking, and, potentially, physical harm. For as much as social networking sites like Facebook and Twitter can bring out the best in human nature, they can also sometimes bring out the worst.

A severe yet all-too-common example of this darker side of human nature occurs when a person is in a relationship with someone who is physically abusive towards her. She may be too afraid to obtain a restraining order and want to hide her physical location as much as possible—including on social networking sites. This is probably a worst case scenario, but one worth considering since you never want to break the trust of your users (or even the law in some places).

When planning to employ your user's location within your application, it's always best to follow these rules:

- Let users opt out of having your application use their location.

- Make full disclosure of how you intend to use location information.

- Let users destroy any past records of their location that your application stores locally or remotely.

Fortunately, iOS itself has all of the plumbing built in to allow or disallow the use of its location services on a per-app basis. It also automatically prompts a user for permission to use location the first time that your application runs and starts CoreLocation services. This is key because it prompts the user immediately. It's sometimes tempting to tuck things like this away in a Settings screen within your application, but we strongly advise against that approach for location-related settings. In this case on iOS, it's a bit of a non-issue since it is out of your hands as a developer. In case you are new to iOS, the standard prompt includes the name of the application requesting permission to use location services and shows Don't Allow and OK buttons, as shown in Figure 9–1.

Figure 9–1. *The iOS location permission prompt*

Once the user makes his selection, iOS stores it and doesn't prompt the user for it again. This is a great feature of iOS because it standardizes the look and feel of this prompt, giving users a consistent experience and saving individual developers from implementing all of this logic themselves. If the user chooses not to allow an application location access, attempts to obtain the location from within iOS code result in a location unavailable error.

Another great feature of iOS's implementation of location services is that it doesn't require you to do anything in your application to account for the fact that users often change their minds or may temporarily restrict your application from using location services. For instance, if a user initially granted your application permission to use location services, but no longer wants to grant your application such permission, she can go to the main Settings application on her device and use the Location Services section to turn off location services for all applications device-wide or on an application-by-application basis (see Figures 9–2 and 9–3).

Figure 9–2. *The iOS Settings application*

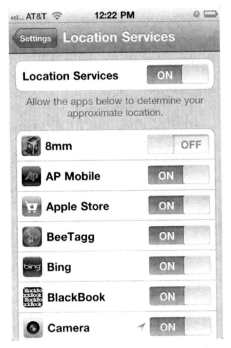

Figure 9–3. *The iOS Location Services settings*

iOS also has another nifty feature that lets you reset the display of the prompt that asks users of applications if they want to grant the application use of location services. This is a device-wide setting that will revoke the permission to use locations services for all applications on the device. This setting is accessed via the main Settings application on an iOS device under General ➤ Reset (as seen in Figure 9–4).

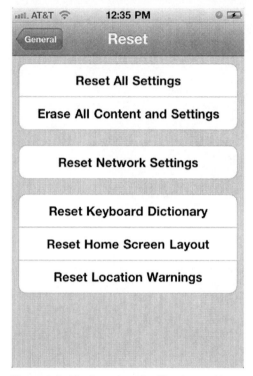

Figure 9–4. *The Reset Location Warnings setting*

Figure 9–5. *Confirmation from the system to reset location warnings*

If you choose Reset Warnings (see Figure 9–5), run the main Maps application on the device, choose OK at the location prompt, and then go back to the main Location Services setting screen, you will see the screen shown in Figure 9–6.

Figure 9–6. *The Locations Services settings after resetting warnings and running the Maps application*

As we mentioned before, prompting users to opt in or out of using their location is just one of three essential parts of working with location. If it's unclear how your application will use a user's location, then we highly recommend displaying your own prompt or information screen with additional information. As of iOS 4, iOS makes this easy to do, and we will show you how in the following sections. If you store location history within your application on the user's device, you should also provide a Settings screen that lets the user flush this history. Alternatively, you could provide a way to have your application only keep records for the past week, automatically flushing this history for the user based on a setting.

Now that we've covered the device side of things and what to understand with respect to location and privacy within your iOS application, let's take a quick look at what Twitter and Facebook do on their ends with respect to location.

Twitter and Facebook have come a long way with respect to the three best practices that we mentioned previously. Let's take a quick look at both of their approaches.

Facebook Places

Facebook has followed Foursquare's lead and created the Places feature. When you *check in* from a place, you are letting your friends on Facebook know where you are and what you are doing, such as eating at a particular restaurant or attending a concert. For a quick overview of what the Places feature can do, check out this link:

www.facebook.com/places/

Note that Facebook lets you control whether or not friends can see where you check into. We recommend reading Facebook's FAQ for a full account of how it deals with privacy:

www.facebook.com/help/?page=18839

In short, you can control whether or not you show up in the Here Now section of a Facebook place page when you check into that place. Do so by going to the Privacy settings section on Facebook (see Figure 9–7).

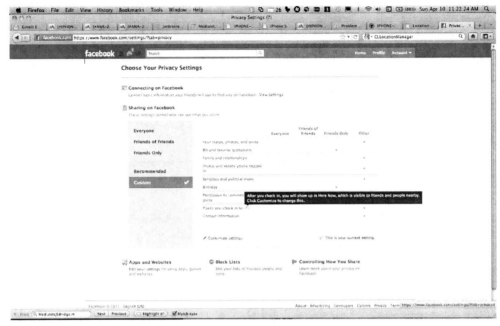

Figure 9–7. *Control whether Facebook check-ins display in the Here Now section.*

Choose Customize settings, and then, under Things I share, choose whether you want
Everyone, Friends and Networks, Friends of Friends, or Friends Only to see your check-ins.
You can also create your own custom setting for Places you check into (see Figure 9–8).

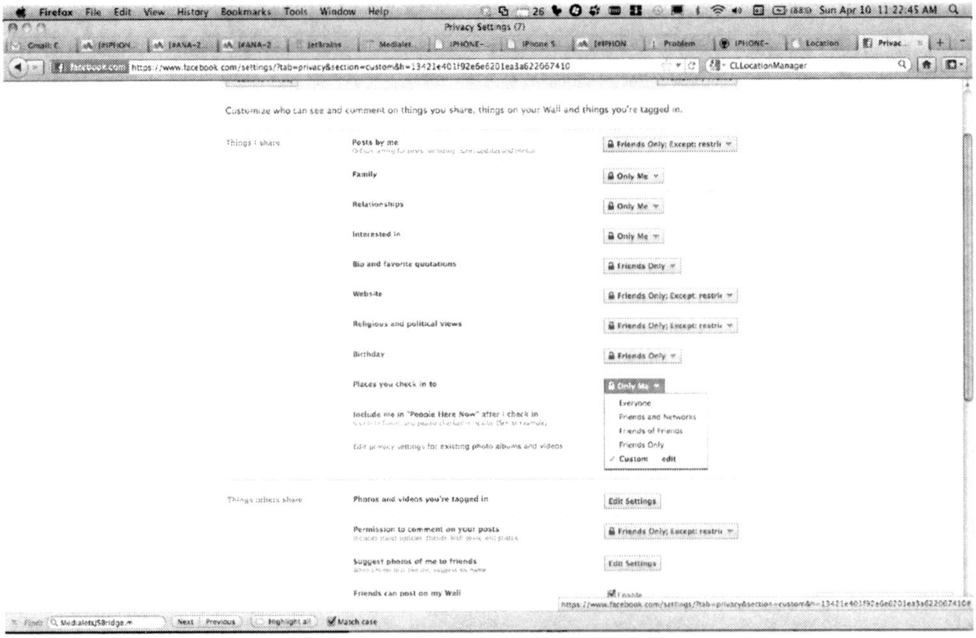

Figure 9–8. *Customize Facebook's check-in settings.*

In this same section, you can adjust the setting for this option:

`Include me in "People Here Now" after you check in`

Clicking the See example link displays what it looks like when you are shown on People Here Now (see Figure 9–9).

Figure 9–9. *The Facebook People Here Now example*

In the Things others share section, you can edit the settings for this option (see Figure 9–10):

Friends can check me in to Places

Figure 9–10. *Facebook lets users give friends permission to check them into places.*

In the Apps and Websites section of the Privacy settings, you can revoke access to Places to applications that you previously granted this access to via OAuth (see Figure 9–11).

Figure 9–11. *Revoke permission for an application to check into places.*

Facebook also lets you see an access log for each application (see Figure 9–12).

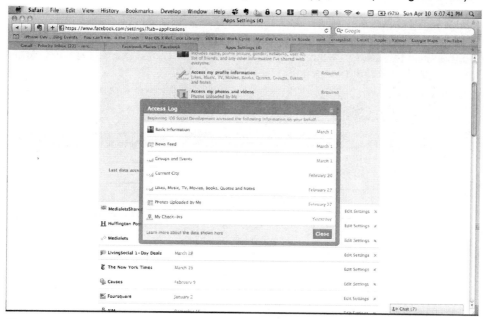

Figure 9–12. *View when an application last performed a check-in.*

If you go to the Info accessible through your friends setting, you can control friends' access to Places information (see Figure 9–13).

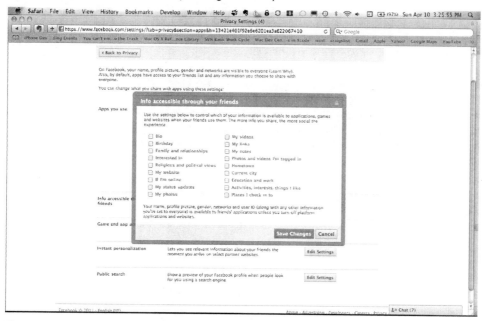

Figure 9–13. *Control friends' access to Places information.*

Adding Locations to Tweets

Since Twitter has a somewhat more limited amount of functionality, it's very straightforward to manage how Twitter uses your location. When you log into your Twitter account, go to Settings ➤ Account (http://twitter.com/settings/account) and scroll down to the Tweet Location section (see Figure 9–14).

Figure 9–14. *Configure the display of location with Tweets.*

Checking the Add a location to your tweets box lets you give Twitter permission to show a location associated with each of your Tweets, allows your Tweets to show up in searches of Tweets by location, and stores the location of your Tweets indefinitely. Remember to be careful with turning this setting on since Twitter, by its nature, encourages people to share their Tweets with the entire Twitter community. This means that anyone on Twitter can see where you are, unless your account is private. If you want to later stop showing your location with your new Tweets, uncheck this box. If you want to erase all records of your location for past Tweets, click the link in the sentence, "You may delete all location information from your past tweets." If you do this, you will be prompted to give Twitter permission to delete all of your location information (see Figure 9–15).

Figure 9–15. *Delete all location history associated with Tweets.*

If you choose to delete all of the location records for your Tweets, then anytime someone views one of your past Tweets, the location information will no longer appear. For a thorough description of the issues involved when sharing your location on Twitter, check out this link:

http://support.twitter.com/forums/26810/entries/78525

Power Hungry

Modern location services on mobile platforms use GPS, WiFi, and cellular data to try to determine the location of a device and return it via their respective APIs. The location service on iOS is no exception. Indeed, this feature is very power hungry, and it can quickly drain the battery of a user's device if not used wisely within your application.

Prior to iOS 4.0, there was only one method for obtaining the location of the device from the CoreLocation framework in iOS. With this method, which Apple refers to as the Standard method in its documentation, you can set accuracy and distance filters to control how often you want to access location information. Unfortunately, it's easy to abuse accessing location services with the Standard method and drain a device's battery. Apple's developers recognized this, so iOS 4 introduced a new Significant Change method for obtaining a device's location. This is a much more power friendly method of obtaining location and sends location updates on a less frequent basis. We will delve into this in greater detail in the next section, where we will show you how to use the Significant Change method in your application. Needless to say, we recommend using this method for the majority of applications, and especially for social applications that do not require a new location reading every second.

CoreLocation

IOS's CoreLocation framework is a very well thought out framework that is relatively easy to incorporate into an application. There is a ton of information available on Apple's iOS Developer site about the framework; however, we'll run through the most important stuff here. We'll also show one way of incorporating the framework into an application that makes it easy to get the device's current location. For total beginners, a thorough reading of Apple's documentation about location in iOS apps might be a good idea; you can find the documentation, entitled "iOS Location Awareness Guide," at this URL:

```
http://developer.apple.com/library/ios/#documentation/UserExperience/Conceptual/Location
AwarenessPG/Introduction/Introduction.html#//apple_ref/doc/uid/TP40009497
```

In the sample applications for this chapter, there is a new class entitled LocationController that exists within LocationController.h/.m. We have designed this class to act as a wrapper or façade for iOS's CoreLocation framework. We've done this in order to accomplish several goals:

- Make it easier to demonstrate how CoreLocation works by having it within one class within our application.

- Make the code easier to maintain in the future since we will only have to make changes for CoreLocation in one class.

- Prevent other classes from having to use CoreLocation individually.

Let's take a look at the header for LocationController to see what CoreLocation objects it uses and what its API looks like:

```objc
#import <CoreLocation/CoreLocation.h>

#ifdef FAKE_CORE_LOCATION
@class FTLocationSimulator;
#endif
@interface LocationController : NSObject <CLLocationManagerDelegate> {
#ifdef FAKE_CORE_LOCATION
    FTLocationSimulator *locationManager;
#else
    CLLocationManager *locationManager;
#endif
    CLLocation *location;
    CLHeading *heading;
    BOOL inPowerSavingMode;
}

#ifdef FAKE_CORE_LOCATION
@property(nonatomic, retain)FTLocationSimulator *locationManager;
#else
@property(nonatomic, retain)CLLocationManager *locationManager;
#endif
@property(nonatomic, retain)CLLocation *location;
```

```
@property(nonatomic, retain)CLHeading *heading;

- (void)startWithPowerSaving:(BOOL)savingPower;
- (void)stop;
- (BOOL)registerRegion:(CLLocationCoordinate2D)center;

@end
```

The main idea behind the LocationController class is that it owns and controls the operation of a CLLocationManager, which is the primary class within CoreLocation. LocationController makes the current location reading available via a location property that is a CoreLocation CLLocation object. LocationController provides methods for starting and stopping the underlying CoreLocation service, and it notifies its delegate when it has new location information. Since we need to receive updates from CLLocationManager, the LocationController is declared as a CLLocationManagerDelegate.

When starting the LocationController, you can elect to take one of two approaches. First, you can start it with power saving, which uses CoreLocation's Significant Change method for determining location. Second, you can use the Standard method. Also, LocationController has a method for registering a region for CoreLocation to monitor, which we will discuss shortly. We're sure that you noticed the references to FTLocationSimulator, and you're probably wondering what it's all about. FTLocationSimulator lets you generate location readings on the iOS simulator, which we will also be covering later in this section.

Let's switch over to LocationManager.m, so we can take a look at what LocationController's methods are doing. The startWithPowerSaving: method begins by stopping the LocationController, in case it has already been started. If you prefer, you could keep track of whether you've already started the CoreLocation services yourself and just exit this method immediately if it's already started. If the CLLocationManager locationManager does not exist yet, it is created, and we set LocationController as its delegate. Next, we check to see if location services are enabled on the device. Note that this changed from a property named locationServicesEnabled to a method of the same name in iOS 4.0, so we check for this, as well.

If location services are enabled, we start the locationManager in one of two ways, depending on the value of the savingPower parameter. If savingPower is YES, we start the locationManager via the startMonitoringSignificantLocationChanges method and store the fact that we are in power saving mode. If savingPower is NO, we use the Standard startUpdatingLocation method and configure our desired level of accuracy and distance filter. You can read more about the different values available for these properties in Apple's documentation or header files:

```
- (void)startWithPowerSaving:(BOOL)savingPower
{
    [self stop];

    if (nil == self.locationManager) {
#ifdef FAKE_CORE_LOCATION
```

```
        self.locationManager =
                    [[[FTLocationSimulator alloc] init] autorelease];
#else
        self.locationManager =
                    [[[CLLocationManager alloc] init] autorelease];
#endif
    }

    self.locationManager.delegate = self;

    //Available in 3.2 and later
    self.locationManager.purpose = @"Big brother is watching.";

    BOOL locationServicesEnabled = NO;
    if ([CLLocationManager
            respondsToSelector:@selector(locationServicesEnabled)]) {
        locationServicesEnabled =
            [CLLocationManager locationServicesEnabled];
    } else {
        locationServicesEnabled =
            self.locationManager.locationServicesEnabled;
    }

    if (locationServicesEnabled) {

        inPowerSavingMode = NO;
        if (savingPower
            && [CLLocationManager respondsToSelector:@selector
                (significantLocationChangeMonitoringAvailable)]) {
            if ([self.locationManager respondsToSelector:@selector
                (startMonitoringSignificantLocationChanges)]) {
                [self.locationManager
                    startMonitoringSignificantLocationChanges];
                inPowerSavingMode = YES;
            }

        } else {
            self.locationManager.desiredAccuracy =
                                        kCLLocationAccuracyBest;
            self.locationManager.distanceFilter = kCLDistanceFilterNone;
            [self.locationManager startUpdatingLocation];
        }
    }
}
```

LocationController's stop method checks to see if we are in power saving mode via the boolean, inPowerSavingMode (we saved this value earlier in our startWithPowerSaving: method). It then calls stopMonitoringSignificantLocationChanges or stopUpdatingLocation, depending on which mode we are in:

```
- (void)stop
{
    if (inPowerSavingMode
        && [CLLocationManager respondsToSelector:@selector
                (significantLocationChangeMonitoringAvailable)]) {
        if ([self.locationManager respondsToSelector:@selector
```

```
                (stopMonitoringSignificantLocationChanges)]) {
            [self.locationManager
                stopMonitoringSignificantLocationChanges];
        }
    } else {
        [self.locationManager stopUpdatingLocation];
    }
}
```

As of iOS 4.0, CoreLocation's CLLocationManager has the ability to notify an application via delegate callbacks when the device enters or leaves a pre-specified geographic region. This is known as *region monitoring*. LocationController supports region monitoring through its registerRegion: method, which directs CLLocationManager to monitor a specified region around a single center point and notify the application when the device enters or leaves the region.

Using CLLocationManager

Next, we'll go over how to use CLLocationManger. First, we need to see if this feature is available. If it is, then we set the radius of the region we want to monitor; create the region to monitor with the center point, radius, and name; and finally, hand it off to CLLocationManager to monitor via its startMonitoringForRegion:desiredAccuracy: method. The desiredAccuracy value controls the size of the buffer around the edge of the region's boundary that CLLocationManager uses to determine if the device has left and reentered a region. Monitoring regions can be a really useful way to incorporate some nice features into your app, such as automatically checking in a user to certain places:

```
- (BOOL)registerRegion:(CLLocationCoordinate2D)center
{
    // Check to see if support is available
    if (![CLLocationManager regionMonitoringAvailable] ||
        ![CLLocationManager regionMonitoringEnabled] )
        return NO;

    CLLocationDegrees radius =
            self.locationManager.maximumRegionMonitoringDistance;

    // Create the region and start monitoring it.
    CLRegion *region = [[CLRegion alloc]
                        initCircularRegionWithCenter:center
                                        radius:radius
                                        identifier:@"test"];
    [self.locationManager startMonitoringForRegion:region
        desiredAccuracy:kCLLocationAccuracyNearestTenMeters];

    [region release];

    return YES;

}
```

When the CLLocationManager acquires a location reading that falls within the criteria for its current mode of operation, it notifies its delegate via the CLLocationManagerDelegate's locationManager:didUpdateToLocation:fromLocation: method. When this delegate method is called, we save the current location reading in our own location property, so that any other parts of our application can access the device's current location reading:

```
- (void)locationManager:(CLLocationManager *)manager
    didUpdateToLocation:(CLLocation *)newLocation
           fromLocation:(CLLocation *)oldLocation
{
    self.location = newLocation;
}
```

If there was a problem initializing the location services, CLLocationManagerDelegate's locationManager:didFailWithError: method is called:

```
- (void)locationManager:(CLLocationManager *)manager
       didFailWithError:(NSError *)error
{
    NSLog(@"didFailWithError");
}
```

When the device enters or leaves a designated region, CLLocationManagerDelegate's locationManager:didEnterRegion: and locationManager:didExitRegion: methods are called:

```
- (void)locationManager:(CLLocationManager *)manager
         didEnterRegion:(CLRegion *)region
{
    NSLog(@"didEnterRegion");
}

- (void)locationManager:(CLLocationManager *)manager
          didExitRegion:(CLRegion *)region
{
    NSLog(@"didExitRegion");
}

- (void)locationManager:(CLLocationManager *)manager
monitoringDidFailForRegion:(CLRegion *)region
              withError:(NSError *)error
{
    NSLog(@"monitoringDidFailForRegion");
}
```

As of iOS 4.2, CLLocationManager can also notify its delegate if the authorization status for the application was changed by the user via the main Settings application on the device:

```
- (void)locationManager:(CLLocationManager *)manager
didChangeAuthorizationStatus:(CLAuthorizationStatus)status
{
    NSLog(@"didChangeAuthorizationStatus");
}
```

Before we move onto other topics, it's worth mentioning location services on iOS and backgrounding. Note that the Significant Change method will periodically wake up your app and provide location updates. If you are using the Standard location method, then you will have to set some values in your application's plist. You can find more information on this in Apple's "iOS Location Awareness Guide," which we referred you to earlier in this chapter.

One final note: When using CoreLocation in your application, you have to link your application against the CoreLocation framework (see Figure 9–16).

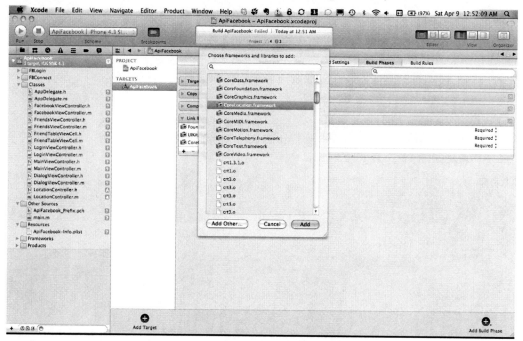

Figure 9–16. *Linking against the CoreLocation framework when using CoreLocation*

Generating Locations in the iOS Simulator

Although Apple has done an outstanding job with its CoreLocation framework, one glaring omission was the ability to generate a sequence of location updates in the iOS simulator. With iOS 5, Apple has added location simulation so that developers can test location-aware apps without needing to leave their desks. In the event that Apple's solution doesn't satisfy, here are two alternative ways to test location apps within the developer environment: iSimulate and FTLocationSimulator. These solutions are very different in their approaches, so we're going to give a quick run-through on how to get set up with them and how they work.

iSimulate

You can acquire iSimulate at the following URL:

www.vimov.com/isimulate/

The iSimulate app runs on your actual iOS device and allows you to interact with an application running in the iOS Simulator on your desktop. Most importantly, it also lets you share the location of your device with the Simulator. You can find a free Lite version of the app in iTunes at this URL:

http://itunes.apple.com/us/app/isimulate-lite/id351339630?mt=8

To get up and running with iSimulate, you also have to configure a few things in your application's project in Xcode:

1. First, download the latest version of the iSimulate SDK from www.vimov.com/isimulate/sdk/.

2. Now add the iSimulate library's .a file (at the time of writing, this is called libisimulate-4.x-opengl.a) to your application target's Frameworks (see Figure 9–17).

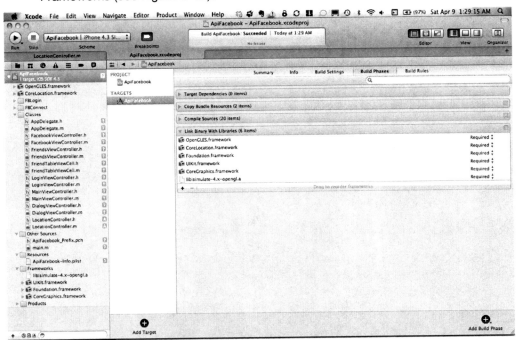

Figure 9–17. *Link against the iSimulate library file.*

3. Next, link your application against the OpenGLES framework (see Figure 9–18).

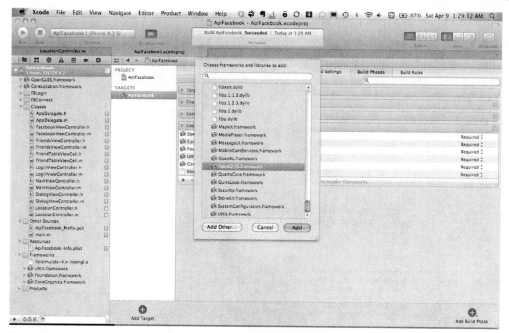

Figure 9–18. *Link against OpenGLES when using iSimulate.*

4. Finally, add an additional -ObjC linker flag to your application target under Build Settings (see Figure 9–19).

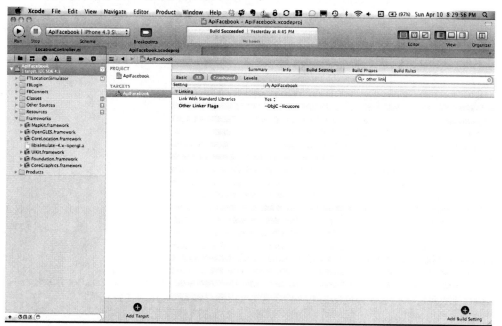

Figure 9–19. *Set additional linker flags when using iSimulate.*

All of this information is also available here:

www.vimov.com/isimulate/documentation/

Now that we have configured iSimulate, it's time to put it into action. On your device, make sure that you are on the same WiFi network as the machine that you are running the iOS Simulator on, and then start iSimulate. You should see a screen like the one shown in Figure 9–20.

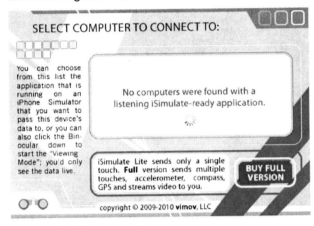

Figure 9–20. *iSimulate on iOS*

Now run your application in the iOS Simulator, and the iSimulate application on your device will detect that the application is running and let you link with it on your device (see Figure 9–21).

Figure 9–21. *iSimulate on iOS: Select the machine to connect to.*

Choose the name of your machine from the list and you will be brought to the main iSimulate screen. You are now ready to rock and roll (see Figure 9–22).

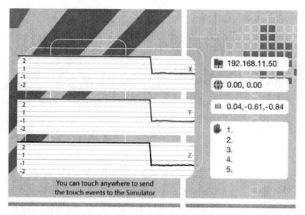

Figure 9–22. *iSimulator on iOS: View the information that iSimulate is sharing.*

futuretap's FTLocationSimulator

You can acquire FTLocationSimulator from the following URL:

```
https://github.com/futuretap/FTLocationSimulator
```

Unlike iSimulate, FTLocationSimulator is code that you build into your app that overrides CLLocationManager. FTLocationSimulator then generates location information by reading in coordinates from a .kml file that you include in your application. There is a little more setup here and some code to discuss, but we are going to walk you through it.

First, you will want to set up a submodule to the FTLocationSimulator source code via Git:

```
$ git submodule add git://github.com/futuretap/FTLocationSimulator.git↵
  FTLocationSimulator
```

Then, within the FTLocationSimulator directory for the submodule, drag the FTLocationSimulator directory to your Xcode project. Next, add the following additional linker flag to your project's target: -licucore. The final step is to adjust your code so that it creates and uses an instance of FTLocationSimulator instead of CLLocationManager whenever FAKE_CORE_LOCATION is defined:

```
#ifdef FAKE_CORE_LOCATION
    self.locationManager =
        [[[FTLocationSimulator alloc] init] autorelease];
  #else
    self.locationManager =
        [[[CLLocationManager alloc] init] autorelease];
  #endif
```

FAKE_CORE_LOCATION is located in FTLocationSimulator.h, and it is defaulted to 1 when targeting the iOS Simulator:

```
#if TARGET_IPHONE_SIMULATOR
#define FAKE_CORE_LOCATION 1
#endif
```

As we noted before, `FTLocationSimulator` overrides `CLLocationManager`. Therefore, if `FAKE_CORE_LOCATION` is defined and `startUpdatingLocation` is called, `FTLocationSimulator`'s `startUpdatingLocation` will be called. This method calls `FTLocationSimulator`'s `fakeNewLocation`, which reads a new location out of the file `fakeLocations.kml` included. It then calls itself again after an update interval:

```
- (void)startUpdatingLocation {
        updatingLocation = YES;
        [self fakeNewLocation];
}
```

You can change the update interval in `FTLocationSimulator.h`:

```
#define FAKE_CORE_LOCATION_UPDATE_INTERVAL 0.3
```

You can also create your own `.kml` file or update the coordinates in `fakeLocations.kml`. We encourage you to read up on generating `.kml` files. Google has some facilities that make it easy to generate these files, which should help your testing.

MapKit

When working with location, it's incredibly useful to be able to visualize what's happening. Therefore, we're going to cover another framework available to us in iOS called *MapKit*. The main class available via MapKit is `MKMapView`. `MKMapView` makes it incredibly easy to incorporate maps into an application. To see this in action, open the file called `MapViewController.m` in the sample projects for this chapter. In the `loadView` method of `MapViewController`, we simply create an `MKMapView` object with a given rectangle, set ourselves as an `MKMapViewDelegate`, tell the `MKMapView` to display our current location on the map by setting its `showUserLocation` property to YES, and then add it to our view controller's view:

```
- (void)loadView {
   [super loadView];

   CGRect rect = CGRectMake(0.0f, 0.0f, 320.0f, 411.0f);
   MKMapView *mapView = [[MKMapView alloc] initWithFrame:rect];
   mapView.delegate = self;
   mapView.showsUserLocation = YES;

   [self.view addSubview:mapView];
   [mapView release];
}
```

Note that, since we've set ourselves as the `MKMapVew`'s delegate, we need to declare our `MapViewController` as an `MKMapViewDelegate` in `MapViewController.h`:

```
@interface MapViewController : UIViewController <MKMapViewDelegate> {

}
@end
```

Also, don't forget to link your application against the MapKit framework (see Figure 9–23).

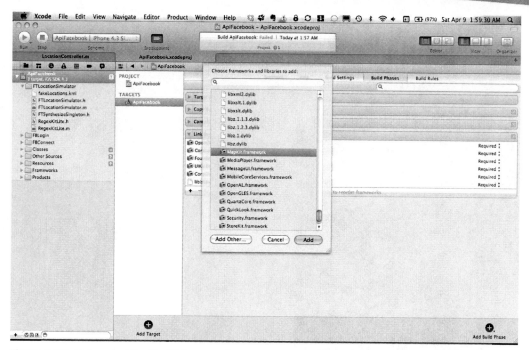

Figure 9–23. *Link against the MapKit framework.*

We also need to implement a few methods from `MKMapViewDelegate`; however, before we describe these methods, we need to address the topic of annotations. There is a lot to cover with annotations, so we won't go into too much detail. The short version is that annotations are visual elements, such as pins that you can place on an `MKMapView`. In Figure 9–24, we have placed an annotation for a location point on the map and represented it as a pin.

Figure 9–24. *Display a pin on a map.*

The code for adding this annotation to the map is in the implementation of
MKMapViewDelegate's mapView: didUpdateUserLocation. This method is called whenever
the map displays an updated location from the CoreLocation framework. This delegate
method is called because we set showsUserLocation to YES on our MKMapView, and we
are simulating position updates. For simplicity's sake, we add the first position reading
that we receive as an MKPointAnnotation, which is a predefined type of annotation via
MKMapView's addAnnotation: method. We also use our LocationController's
registerRegion: method to register a region around this first position:

```
- (void)mapView:(MKMapView *)mapView didUpdateUserLocation:↵
(MKUserLocation *)userLocation
{
    static int once = 0;
    if (0 == once) {
        once = 1;

        // create the pin annotation
        MKPointAnnotation *annotation = [[MKPointAnnotation alloc] init];
        annotation.coordinate = userLocation.coordinate;
        [mapView addAnnotation:annotation];
        [annotation release];

        [locationController registerRegion:userLocation.coordinate];
    }

    NSLog(@"didUpdateUserLocation");
}
```

Displaying an annotation on an MKMapView is a two-step process. First, we add an annotation to the MKMapView (as we did in the preceding code). Second, we provide an annotation view that is responsible for displaying the annotation. When the MKMapView has determined that it needs to display an annotation, it calls its delegate's mapView:viewForAnnotation: method. In the code that follows, you will see that if MKMapView is requesting a view for an MKPointAnnotation, we create an MKPinAnnotationView and animate its display on the map. The animation will make the pin look like it's falling from the sky and dropping into place on the map:

```
- (MKAnnotationView *)mapView:(MKMapView *)mapView
        viewForAnnotation:(id <MKAnnotation>)annotation {

    if ([annotation isMemberOfClass:[MKUserLocation class]]) {
#ifdef FAKE_CORE_LOCATION
        //get the app delegate's location manager;return it's fake user
        //location view
        return locationController.locationManager.fakeUserLocationView;
#else
        return nil;
#endif
    } else {
        if ([annotation isKindOfClass:[MKPointAnnotation class]]) {
            // Try to dequeue an existing pin view first.
            MKPinAnnotationView *pinView =
            (MKPinAnnotationView*)[mapView
            dequeueReusableAnnotationViewWithIdentifier:@"PinView"];
            if (!pinView) {
                // If an existing pin view was not available, create one.
                pinView = [[[MKPinAnnotationView alloc]
                initWithAnnotation:annotation
                    reuseIdentifier:@"PinAnnotation"] autorelease];
                pinView.pinColor = MKPinAnnotationColorRed;
                pinView.animatesDrop = YES;
            } else {
                pinView.annotation = annotation;
            }

            return pinView;
        }
    }

    // code to create views for other annotations
    return nil;
}
```

This code is also checking for MKUserLocation annotations. We won't go into too much detail here, but you should note that the FTLocationSimulator class that we discussed earlier is designed to show the user's location moving along the map by providing an MKAnnotationView for the map. You can see this in action in FTLocationSimulator's fakeUserLocationView method:

```
- (MKAnnotationView*)fakeUserLocationView {
    if (!self.mapView) {
        return nil;
    }
```

```
[self.mapView.userLocation setCoordinate:self.location.coordinate];
MKAnnotationView *userLocationView = [mapView
    dequeueReusableAnnotationViewWithIdentifier:@"fakeLocationView"];
if (nil == userLocationView) {
    userLocationView = [[MKAnnotationView alloc]
                    initWithAnnotation:self.mapView.userLocation
                    reuseIdentifier:@"fakeLocationView"];
}
UIImage *image = :[UIImage imageNamed:@"TrackingDot.png"];
UIImageView *imageView =
            [[UIImageView alloc] initWithImage:image];
[userLocationView addSubview:imageView];
[imageView release];
  userLocationView.centerOffset = CGPointMake(-10, -10);
  return userLocationView;
}
```

The final piece of the puzzle that we need to implement is the code that handles what happens when the user selects an annotation on the map. When this happens, MKMapView calls its delegate's mapView: didSelectAnnotationView: method. We will use this method in our Facebook example to show how to check in a user to a place. Let's take a look at that now.

Facebook Places (Search), Check-ins (Getting and Posting), and Friends Nearby

Within the Facebook app itself, checking into Places is done via the Nearby screen, which automatically searches for Places near your current location. If permission to use location services has not been granted to the Facebook application, it displays the following screen (see Figure 9–25).

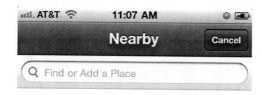

Location unavailable.

Location Services are disabled. You must enable
Location Services to view nearby places and check-
ins.

Figure 9–25. *Location unavailable in the Check-Ins section of the Facebook iOS application*

Assuming that permission to use location services has been granted to the Facebook
application, you will see a list of returned place matches (see Figure 9–26), as well as
detailed information for a place. This is how the Facebook application lets its user
community manage places. A Place profile (which is essentially similar to a Facebook Page)
is shown in Figure 9–27; users can act upon places in the ways shown in Figure 9–28.

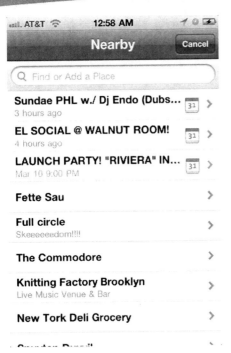

Figure 9–26. *Searching for nearby places and events in Facebook's iOS application*

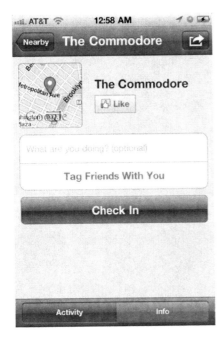

Figure 9–27. *Detailed information about a place in Facebook's iOS application*

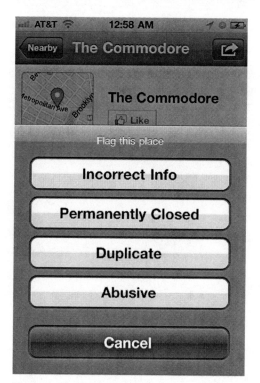

Figure 9–28. *Flag a place in Facebook's iOS application.*

Within our sample app, we want to make it possible to let someone check into a place on Facebook. Recall that we set up our application to display a pin on the map. When the pin is selected by the user, MKMapViewDelegate's mapView:didSelectAnnotationView: method is called. In our implementation of this in MapViewController, we issue a search request to Facebook to ask for a list of places around the location of the annotation. To issue a search request to Facebook, we simply set the graph path for Facebook's requestWithGraphPath:andParams:andDelegate: method to search. The additional parameter to supply is a dictionary with values for type, center, and distance keys. The MapViewController class is an FBRequestDelegate, so we supply it as the delegate:

```
- (void)mapView:(MKMapView *)mapView
    didSelectAnnotationView:(MKAnnotationView *)view
{
    NSString *centerString = [NSString stringWithFormat: @"%f,%f",
        view.annotation.coordinate.latitude,
        view.annotation.coordinate.longitude];

    NSMutableDictionary *params =
            [NSMutableDictionary dictionaryWithObjectsAndKeys:
            @"place", @"type",
            centerString, @"center",
            @"1000", @"distance", // In Meters (1000m = 0.62mi)
        nil];

    [facebook requestWithGraphPath:@"search"
```

```
                          andParams:params
                          andDelegate:self];
    }
```

When the `FBRequestDelegate`'s `request:didLoad:` is called, the result parameter is a dictionary with an array of place dictionaries. Each `place` dictionary has an id; a category; a name; and a `location` dictionary with a city, country, state, latitude, and longitude:

```
{
    data =      (
                {
            category = "Local business";
            id = 151247078226083;
            location =              {
                city = "Monta Vista";
                country = "United States";
                latitude = "37.3316086";
                longitude = "-122.05885";
                state = CA;
            };
            name = "Somerset Square Park";
        }
    );
}
```

In the following code, we take the first match from the array of dictionaries in the result and post a check-in to Facebook via this graph path:

`"me/checkins"`

We set the parameters for the post request in a dictionary with values for `place`, `coordinates`, and `message` keys. Note that the latitude and longitude values for the `coordinates` key need to be in JSON format, so we use SBJSON (which is included in the Facebook SDK) to convert these values to a JSON string:

```
- (void)request:(FBRequest *)request didLoad:(id)result {
    NSLog(@"didLoad:");

    NSArray *places = [(NSDictionary*)result objectForKey:@"data"];
    if (0 < [places count]) {
        NSDictionary *dictionary = [places objectAtIndex:0];
        if (nil != dictionary) {
            NSDictionary *locDictionary =
                [dictionary objectForKey:@"location"];

            NSMutableDictionary *coordinatesDictionary =
                [NSMutableDictionary dictionaryWithObjectsAndKeys:
                [locDictionary objectForKey:@"latitude"], @"latitude",
                [locDictionary objectForKey:@"longitude"], @"longitude",
                nil];

            SBJSON *jsonWriter = [[SBJSON new] autorelease];
            NSString *coordinates =
                [jsonWriter stringWithObject:coordinatesDictionary];

            NSMutableDictionary *params =
```

```
                [NSMutableDictionary dictionaryWithObjectsAndKeys:
                [dictionary objectForKey:@"id"], @"place",
                coordinates, @"coordinates",
                @"This is a test checkin", @"message",
                nil];

            [facebook requestWithGraphPath:@"me/checkins"
                            andParams:params
                        andHttpMethod:@"POST"
                            andDelegate:self];
        }
    }
}
```

Note that you can also include a user's friends in a check-in by tagging them in the checkin POST. To do this, add an additional key entitled tags to the params dictionary and set its value to a comma-delimited list of Facebook user ids.

Posting check-ins to a user's Facebook account requires publish_checkins permissions, so we have to update our login code to include this additional permission:

```
- (void)login {
    [facebook authorize:[NSArray arrayWithObjects:
                    @"user_groups", @"user_events",
                    @"offline_access", @"publish_checkins", nil]
            delegate:self];
}
```

When logging in with this additional permission, the following OAuth screen is displayed (see Figure 9–29).

Figure 9–29. *Permission via OAuth to check into places on Facebook*

Once the check-in is posted, it will show up in the user's Facebook iOS app (and on Facebook.com, of course), as shown in Figure 9–30.

Figure 9–30. *Check-ins in Facebook's iOS application*

Selecting a check-in shows a small map and description of the place, as well as any comments on the check-in (see Figure 9–31).

Figure 9–31. *Details about a Facebook check-in*

The place can be viewed on a larger map within the Facebook iOS app (see Figure 9–32).

Figure 9–32. *A larger map view of a Facebook check-in*

Next, you are given the choice to view the map in the main Maps application on the device or to get directions (see Figure 9–33).

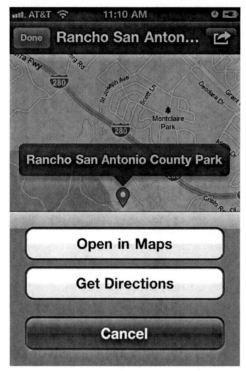

Figure 9–33. *Actions that can be taken on a check-in in Facebook's iOS application*

Just as we can post check-ins for a user, we can also retrieve a user's check-ins via the Facebook graph path, "me/checkins":

```
[facebook requestWithGraphPath:@"me/checkins"
                    andParams:nil
                  andDelegate:self];
```

The returned result is an array of dictionaries where each dictionary contains information about an individual check-in. This information includes the application that posted the check-in, the time of creation, the user who posted the check-in, the Facebook id for the check-in, the message associated with the check-in, and the place associated with the check-in:

```
(
    {
    application =        {
        id = 114442211957627;
        name = "Beginning iOS Social Development";
    };
    "created_time" = "2011-04-09T16:14:19+0000";
    from =        {
        id = 623441509;
        name = "Christopher White";
```

```
        };
    id = 10150149394136510;
    message = "This is a test checkin";
    place =        {
        id = 144940418859769;
        location =        {
            latitude = "37.332301584174";
            longitude = "-122.08672354097";
        };
        name = "Rancho San Antonio County Park";
    };
    };
}
)
```

Retrieving check-ins from a user's Facebook account requires `user_checkins`
permissions, so we have to update our login code to include this additional permission:

```
- (void)login {
    [facebook authorize:[NSArray arrayWithObjects:
                    @"user_groups", @"user_events",
                    @"offline_access", @"publish_checkins",
                    @"user_checkins", nil]
            delegate:self];
}
```

When logging in with this additional permission, the following 0Auth screen is displayed
(see Figure 9–34).

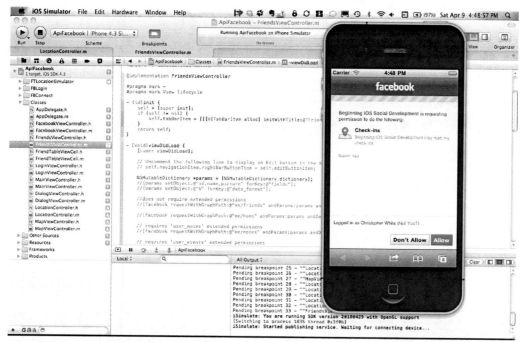

Figure 9–34. *Facebook check-in permissions*

Tweetin' With Location

When it comes to Twitter, the main thing that you will want to enable in your application is the ability to let users associate a location with their Tweets. We've set up the ApiTwitter example for this chapter to resemble the ApiFacebook application, so we're going to skip over some setup since it was covered in the previous sections. At this point, the `LocationController` class has been incorporated, we are simulating locations via `FTLocationSimulator`, and we're using our `MapViewController` to display a map with an annotation. The only difference is what we do when the user selects the annotation.

Twitter has done a great job documenting its geo-location API, and we encourage you to familiarize yourself with Twitter's underlying HTTP API here:

`http://dev.twitter.com/doc/get/geo`

Until now, we've been using XML as our format when working with Twitter's APIs; however, the Twitter geo-location APIs only return results in JSON format. In addition, the base URL for a location is the updated Twitter URL that follows, where 1 is the version of the API:

`http://api.twitter.com/1/`

In order to get a feel for working with these APIs, open up a browser to apigee.com's Twitter console (see Figure 9–35). This is a very useful tool for experimenting with Twitter's API and getting your feet wet:

`https://apigee.com/console/twitter`

Figure 9–35. *Apigee's Twitter console*

Since Twitter's geo-location API only returns results in JSON format, we have to update MGTwitterEngine to work with the SBJSON library, which is an easy to use Objective-C drop-in for working with JSON. First, in MGTwitterEngine.m, we have to make sure that we set the URL format to JSON and import JSON.h:

```
#elif SBJSON_AVAILABLE
        #define API_FORMAT @"json"
        #import "JSON.h"
#else
```

We also have to update the default Twitter domain:

```
#define TWITTER_DOMAIN          @"api.twitter.com/1"
```

Next, we have to tell MGTwitterEngine to work with JSON when it parses the data for a connection. The data in the response is first converted to its JSON string representation, and the JSON is converted into an NSArray or NSDictionary using the NSString category method JSONValue, which is defined in the SBJSON library:

```
#elif SBJSON_AVAILABLE
- (void)_parseDataForConnection:(MGTwitterHTTPURLConnection *)connection
{
    NSString *identifier = [[[connection identifier] copy] autorelease];
    NSData *jsonData = [[[connection data] copy] autorelease];
    MGTwitterResponseType responseType = [connection responseType];
    NSString *json_string =
        [[[NSString alloc] initWithData:jsonData
                              encoding:NSUTF8StringEncoding]
                            autorelease];

    id json = [json_string JSONValue];

    NSArray *parsedObjects;

    if ([json isKindOfClass:[NSArray class]]) {
            parsedObjects = [NSArray arrayWithArray:json];
    } else if ([json isKindOfClass:[NSDictionary class]]) {
            parsedObjects = [NSArray arrayWithObject:json];
    }

    [self parsingSucceededForRequest:identifier
                      ofResponseType:responseType
                   withParsedObjects:parsedObjects];

}
#else
```

In MGTwitterEngineGlobalHeader.h, we store the #define that determines if JSON should be used as the default return format. Setting this to 1 will enable this:

```
#define SBJSON_AVAILABLE 0
```

In order to compile this code, you will also have to create a new group in your Xcode project entitled SBJSON and drag the SBJSON files to the group folder. If you don't already have the SBJSON files on your machine, you should clone the Github repository for it or create a submodule. We recommend using a submodule:

```
$ git submodule add git://github.com/stig/json-framework.git json-framework
```

Now that we have SBJSON incorporated into MGTwitterEngine, we have to add support for Twitter's geo API and for POSTing status updates with `location` parameters. Twitter's HTTP geo APIs use the following format:

`geo/<action>.json`

We've therefore created a geoResultsForPath:withParams: method that lets you set the action that you want to perform, as well as the parameters. The four available path actions are as follows:

- `geo/search`
- `geo/reverse_geocode`
- `geo/similar_places`
- `geo/id`

The parameters consist of `latitude` and `longitude` values, place names, and so on:

```
- (NSString *)geoResultsForPath:(NSString *)path
                    withParams:(NSDictionary*)params
{
    NSString *path1 =
        [NSString stringWithFormat:@"geo/%@.%@", path, API_FORMAT];

    return [self _sendStandardRequestWithMethod:nil
                            path:path1
                  queryParameters:params
                             body:nil
                      requestType:MGTwitterAccountRequest
                     responseType:MGTwitterMiscellaneous];
}
```

Now we're finally ready to put this into action. In MapViewController.m, go to the mapView:didSelectAnnotationView: method:

```
- (void)mapView:(MKMapView *)mapView
      didSelectAnnotationView:(MKAnnotationView *)view
{
    NSNumber *lat =
        [NSNumber numberWithDouble:view.annotation.coordinate.latitude];
    NSNumber *lon =
        [NSNumber numberWithDouble:view.annotation.coordinate.longitude];

    NSMutableDictionary *params = [NSMutableDictionary dictionary];
    [params setObject:[lat stringValue] forKey:@"lat"];
    [params setObject:[lon stringValue] forKey:@"long"];
    NSString *identifier =
        [sa_OAuthTwitterEngine geoResultsForPath:@"reverse_geocode"
                                 withParams:params];

    //listen for a notification with the name of the identifier
    [[NSNotificationCenter defaultCenter]
        addObserver:self
            selector:@selector(twitterPlacesRequestDidComplete:)
               name:identifier
             object:nil];
}
```

When the pin on the map is selected, we call Twitter's geo/reverse_geocode API with parameters for latitude and longitude. We get the latitude and longitude values from the annotation that is associated with the pin. The concept of *reverse geocoding* refers to taking a location in latitude and longitude coordinates and giving back an address or actual place name for the location. Note that there are additional parameters that you can supply to control the granularity of the reverse geocoding or other location searches.

In Twitter, all places have a Twitter id; and when associating a location with a Tweet, Twitter recommends using its place id values instead of raw latitude and longitude values. This helps to protect user privacy. For more information about how to handle this in your application and to adhere to Twitter's geo guidelines, we strongly urge you to read the information posted here:

http://dev.twitter.com/pages/geo_dev_guidelines

Let's recap what we have thus far. We are asking Twitter to reverse geocode a location for us, and we're then setting ourselves up to be notified when the response comes back. The raw JSON response data uses the following format:

```
{
    query = {
        params = {
            accuracy = 0;
            autocomplete = 0;
            granularity = neighborhood;
            query = London;
            "trim_place" = 0;
        };
        type = search;
        url = "URL";
    };
    result = {
        places = (
            {
                attributes = {
                };
                "bounding_box" = {
                    coordinates = (
                        (
                            (
                                "-0.5093057",
                                "51.286606"
                            ),
                            (
                                "0.334433",
                                "51.286606"
                            ),
                            (
                                "0.334433",
                                "51.691672"
                            ),
                            (
                                "-0.5093057",
                                "51.691672"
```

```
                    )
                )
            );
            type = Polygon;
        };
        "contained_within" = (
                    {
                attributes = {
                };
                "bounding_box" = {
                    coordinates = (
                        (
                            (
                                "-6.3651943",
                                "49.8825312"
                            ),
                            (
                                "1.768926",
                                "49.8825312"
                            ),
                            (
                                "1.768926",
                                "55.8116485"
                            ),
                            (
                                "-6.3651943",
                                "55.8116485"
                            )
                        )
                    );
                    type = Polygon;
                };
                country = "United Kingdom";
                "country_code" = GB;
                "full_name" = "England, United Kingdom";
                id = 8ef32ff56ef11c22;
                name = England;
                "place_type" = admin;
                url = "URL";
            }
        );
        country = "United Kingdom";
        "country_code" = GB;
        "full_name" = "London, England";
        id = 5d838f7a011f4a2d;
        name = London;
        "place_type" = admin;
        url = "URL";
    }
    );
    };
}
)
```

Notice that the actual array of places is in a dictionary entitled result. Each place is itself a dictionary of values, but the value that we are most interested in is the value for the id key. When we get a notification that we have received place results from Twitter, we take the dictionary for the first place in the array, extract its place id, and then submit a status update with an additional dictionary of params. In conforming with Twitter's API, we supply a parameter with the key place_id:

```
- (void)twitterPlacesRequestDidComplete:(NSNotification*)notification {

    [[NSNotificationCenter defaultCenter] removeObserver:self];

    NSArray *places = [notification.userInfo objectForKey:@"places"];
    if (0 < [places count]) {
        //grab the first place
        NSDictionary *placesDict = [places objectAtIndex:0];
        NSDictionary *resultDict = [placesDict objectForKey:@"result"];
        NSArray *resultPlaces = [resultDict objectForKey:@"places"];
        if (0 < [resultPlaces count]) {
            NSDictionary *firstPlace = [resultPlaces objectAtIndex:0];

            NSMutableDictionary *params =
                [NSMutableDictionary dictionary];
            [params setObject:[firstPlace objectForKey:@"id"]
                    forKey:@"place_id"];
            [sa_OAuthTwitterEngine sendUpdate:@"location tweet!"
                            withParams:params];
        }
    }
}
```

If we then go to Twitter on the Web, lo and behold, we see our Tweet with a location (see Figure 9–36). Note that you have to enable location with Tweets in your settings on Twitter, as discussed earlier in this chapter.

There are a lot of fun things that you can do with location in Twitter, so give this code a go. The actual sample code has some other example code that you can uncomment to see how the other Twitter geo APIs work. They are all closely related and take almost identical parameters.

Before we close out this chapter, we'd also like to note that you can use MapKit's MKReverseGeocoder class if you don't want to use Twitter or Facebook to look up places for coordinates. It's up to you. The sample code also has MKReverseGeocoder implemented, so that you can tinker with this at your leisure.

Figure 9–36. *A Tweet with location information*

Conclusion

Working with location is a lot of fun, but it also has its perils. When working with location in your application and with social networks like Facebook and Twitter, it is paramount for you to put yourself in your user's shoes and ask yourself important questions about how you are using her location. Every application has a unique user interface design, but we encourage you to incorporate a disclosure about what you are doing with a user's location in your application and to display it immediately on the first run of your application or the first time that a user is going to perform an action where her location will be used.

This is just one of the many design and interface guidelines you should follow. You'll read more about them in Chapters 11 through 14.

That's it for location. We've given you the basic building blocks, so have some fun. In the next chapter, we cover a grab bag of technical issues that will improve your applications overall integration with Facebook and Twitter.

Chapter 10

Using Open Source Tools and Other Goodies

The world of mobile software moves incredibly fast, and it can sometimes seem like a daunting undertaking to stay abreast of all the latest developments. While this book is intended as an introduction to integrating Facebook and Twitter into your application, there are a host of related technologies that can make life easier or reveal how other applications accomplish certain tasks. In addition, there are some cross-posting libraries available that can save you the trouble of integrating directly with the Facebook and Twitter SDKs. These topics are explored in this chapter.

This chapter also includes a discussion of data and trends that are available from Twitter. In addition to its standard client APIs, Twitter makes data and trends available to developers. Twitter Trends is the site's tool for measuring topics (i.e., hash tags) that are quickly becoming popular (that are hot news, in other words). If you haven't heard of the Trends tool, check out this compendium on Twitter.com:

```
http://yearinreview.twitter.com/trends/
```

It may not always make sense to access these trends directly from within your application, and Twitter's terms restrict some of the ways you can use its data; however, it might prove useful to look at this server-to-server transaction. Later, you'll learn how to do some of your own number crunching with this data and serve what you need to your application.

The Shorter, the Better

A common problem with referencing resources on the Web is that URLs for these resources can sometimes be incredibly long. This presents a problem when incorporating services like Twitter into an application because Tweets need to be short in length. For instance, it is not good from a user's perspective if an application wants to let a user Tweet an article, but the length of the URL for the article takes up almost the entire Tweet or is entirely too long to fit in a Tweet.

This is where URL shorteners come into play. There are a number of URL shortening services available, inclding Twitter's own, which was announced as this book was going to press. However, third party URL shorteners offer functionality Twitter doesn't (such as analytics) so we'll spent some time talking about two of them. We will also cover how they work and how to integrate them into an iOS application. Note that not all these services may be in business in perpetuity; if you're interested in the archival quality of your links, use Twitter's own shortener, T.co.

Here are two common third-party URL shortening services:

- `http://bit.ly`
- `http://TinyURL.com`

Both services are entirely free to use, and they work on the same premise: you supply a URL to the service, and it returns a shortened URL back to you.

A handy tool for experimenting with these services is a command-line utility known as *cURL*, which you can learn more about at this URL:

`https://secure.wikimedia.org/wikipedia/en/wiki/CURL`

cURL is designed to support a number of Internet protocols, but HTTP is the only protocol that is relevant in this case. To see curl in action, open up Terminal on a Mac and type the following at the command line:

`$ curl http://www.apress.com`

This writes out to the command line all of the HTML for the Apress homepage that would normally be processed and displayed by a web browser.

For URL shortening, you need more than just a URL. The URL shortening services require that the URL to be shortened be set as a parameter with the request. To send parameters along with a URL request, use cURL's -d option:

`$ curl -d "<request parameters>" URL`

TinyURL has a simple protocol in place. Simply submit a request to `http://tinyurl.com/api-create.php` with a url parameter that is set to the URL that you want to shorten:

`$ curl -d "url=http://www.apress.com" http://tinyurl.com/api-create.php`

This will return a shortened URL that uses this form:

`http://tinyurl.com/9qths`

Of course, `www.apress.com` isn't a URL that really needs shortening—but this is just an example.

Bit.ly, like TinyURL, shortens URLs; however, it also provides tracking, analytics, search history, and a lot more on the shortened URLs that it generates. To get the best usage out of bit.ly, you need to sign up for an account on its site. After completing the sign up, bit.ly will associate an apiKey with the account. This apiKey is needed to use its service. The bit.ly protocol requires a request to `http://api.bitly.com/v3/shorten` with the following parameters:

- login: A bit.ly username (chosen when you create an account)

- apiKey: The api key that is associated with the username provided (this api key is generated by bit.ly upon successful registration)

- longUrl: The URL to shorten

- format: The desired format for the response; supported values are json (default), xml, and txt

Therefore, a request for bit.ly to shorten a URL would look like the following when using cURL:

```
$ curl -d "login=<bit.ly username>&apiKey=<bit.ly API
         key>&longUrl=http://www.apress.com&format=txt"
         http://api.bitly.com/v3/shorten
```

This will return a shortened URL that uses this form:

```
http://bit.ly/dIB3mD
```

For more detailed information about the bit.ly API, go here:

```
https://code.google.com/p/bitly-api/wiki/ApiDocumentation#/v3/shorten
```

For a quick read on some of the underlying theory involved with URL shortening, read the article, "URL Shortening: Hashes In Practice," at this URL:

```
www.codinghorror.com/blog/2007/08/url-shortening-hashes-in-practice.html
```

For more detailed information about curl and what it can accomplish, go to the following page:

```
http://curl.haxx.se/docs/manpage.html
```

Or, you can just type the following from a command line:

```
$ man curl
```

Using URL Shorteners in iOS

curl is a great tool to perform a quick test with; however, it's of no use within an iOS app. While there are a number of ways to integrate with URL shorteners in an iOS app, the quickest way is to use NSString's stringWithContentsOfURL method. This method takes a URL, does all of the work to issue a request for the URL, and returns the response as an NSString. So, in the case of TinyURL, a request to shorten a URL via this service would look as follows within Objective-C code when using NSString's stringWithContentsOfURL:

```
NSString *longURL = @"http://www.apress.com";

NSString *format = @"http://tinyurl.com/api-create.php?url=%@";
NSString *apiEndpoint = [NSString stringWithFormat:format,longURL];

NSString *shortURL =
[NSString stringWithContentsOfURL:[NSURL URLWithString:apiEndpoint]
                    encoding:NSASCIIStringEncoding error:nil];
```

Note that `stringWithContentsOfURL` blocks until it receives a response. Therefore, depending on the requirements of the application using this method, it may be worthwhile to call this method on a background thread or to skip over the use of NSString's `stringWithContentsOfURL`, and then issue the request via `NSURLRequest`.

ShareKit: Sometimes Quick and Dirty Does the Trick

One of the main problems with integrating social services into an application is that there are so many social services proliferating online. Others have recognized this same problem and have gone through the trouble of aggregating all of these services into one library that applications can integrate with. One of the better aggregation libraries out in the wild is ShareKit, which you can acquire at this URL:

`http://getsharekit.com/`

ShareKit is an open source Objective-C library that makes it easy to integrate with the following services in our application:

- Delicious
- Email
- Facebook
- Google Reader
- Instapaper
- Pinboard
- Read It Later
- Tumblr
- Twitter

Since ShareKit is open source and hosted on Github, the code can be cloned, forked, or reviewed at any time:

`https://github.com/ideashower/sharekit/`

Note that the latest code on Github may not reflect what is in the current, official release of ShareKit, so be careful. Downloading and using the official version from the ShareKit site is highly recommended. At the time of writing, the latest official release of ShareKit is version 0.2.1. The download for this has been added to the source code repository for this book on Github, and it can be found in the `ShareKit` directory.

You can also find a ShareKit sample application in the source code repository (in the `Chapter10` directory). This sample application uses the version of ShareKit that is also in the repository we previously mentioned (0.2.1). The instructions that follow for integrating with ShareKit refer to the sample application.

Getting Started with ShareKit

To get started with ShareKit, first drag the `ShareKit` source code directory into your project. This directory is located at the following path in the `Git` repository for this book:

`ShareKit/Classes/ShareKit`

When dragging the ShareKit folder into a project, choose the default options in the pop-up dialog, as shown in Figure 10–1.

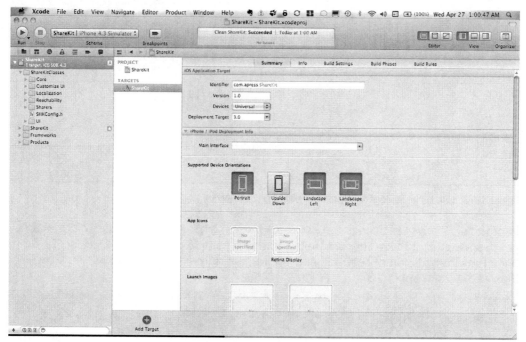

Figure 10–1. *Choose the default options when dragging ShareKit into an Xcode project.*

Next, link the application against the following frameworks (see Figure 10–2):

- `SystemConfiguration.framework`
- `Security.framework`
- `MessageUI.framework`

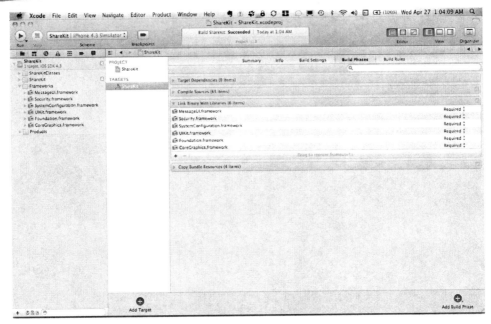

Figure 10–2. *Link the application against the appropriate frameworks.*

In order for ShareKit to access the desired services, it has to know certain information about accounts for those services. In the ShareKit sample project, go to `SHKConfig.h,` enter the information for Facebook and Twitter, and turn on debugging, as shown in Figures 10–3 through 10–5.

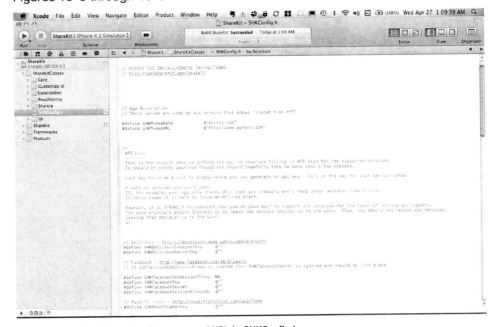

Figure 10–3. *Set the application name and URL in SHKConfig.h.*

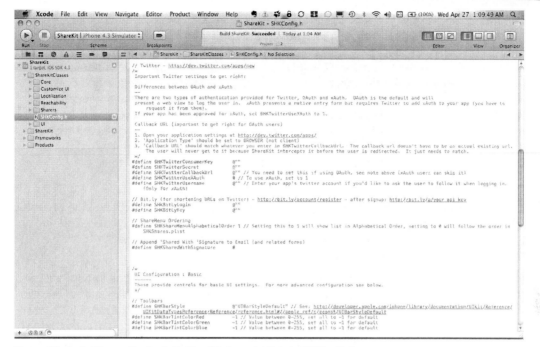

Figure 10–4. *Set the application's Twitter OAuth credentials in SHKConfig.h.*

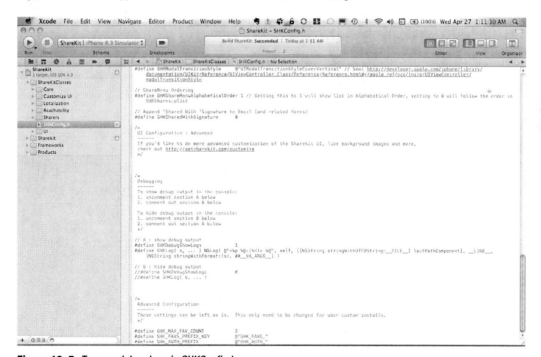

Figure 10–5. *Turn on debug logs in SHKConfig.h.*

Integrating ShareKit with Facebook requires the Facebook OAuth consumer key and secret for an application; similarly, integrating ShareKit with Twitter requires the Twitter OAuth consumer key and secret for an application. In addition, Twitter requires a callback URL. In order to set a callback URL for a Twitter application, the application has to be created on Twitter as a browser application. This means that, if an application was previously created on Twitter as a client application, that application needs to be reconfigured as a browser application. Otherwise, you'll need to create a new application. The actual URL that is entered for the Twitter application does not matter. The only thing that matters is that the URL specified in SHKConfig.h must match the URL specified on Twitter.com. An example would look something like this:

```
www.apress.com/callback
```

When working with Twitter, integration with bit.ly is required to post URLs since ShareKit uses bit.ly under the covers to shorten URLs before posting them to Twitter. Creating an application on bit.ly was covered previously in this chapter, so please refer to that section for additional instructions.

With the account information configured in the ShareKit header file, it's time to add code to the project to use ShareKit to post to Facebook and Twitter. Go to `MainViewController.m` in the ShareKit sample project and examine the `loadView` method. In this method, a `UIToolbar` is added to the view controller's view and is given a `UIBarButtonSystemItem` with the default action icon on the button, as shown in Figure 10–6:

Figure 10–6. *The UIToolBar in ShareKit with its default button*

```objc
- (void)loadView
{
    [super loadView];

    self.view.backgroundColor = [UIColor whiteColor];

    UIBarButtonItem *item = [[UIBarButtonItem alloc]
        initWithBarButtonSystemItem:UIBarButtonSystemItemAction
                        target:self
                        action:@selector(share)];

    NSArray *items = [NSArray arrayWithObject:item];
    [items addObject:item];
    [item release];

    CGRect frame = CGRectMake(0.0f,
                        self.view.bounds.size.height-40.0f,
                        self.view.bounds.size.width,
                        40.0f);
    toolbar = [[UIToolbar alloc] initWithFrame:frame];

    [toolbar setItems:items animated:YES];
    [self.view addSubview:toolbar];
    [toolbar release];
```

```
    [SHK flushOfflineQueue];
}
```

Selecting the bar button calls the share method, which displays an SHKActionSheet to the user:

```
- (void)share
{
    // Create the item to share (in this example, a url)
    NSURL *url = [NSURL URLWithString:@"http://www.apress.com"];
    SHKItem *item = [SHKItem URL:url title:@"Apress is Awesome!"];

    // Get the ShareKit action sheet
    SHKActionSheet *actionSheet =
        [SHKActionSheet actionSheetForItem:item];

    // Display the action sheet
    [actionSheet showFromToolbar:toolbar];
}
```

An SHKActionSheet is a nice pop-up presented to the user that displays options for sharing information (see Figure 10–7).

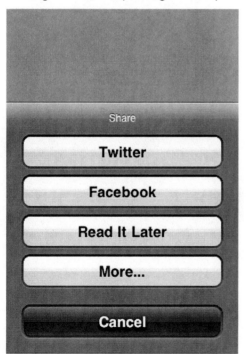

Figure 10–7. *The SHKActionSheet pop-up*

Clicking the Facebook button displays the familiar Facebook mobile web page for posting (see Figure 10–8).

Figure 10–8. *You'll recognize the Facebook mobile web page for posting.*

Clicking the Twitter button displays a nice dialog with a shortened URL (see Figure 10–9).

Apress is Awesome! http://bit.ly/dlB3mD

Figure 10–9. *ShareKit's Twitter dialog*

ShareKit supports more than just posting URLs and text, so it is worth exploring more of what it offers. It's a very nicely crafted solution for integrating quickly with Facebook and Twitter.

All the Latest Twitter Trends

It's always interesting to think about what people are Tweeting about in general within a specific geographic area or during a given time period. Twitter makes this data available via its trends API. Accessing these trends is very straightforward and does not require any authentication; however, be aware that the usage of these APIs is always subject to Twitter's rate limiting. This data can be accessed directly from within an iOS app or from server-to-server, depending on the needs of your application.

Twitter returns trends based on Twitter hash tags. Recall that Twitter hash tags are a means for Twitter users to associate or group Tweets together. For instance, assume a Twitter user wanted to Tweet about unicorns, so that his Tweet would be included whenever someone wanted to search for or see trends for Tweets about unicorns. In this case, he would include the hash tag #unicorns in his Tweet.

There are a few different ways to use the trends API. To obtain the top ten topics that are currently trending on Twitter, you can use the following request:

```
http://api.twitter.com/1/trends.json
```

The quickest way to see what this returns is to use curl again:

```
$ curl http://api.twitter.com/1/trends.json
{"trends":[
{"url":"http:\/\/search.twitter.com\/search?q=%23thatminiheartattackwhen","name":"#thatm
iniheartattackwhen"},
{"url":"http:\/\/search.twitter.com\/search?q=%23urnotmytypeif","name":"#urnotmytypeif"}
,
{"url":"http:\/\/search.twitter.com\/search?q=%23starship","name":"#starship"},
{"url":"http:\/\/search.twitter.com\/search?q=Seth+Meyers","name":"Seth Meyers"},
{"url":"http:\/\/search.twitter.com\/search?q=Jos%C3%A9+Aldo","name":"Jos\u00e9Aldo"},
{"url":"http:\/\/search.twitter.com\/search?q=Catcher+Freeman","name":"CatcherFreeman"},
{"url":"http:\/\/search.twitter.com\/search?q=Green+Men","name":"Green Men"},
{"url":"http:\/\/search.twitter.com\/search?q=Steven+Seagal","name":"StevenSeagal"},
{"url":"http:\/\/search.twitter.com\/search?q=Glenn+Healy","name":"Glenn Healy"},
{"url":"http:\/\/search.twitter.com\/search?q=Karate+Kid","name":"Karate
Kid"}],"as_of":"Sun, 01 May 2011 03:35:42 +0000"}
```

This returns a dictionary that contains an array of trends and an as_of date for when this trend snapshot was taken. Each trend in the array of trends contains the following:

- name: The hash tag for the trend.
- url: The URL to the Twitter search results page for that topic.

The same information can be obtained via the following request:

```
$ curl http://api.twitter.com/1/trends/current.json?exclude=#unicorns
```

Note that the trends/current API allows for excluding Twitter hash tags from the results. Also note that the Twitter search URL is not included with each individual trend:

```
{"trends":{"2011-05-01 03:32:19":[
{"promoted_content":null,"events":null,"query":"#thatminiheartattackwhen","name":"#thatm
iniheartattackwhen"},
{"promoted_content":null,"events":null,"query":"#urnotmytypeif","name":"#urnotmytypeif"}
,
{"promoted_content":null,"events":null,"query":"#starship","name":"#starship"},
{"promoted_content":null,"events":null,"query":"Seth Meyers","name":"Seth Meyers"},
{"promoted_content":null,"events":null,"query":"Jos\u00e9 Aldo","name":"Jos\u00e9Aldo"},
{"promoted_content":null,"events":null,"query":"Catcher
Freeman","name":"CatcherFreeman"},
{"promoted_content":null,"events":null,"query":"Green Men","name":"Green Men"},
{"promoted_content":null,"events":null,"query":"StevenSeagal","name":"Steven Seagal"},
{"promoted_content":null,"events":null,"query":"Glenn Healy","name":"GlennHealy"},
{"promoted_content":null,"events":null,"query":"Karate Kid","name":"Karate
Kid"}]},"as_of":1304220739}
```

Trending Topics

Twitter also makes available the top 20 trending topics for each hour in a given day:

```
$ curl http://api.twitter.com/1/trends/daily.json?date=2011-04-29&exclude=#unicorns
```

The response includes a trends dictionary, where each trend is a dictionary where the key is a given hour for the day in question, the value of which is the array of trends for that time of the given day:

```
{"trends":{
"2011-04-29 07:00":[<array of trends>],
"2011-04-29 20:00":[<array of trends>]},
"as_of":1304223220}
```

Note that Twitter only makes this data available as far back as the last seven to ten days. If the date parameter of the request is set to a day for which no data is available, Twitter returns the following:

```
{"errors":[{"code":35,"message":"Trend data not available"}]}
```

Similarly, Twitter makes available the top 30 trending topics for each day in a given week, going back three to four weeks:

```
$ curl curl http://api.twitter.com/1/trends/weekly.json?date=2011-04-
21&exclude=#unicorns
```

The response includes a trends dictionary where each trend is a dictionary and where the key is a given week, the value of which is the array of trends for that week:

```
{"trends":{
"2011-04-16":[<array of trends>],
"2011-04-17":[<array of trends>]},
"as_of":1304223220}
```

For daily and weekly trends, if a date in the future is specified, Twitter will return the trends for the current date.

Where On Earth ID

As previously mentioned, Twitter trends can also be obtained based on location. However, the Twitter trends API does not use latitude and longitude for locations; instead, it uses Where on Earth IDs (WOEID), which are maintained by Yahoo! A *WOEID* is a unique identifier for any named place on the planet. You can find more information on this topic at the following URLs:

- http://developer.yahoo.com/geo/geoplanet/
- http://developer.yahoo.com/geo/geoplanet/guide/concepts.html

Twitter can return the WOEIDs that it has trending topic information for:

```
$ curl http://api.twitter.com/1/trends/available.json
```

This request can take optional lat and long parameters to narrow the result set that is returned. The request returns an array of places, where each place is represented by a dictionary with values for different keys. One of these keys is the WOEID:

```
[{"countryCode":"TR","country":"Turkey","url":"http:\/\/where.yahooapis.com\/v1\/place\/
23424969","parentid":1,"name":"Turkey","woeid":23424969,"placeType":{"code":12,"name":"C
ountry"}},...]
```

You can obtain the top 10 current trending topics within the geographical area for a given WOEID (assuming trending information is available) by issuing a request that uses the following form:

```
http://api.twitter.com/1/trends/WOEID.json
```

So, to obtain the top 10 trending topics for the WOEID of 1, the request looks like this:

```
$ curl http://api.twitter.com/1/trends/1.json
```

Like the other trends request, this returns a dictionary with an array of trends:

```
[{"as_of":"2011-05-01T03:39:32Z","trends":[
{"url":"http:\/\/search.twitter.com\/search?q=%23thatminiheartattackwhen","query":"%23th
atminiheartattackwhen","events":null,"promoted_content":null,"name":"#thatminiheartattac
kwhen"},
{"url":"http:\/\/search.twitter.com\/search?q=%23urnotmytypeif","query":"%23urnotmytypei
f","events":null,"promoted_content":null,"name":"#urnotmytypeif"},
{"url":"http:\/\/search.twitter.com\/search?q=%23starship","query":"%23starship","events
":null,"promoted_content":null,"name":"#starship"},
{"url":"http:\/\/search.twitter.com\/search?q=Seth+Meyers","query":"Seth+Meyers","events
":null,"promoted_content":null,"name":"Seth Meyers"},
{"url":"http:\/\/search.twitter.com\/search?q=Jos%C3%A9+Aldo","query":"Jos%C3%A9+Aldo","
events":null,"promoted_content":null,"name":"Jos\u00e9 Aldo"},
{"url":"http:\/\/search.twitter.com\/search?q=Catcher+Freeman","query":"Catcher+Freeman"
,"events":null,"promoted_content":null,"name":"Catcher Freeman"},
{"url":"http:\/\/search.twitter.com\/search?q=Green+Men","query":"Green+Men","events":nu
ll,"promoted_content":null,"name":"Green Men"},
{"url":"http:\/\/search.twitter.com\/search?q=Steven+Seagal","query":"Steven+Seagal","ev
ents":null,"promoted_content":null,"name":"Steven Seagal"},
{"url":"http:\/\/search.twitter.com\/search?q=Glenn+Healy","query":"Glenn+Healy","events
":null,"promoted_content":null,"name":"Glenn Healy"},
{"url":"http:\/\/search.twitter.com\/search?q=Karate+Kid","query":"Karate+Kid","events":
null,"promoted_content":null,"name":"Karate Kid"}],
```

`"created_at":"2011-05-01T03:28:09Z","locations":[{"name":"Worldwide","woeid":1}]}]`

There are also other services that provide Twitter trend information. One of these is letsbetrends.com, which has its own API. For more information on this service, go here:

`http://letsbetrends.com/`

Also, if your application needs to show hints or information about hash tags, a service like tagalus (`http://tagal.us/`) can be used. Here is a good article on making sense of Twitter hash tags:

`http://blog.programmableweb.com/2009/03/20/make-sense-of-confusing-twitter-hash-tags/`

Offline Storage Revisited: SQLite

Part of Chapter 8 explored the topic of storing Tweets offline using iOS's Core Data. It's worth mentioning that, under the hood, Core Data saves the data for its data model in a SQLite database. *SQLite* is a "cross-platform C library that implements a self-contained, embeddable, zero-configuration SQL database engine." You can learn more about this database at `www.sqlite.org/`.

Core Data creates the SQLite database file in an application's `Documents` directory. When using the simulator, the `Documents` directory is accessed from the following path, where "4.3" will vary depending on which version of iOS the application is targeting, and `<app id>` is a unique application identifier created by iOS that varies by application:

`Library/Application Support/iPhone Simulator/4.3/Applications/<app id>/Documents`

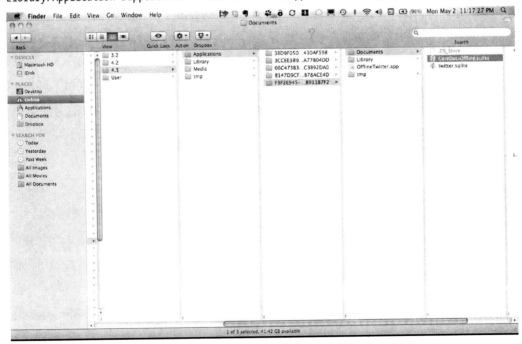

Figure 10–10. *The Mac OS X File System path to iOS simulator applications*

To determine which directory belongs to a given application, examine the contents of each of the <app id> directories and find the one that contains the .app file for the application in question. In the case of the Chapter 8 offline application, the file is OfflineTwitter.app. In the Documents directory for this application, there is a SQLite database file entitled CoreDataOffline.sqlite. The name of this file matches the name of the xcdatamodeld that represents the Core Data model, CoreDataOffline.

Viewing the contents of a SQLite database requires database software. One of the better database software products available for Mac OS X is MesaSQLite (www.desertsandsoftware.com/?realmesa_home). MesaSQLite is free, and it's invaluable when working with databases in an iOS application. After installing MesaSQLite or another database application, open the CoreDataOffline.sqlite file mentioned previously, and then view the contents of the ZTWEET table. (In MesaSQLite, choose the ZTWEET table from the Table Name drop-down list and click Show All to query for all of the Tweets in the database.) The ZTWEET table is where Core Data stores the Tweet objects that the application creates and saves. Note that there are ZID and ZTEXT columns that correspond to the id and text properties, respectively, for each Tweet object in the data model.

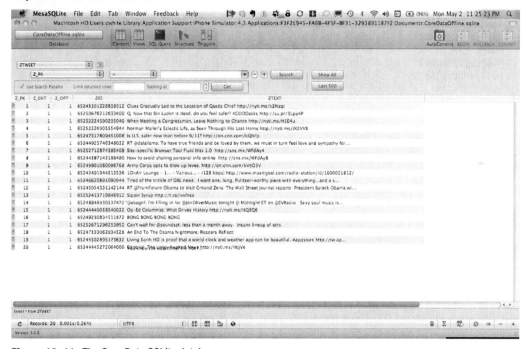

Figure 10–11. *The Core Data SQLite database*

Working with SQLite can be a little tricky, so it's worthwhile to get some hands-on experience with it. Therefore, the rest of this section will show how to reimplement the OfflineTwitter application from Chapter 8 using SQLite directly instead of Core Data. All of the code that follows is in the Github repository in the Chapter10/OfflineTwitter directory.

Reimplementing OfflineTwitter Without Core Data

Since the original architecture for the OfflineTwitter application kept all of the data access code in the `TwitterDataStore` class, almost all of the user interface views and controllers can be left as-is. The only work to do is to create a version of `TwitterDataStore` that uses SQLite directly to store, retrieve, and delete Tweets instead of Core Data.

First, the Tweet class is adjusted slightly, so that it's no longer a managed object:

```
@interface Tweet : NSObject {
}

@property (nonatomic, retain) NSNumber * id;
@property (nonatomic, retain) NSString * text;

@end
```

Next, `TwitterDataStore` is stripped down, so it's now a base class that any type of `TwitterDataStore` can be derived from:

```
@interface TwitterDataStore : NSObject {
}

- (NSURL *)applicationDocumentsDirectory;
- (NSArray*)tweets;
- (void)deleteTweets;
- (void)synchronizeTweets:(NSArray*)tweets;

@end
```

Now a class entitled `TwitterDataStore_SQLite` is created to do the actual heavy lifting of storing, retrieving, and deleting Tweets using SQLite. The class definition is located in `TwitterDataStore_SQLite.h`:

```
#import "TwitterDataStore.h"

@class sqlite3;
@interface TwitterDataStore_SQLite : TwitterDataStore {
    sqlite3              *database;
}

@end
```

Next, let's look at `TwitterDataStore_SQLite.m` in Xcode. Note that two additional helper methods are declared for the class:

```
- openDatabase
- closeDatabase
```

In the initializer for the class, `sqlite3.h` is imported, so that `TwitterDataStore_SQLite` can use SQLite. It's worth reviewing this header file to gain additional insight into what SQLite makes available to iOS applications since this discussion only touches the surface. Within the code, `openDatabase` is called to create the database (if it doesn't already exist) and set up the table(s) within the database. In `dealloc`, the database is closed when the class is destroyed:

```objc
#import "TwitterDataStore_SQLite.h"
#import "sqlite3.h"
#import "Tweet.h"

@interface TwitterDataStore_SQLite ()
- (void)openDatabase;
- (void)closeDatabase;
@end

@implementation TwitterDataStore_SQLite

- (id)init
{
    if ((self = [super init])) {
        [self openDatabase];
    }
    return self;
}

- (void)dealloc
{
    [self closeDatabase];
    [super dealloc];
}
```

The openDatabase method is tasked with creating the database and populating it with a table to store Tweets. If the database object is already open, this method does nothing. This is accomplished by checking to see if the pointer to the sqlite3 database object is NULL. Opening a database via SQLite is accomplished with the sqlite3_open method. This method requires a path to the SQLite database file that it needs to create if it doesn't already exist or to open if it does already exist. It also requires a pointer to a pointer of a sqlite3 database object.

If the database is opened successfully, the Tweets table for the database is created via the sqlite3_exec method, which executes a SQL query on the database. If the table doesn't exist already, the query creates the table with columns for the id of a Tweet and the actual message content for the Tweet:

```objc
NSString *createTables =
    @"CREATE TABLE IF NOT EXISTS tweets (id INTEGER
                                    PRIMARY KEY,
                                    message TEXT);";
```

Next, using sqlite3_exec again, an index is created for this table on the Tweet id in order to speed up querying Tweets out of the database:

```objc
NSString *createIndex =
    @"CREATE INDEX IF NOT EXISTS tweetIndex ON tweets(id);";

- (void)openDatabase
{
    if (nil == database) {
        NSURL *path =
            [[self applicationDocumentsDirectory]
            URLByAppendingPathComponent:@"twitter.sqlite"];
```

```
        if (SQLITE_OK !=
            sqlite3_open([[path relativePath] UTF8String], &database)) {
            [self closeDatabase];
        } else {
            char *errmsg;

            NSString *createTables =
            @"CREATE TABLE IF NOT EXISTS tweets (id INTEGER PRIMARY KEY,
                                                 message TEXT);";
            if (SQLITE_OK !=
                sqlite3_exec(database,
                [createTables UTF8String],
                NULL,
                NULL,
                &errmsg)) {
                NSLog(@"create table error: '%s'", errmsg);
            }

            NSString *createIndex =
                @"CREATE INDEX IF NOT EXISTS tweetIndex ON tweets(id);";
            if (SQLITE_OK !=
                sqlite3_exec(database,
                            [createIndex UTF8String],
                            NULL,
                            NULL,
                            &errmsg)) {
                NSLog(@"create table index error: '%s'", errmsg);
            }
        }
    }
}
```

closeDatabase is a very straightforward method. It calls sqlite3_close on the sqlite3 database object owned by the class. This closes the database, and then sets the pointer to the database to NULL, so that the openDatabase method will reopen the database if it is subsequently called:

```
- (void)closeDatabase
{
    sqlite3_close(database);
    database = nil;
}
```

Since the goal of this sample project is to store Tweets offline in a SQLite database, the first task to take on is synchronizing the Tweets that are retrieved from Twitter and storing them in the database (see Figure 10–12). As with the Core Data example, this occurs in TwitterDataStore's synchronizeTweets: method, which first deletes any Tweets in the database and then stores the new Tweets.

Recall that the Tweets are passed in as an array of NSDictionary objects, where each NSDictionary in the array represents a Tweet. Let's take a closer look at the for-loop that operates on the Tweets. The first step is to initialize a SQL transaction:

```
sqlite3_exec(database, "BEGIN;", NULL, NULL, NULL);
```

The actual SQL statement that will store a Tweet is as follows:

```
char *text = "INSERT INTO tweets (id, message) VALUES (?, ?);";
```

Note the presence of the ? symbols in the statement. This denotes that the values are going to be bound to the statement after it is prepared via sqlite3_prepare_v2. Note that the Tweet id is being stored as a 64-bit integer and is bound via sqlite3_bind_int64. The contents of the Tweet are stored as text and are bound via sqlite3_bind_text. The transaction is then executed via sqlite3_step. The transaction could fail for some reasons, so steps are taken to roll back the transaction in the case of a failure. This preserves the state of the database if a failure occurs. Here's the code to do this:

```
- (void)synchronizeTweets:(NSArray*)tweets
{
    NSAutoreleasePool *autoReleasePool =
        [[NSAutoreleasePool alloc] init];

    @synchronized(self) {

        [self deleteTweets];

        char *text = "INSERT INTO tweets (id, message) VALUES (?, ?);";

        for (NSDictionary *tweetDictionary in tweets) {

            sqlite3_exec(database, "BEGIN;", NULL, NULL, NULL);

            sqlite3_stmt *stmt = NULL;
            if (SQLITE_OK !=
                sqlite3_prepare_v2(database, text, -1, &stmt, NULL)) {
                NSLog(@"error: '%s'", sqlite3_errmsg(database));
                sqlite3_exec(database, "ROLLBACK;", NULL, NULL, NULL);
            }

            NSNumberFormatter * f = [[NSNumberFormatter alloc] init];
            NSNumber * tweetId =
                [f numberFromString:[tweetDictionary objectForKey:@"id"]];
            sqlite3_bind_int64(stmt, 1, [tweetId longLongValue]);
            [f release];

            NSString *message = [tweetDictionary objectForKey:@"text"];
            sqlite3_bind_text(stmt,
                              2,
                              [message UTF8String],
                              -1,
                              SQLITE_TRANSIENT);

            BOOL result = sqlite3_step(stmt) != SQLITE_ERROR;
            sqlite3_finalize(stmt);

            sqlite3_exec(database, result ? "END;" : "ROLLBACK;",
                         NULL, NULL, NULL);
        }
    }

    //post a notification that the tweets are available...have responder
    //update itself on the main thread
```

```
    [[NSNotificationCenter defaultCenter]
        postNotificationName:@"tweetsDidSynchronize"
                  object:self
userInfo:nil];

    [autoReleasePool release];
}
```

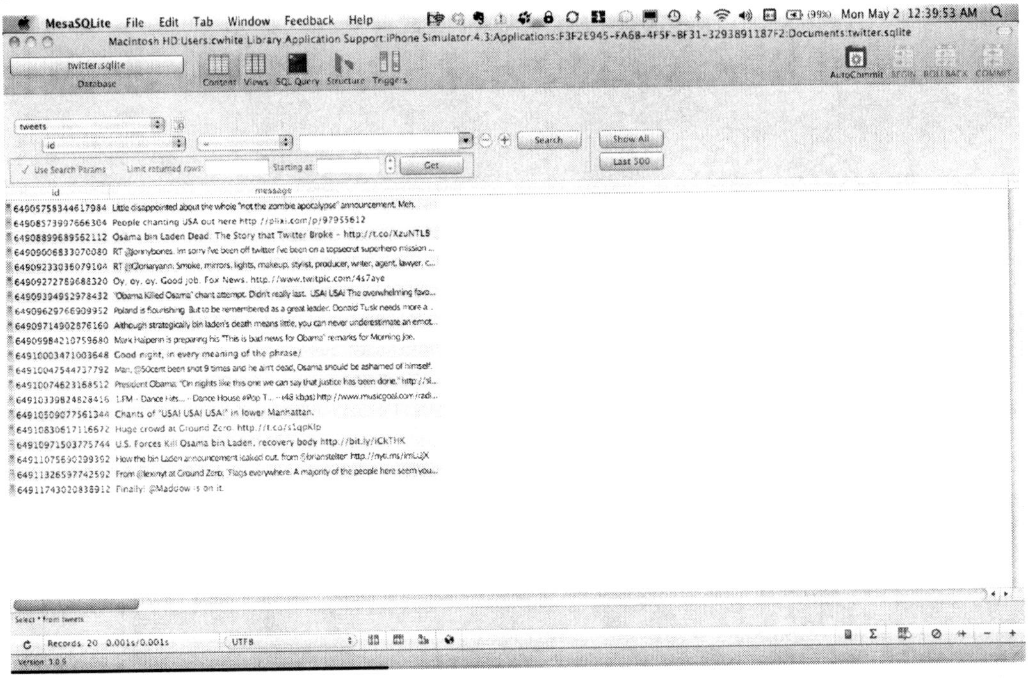

Figure 10–12. *The SQLite database of Tweets*

Now that the Tweets are in the database, the application needs a way to retrieve them. This is accomplished via `TwitterDataStore`'s tweets method. This method uses a standard SQL SELECT statement to get all of the Tweets from the database:

```
NSString *tweetsStatement = @"SELECT id, message FROM tweets";
```

If the statement is prepared successfully, the result set is traversed, and a new Tweet is created and initialized for each row in the result set. The Tweet is then added to an array of Tweets that is returned by the method:

```
- (NSArray*)tweets
{
    NSMutableArray *tweets = [NSMutableArray array];

    @synchronized(self) {

        sqlite3_stmt *queryStatement = nil;
        NSString *tweetsStatement = @"SELECT id, message FROM tweets";
        if (SQLITE_OK != sqlite3_prepare_v2(database,
                [tweetsStatement UTF8String],-1,&queryStatement, NULL)) {
            NSLog(@"error: '%s'", sqlite3_errmsg(database));
```

```
            return nil;
        }

        while(sqlite3_step(queryStatement) == SQLITE_ROW) {

            Tweet *tweet = [[[Tweet alloc] init] autorelease];
            [tweet setId:[NSNumber numberWithLongLong:
                        sqlite3_column_int64(queryStatement, 0)]];
            [tweet setText:[NSString stringWithUTF8String:
                    (const char*)sqlite3_column_text(queryStatement, 1)]];
            [tweets addObject:tweet];
        }
        sqlite3_finalize(queryStatement);
    }

    return tweets;
}
```

The final method to implement to complete the SQLite implementation of TwitterDataStore is deleteTweets. This method simply executes a SQL DELETE statement on the database to delete all of the Tweets:

```
NSString *deleteTweetsStatement = @"DELETE FROM tweets";

- (void)deleteTweets
{
    @synchronized(self) {
        char            *errmsg;

        NSString *deleteStmnt = @"DELETE FROM tweets";
        if (SQLITE_OK !=
            sqlite3_exec(database, [deleteStmnt UTF8String], NULL,
            NULL, &errmsg)) {
            NSLog(@"error: '%s'", sqlite3_errmsg(database));
        }
    }
}
```

The preceding code uses SQLite, so it will not link unless the application's Xcode project is adjusted to link against libsqlite3.0.dylib instead of CoreData.framework (see Figure 10–13).

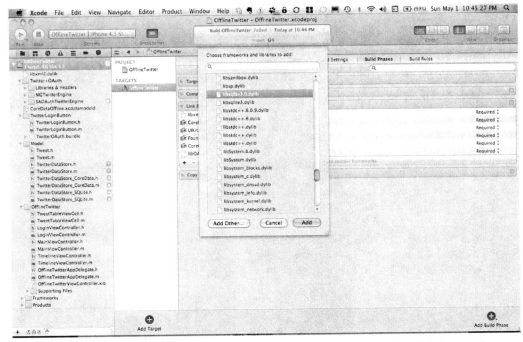

Figure 10–13. *Adjusting the Xcode project to link against libsqlite3.0.dylib instead of CoreData.framework*

To Test or Not to Test, That is the Question

Since code for a data model or layer doesn't require a user interface, it presents a unique opportunity to discuss an often overlooked topic for iOS and mobile development in general, which is Unit Testing. Unfortunately, a lot of projects avoid writing Unit Tests altogether or try to add some tests at the tail end of a project. Part of this is due to how difficult it often is to get a testing environment set up for a project, and some of it may be due to developer laziness. However, when done early and often, Unit Tests actually let developers be lazier than if they hadn't written tests at all because it requires less manual testing. In addition, with Xcode 4, Apple has made it easier than ever to get up and running with Unit Tests for an iOS project.

What follows is a step-by-step tutorial that adds a Unit Test to the OfflineTwitter Xcode for this project. The Unit Test validates the code that synchronizes the Tweets in the database. Of course, it's always best to write tests as code is being written, but the main purpose of this tutorial is to show how easy it is to add Unit Tests to an iOS Facebook or Twitter application.

Adding Unit Tests to a Social iOS App

Apple has configured Unit Tests to build and run as a separate target within an Xcode project. While this may seem a bit cumbersome at first, it has the nice advantage of keeping test code out of the main application target in a project. This means that test files don't get built into the final application binary. It also helps with debugging and setting up an automated test environment.

To add a new Target to a project in Xcode 4, from the File menu choose New ➤ New Target... (see Figure 10–14).

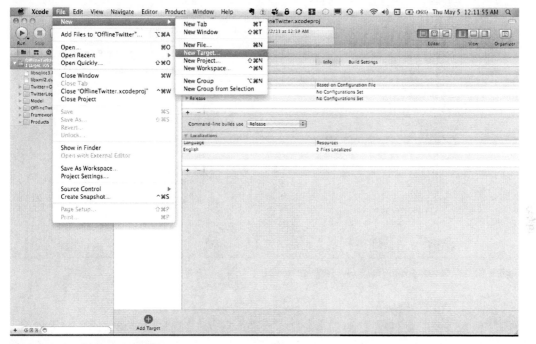

Figure 10–14. *Adding a new target*

In the Target template pop-up window, go to the iOS section, choose Other, and then select Cocoa Touch Unit Testing Bundle (see Figure 10–15).

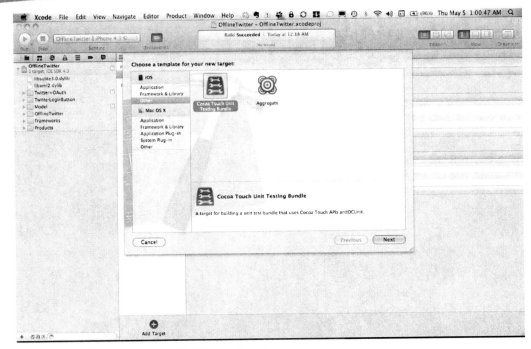

Figure 10–15. *Choose Cocoa Touch Unit Testing Bundle.*

Next, give the new target a name (see Figure 10–16).

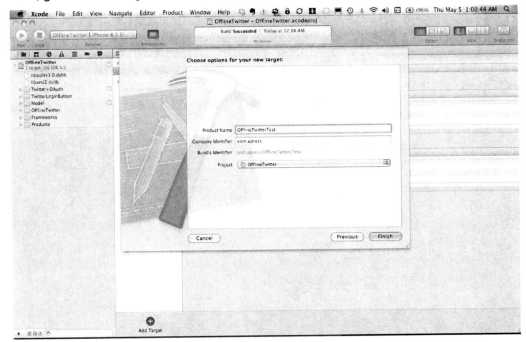

Figure 10–16. *Rename the target.*

Now switch to the new Target in Xcode via the Target drop-down, choose Test from the Product menu to create a build, and then run the test Target (see Figure 10–17).

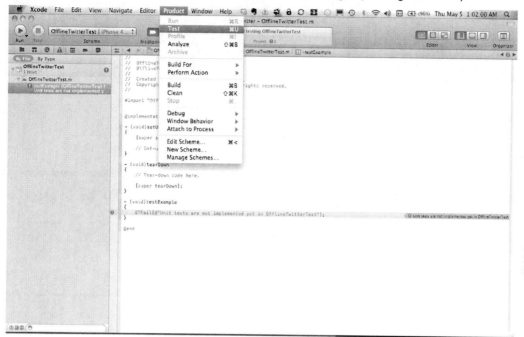

Figure 10–17. *Build and run the test target.*

The default test code created by Xcode is designed to cause a failure out-of-the-box. This illustrates how Xcode highlights test case failures (see Figure 10–18).

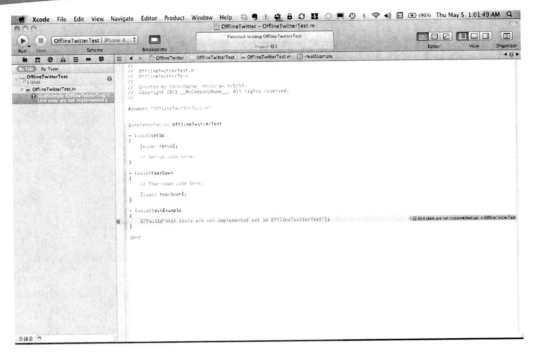

Figure 10–18. *Failure!*

The tests need to be written for the `TwitterDataStore_SQLite` class; therefore, the `TwitterDataStore_SQLite`, `TwitterDataStore`, and `Tweet` classes need to be added to the `OfflineTwitterTest` Target, so that the `OfflineTwitterTest` Target will link when actual test code is added (see Figures 10–19 through 10–21).

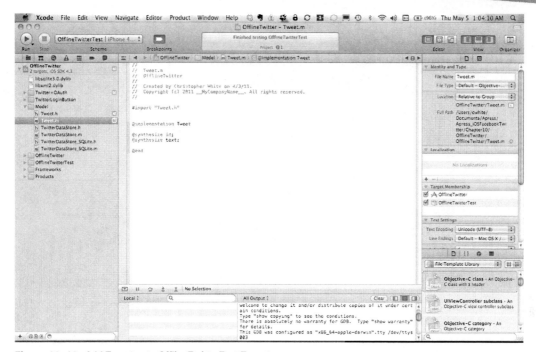

Figure 10–19. *Add Tweet.m to OfflineTwitterTest Target*

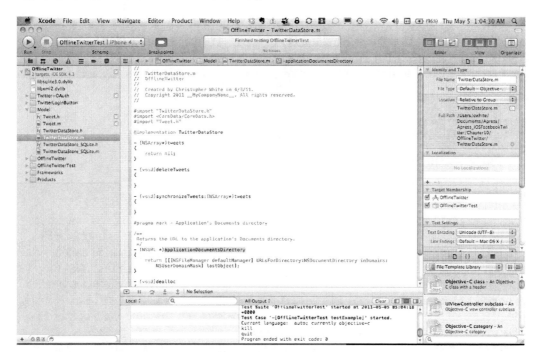

Figure 10–20. *Add TwitterDataStore.m to OfflineTwitterTest Target*

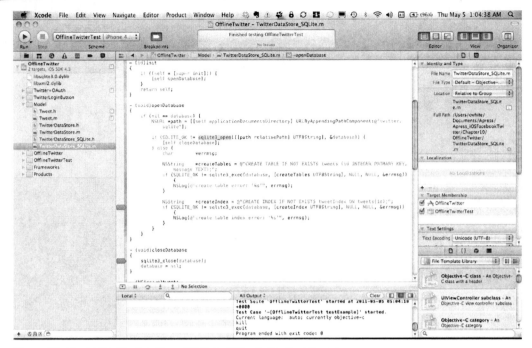

Figure 10–21. *Add TwitterDataStore_SQLite to OfflineTwitterTest Target*

All of the setup is now complete, so it's time to write a simple test to see everything in action. The test class will test functionality in the TwitterDataStore_SQLite class, so it needs to own a TwitterDataStore_SQLite object. Open OfflineTwitterTest.h in the sample project and note the declaration of a TwitterDataStore_SQLite object:

```
#import <SenTestingKit/SenTestingKit.h>

@class TwitterDataStore_SQLite;
@interface OfflineTwitterTest : SenTestCase {
@private
    TwitterDataStore_SQLite *twitterDataStore;
}

@end
```

With most Unit Testing frameworks, test classes are given a chance to do some setup before the test is run and some cleanup after the test is finished. Unit Testing for iOS projects is no different. Before a test is run, the test class's setUp method is called. After the test executes, the tearDown method is called. Open OfflineTwitterTest.m in the sample project and examine the implementation of these methods. Since this is a basic example, setUp instantiates the TwitterDataStore_SQLite object, and tearDown releases the object, so that the test doesn't create a memory leak (which could cause other side effects). Depending on the nature of the code in an application, more code may be required for these methods. Generally, these methods should be reserved for code that is required for every test in the class:

```
- (void)setUp
```

```
{
    [super setUp];

    // Set-up code here.
    twitterDataStore = [[TwitterDataStore_SQLite alloc] init];
}

- (void)tearDown
{
    // Tear-down code here.
    [twitterDataStore release];

    [super tearDown];
}
```

What follows is an actual test for the functionality of the `TwitterDataStore_SQLite` class. While there is the temptation to write Unit Tests for each method of a class, a better approach is to consider what the class is supposed to accomplish as a whole and write tests to validate its functionality. This also brings up the topic of naming tests. It is best to give tests useful, descriptive names so that other developers on a project will immediately know, just from the name, what the test is trying to validate. To that end, the test that follows is entitled `testItShouldSynchronizeTweets` to reflect the fact that one of `TwitterDataStore_SQLite`'s main responsibilities is to store and synchronize Tweets.

The test first deletes any Tweets from `TwitterDataStore_SQLite`, so that it's starting with a clean slate. This approach may not be necessary or desirable in all cases, and it should be adjusted on a class-by-class or application basis. Next, an `NSDictionary` is created to represent a dummy Tweet. Since `TwitterDataStore_SQLite`'s `synchronizeTweets:` method takes an `NSArray` as its only parameter, the `NSDictionary` for the Tweet is added to an `NSArray` object that is passed to `synchronizeTweets:`. `TwitterDataStore_SQLite`'s tweet method is then used to retrieve the stored Tweets, and a simple comparison is made to confirm that the datastore has a single Tweet. Depending on the test or application, additional validation could be added, such as whether or not the contents of the retrieved Tweet match what was put in the dictionary for the Tweet:

```
- (void)testItShouldSynchronizeTweets
{
    [twitterDataStore deleteTweets];

    NSDictionary *tweetDictionary = [NSDictionary
    dictionaryWithObjects:[NSArray arrayWithObjects:@"1", @"Tweet!", nil]
    forKeys:[NSArray arrayWithObjects:@"id", @"text", nil]];

    NSArray *newTweets = [NSArray arrayWithObject:tweetDictionary];
    [twitterDataStore synchronizeTweets:newTweets];

    NSArray *tweets = [twitterDataStore tweets];
    STAssertTrue((1 == [tweets count]), @"Test error message");
}

@end
```

The great thing about tests like this is that they make it very easy to debug code under specific scenarios, without having to run the actual application and perform multiple steps within the user interface. Such an approach also makes testing repeatable, which is excellent when code needs to be refactored or optimized. And of course, it ensures that *regressions* (i.e., bugs introduced into code that was previously working as expected) are not introduced into the code when it is adjusted or goes through a major overhaul.

Applications will need more than just one test. When additional tests are required, they can be added to an existing `test` class, or a new `test` class can be added to the test Target. Don't forget to also add any files from the main application Target to the test Target, depending on which functionality is being tested.

For additional information on this topic from Apple, review the testing sections in the document at this URL:

```
http://developer.apple.com/library/ios/#documentation/ToolsLanguages/Conceptual/Xcode4Us
erGuide/Building/Building.html
```

The tests are built via the `SenTestingKit` framework. The framework makes a number of macros available for validating tests. These macros start with the prefix, `ST`. The preceding example code uses the macro, `STAssertTrue`, but other available macros can be found in `SenTestCase_Macros.h`.

Setting up the test Target is a big part of configuring a project for tests. As mentioned previously, this overview covered Unit Testing from within Xcode 4. If a project is being built using Xcode 3, a different configuration is required.

While the `SenTestingKit` framework is available in Xcode 3, Apple's out-of-the-box offering for setting up tests is less than ideal. However, some engineers at Google were nice enough to expand on Apple's offering and make an updated iOS Unit Testing library available to the general public. Setting this up in Xcode 3 requires a few manual steps, but it's well worth the effort. The code is part of Google's google-toolbox-for-mac initiative, and it can be found here:

```
https://code.google.com/p/google-toolbox-for-mac/wiki/iPhoneUnitTesting
```

Another worthwhile alternative for Xcode 3 is GHUnit, which you can find here:

```
https://github.com/gabriel/gh-unit
```

Another interesting aspect of writing Unit Tests pertains to mocking objects. Learning to mock objects for tests can take test code to the next level. The main offering for mocking objects in Objective-C Unit Tests for iOS projects is OCMock. Note that using OCMock doesn't require a new testing target in an iOS project. Rather, it offers classes and functionality to use in existing test classes and methods or new tests. Explore the information at the following link for an introduction to OCMock, as well as setup instructions:

```
www.mulle-kybernetik.com/software/OCMock/
```

Conclusion

There are a number of great tools available to make life easier when developing iOS projects. These range from free online services to open source tools and software. This chapter touches just the surface of what is available; however, it covers a few that are indispensable for writing great iOS apps in general, as well as for Facebook and Twitter specifically. There is a wealth of information available online and via books and publications with respect to data modeling, testing, and shortening URLs; but writing iOS applications lends itself to the tools and software covered in this chapter due to the nature of mobile development and the constraints of the iOS platform.

Chapter 11

Apps You Can (and Cannot) Build

Sadly, we realized early on in writing this book that we'd need a chapter about all the rules that attend the use of the Facebook and Twitter APIs. Back in 2009, when these apps were exploding in popularity, social APIs were used with relative abandon. The platform makers—and that includes Facebook and Twitter—weren't sure how smartphones were going to change the way people used their tools.

Now that some time has passed, Facebook and Twitter have begun restricting the ways in which you can use their APIs.

In fairness, Facebook's platform policies are sensible and give developers wide latitude. Twitter, on the other hand, is often accused of being more manipulative (to put it diplomatically) about how people use their code.

While we, the authors, would certainly prefer complete freedom to use these APIs however we want, it's important to acknowledge that a brand like Twitter has a reputation to uphold, and (like any company) it is terrified of someone dragging it through the mud or confusing consumers about what Twitter is for.

Treat this section as a filter for your app ideas. If you already have an app that you're adding Twitter or Facebook functionality to, then you'll still want to skim this chapter to make sure none of your app's visual or interactive elements attract any negative attention from the Twitter and Facebook platforms.

After all, the only thing worse than having to obey rules is having to go back and redo your work to comply with them.

Twitter: No Clients Allowed

In March 2011, Twitter platform team member Ryan Sarver (@rsarver) posted a missive to its developer group. In this post, Sarver declared new Twitter fiats meant to corral what and how developers build. You can read his post at this URL:

https://groups.google.com/forum/#!topic/twitter-development-talk/yCzVnHqHIWo/discussion

We won't bother reproducing the note in full, but we'll highlight some areas where the changes in policy have been most acute. These also tend to be areas that developers new to the platform aren't aware of. The main points were as follows:

- Twitter has gotten exceedingly popular since its developer terms were first written.

- The more mainstream the service, the more consistent the UI and UX must be; otherwise, Twitter suffers what is known in the business as *brand dilution*.

- The UI and UX in the official Twitter apps are best, as indicated by their immense popularity compared to that of third-party Twitter apps.

- As a result, Twitter is slowly cracking down on the creation of Twitter clients that only reproduce Twitter functionality (and don't add some other kind of value). It's suggestions for value-added Twitter apps include publishing tools (such as SocialFlow), curation tools (such as Sulia), and data products (such as Klout). Other opportunities include social CRM clients like HootSuite; as well as other unique services like Foursquare, Instagram, and Quora.

In summary: You can still develop freely with the Twitter API. But from now on, you'll have to be more creative about the way your app uses the service. Simply reproducing the Twitter app with a different design or interaction will earn you a scolding from the Twitter team email (and possibly loss of access to the Twitter API).

The Lowdown on the Twitter Terms of Service

When Twitter posted the note just described, it also disseminated a revised Terms of Service that provided more specificity on the changes described in that post. Again, we won't reproduce them in full here, but there are certain areas you should be particularly aware of.

> **NOTE:** The best case scenario is that you will create an app that is wildly popular. If your app ever needs more than 5 million user tokens, you will need to contact Twitter directly about access to the Twitter API.

You can find the complete Twitter Terms of Service here:

http://dev.twitter.com/pages/api_terms

Rules of the Road

We will summarize Twitter's "rules" in the sections that follow. Note that even our summary—which is significantly more terse than the actual document—is still annoyingly long. We've put the most crucial points in boldface, in case you'd like to read those quickly. But don't move *too* fast—it'd be a shame to invest time and energy in a project not endorsed by these terms, since you may have to scrap it later.

Using the API

Here are some of the key rules governing the use of Twitter's API:

- You need written permission from Twitter If you want to sell, rent, lease, sublicense, redistribute, or syndicate the Twitter API, Twitter data, or Twitter content. Here are some additional rules pertaining to these permissions:

    - You face a special restriction if you provide an API that returns Twitter data: it may only return Tweet IDs and user IDs.

    - You may export or extract non-programmatic, GUI-driven Twitter content as a PDF or spreadsheet by using "save as" or similar functionality.

    - You are not permitted to export Twitter content to a datastore as a service or other cloud-based service.

- You aren't allowed to alter any proprietary notices or marks on the Twitter API or content.

- **You can't use the Twitter API for purposes of monitoring the up-time, performance, or functionality of Twitter.**

- **You can't use Twitter trademarks in a manner that suggests you have any association with Twitter.**

- **You can't sell or access the Twitter API to aggregate, cache (except as part of a Tweet), or store geographic location info contained in Tweets.**

- You can't charge a premium for access to any Twitter feature.

What Your App Can Do

According to Twitter, your service "may be an application or client that provides major components of a Twitter-like end user experience"; however, if you build a client app, additional terms apply:

- You must use the Twitter API as the sole source for features in your client that are substantially similar to functionality offered by Twitter. In other words, you can't mix another similar API into your Twitter API project, or the company will write you one of those threatening emails.

- You may not offer payment to third parties for distribution of your app.

- **You cannot frame or reproduce significant portions of the Twitter service in your app; instead, you must use the Twitter API to display Twitter content.**

- Do not store private data or content, or duplicate Twitter's database.

Rules Governing Existing Twitter Clients

Given the new terms of service, it might seem strange that several non-official Twitter clients remain in the app store. When Twitter made the "no more clients" announcement in March 2011, its platform developers said some existing Twitter client apps would be allowed to continue doing business. However, Twitter's Ryan Sarver added[1]:

> "We will be holding you to high standards to ensure you do not violate users' privacy, that you provide consistency in the user experience, and that you rigorously adhere to all areas of our Terms of Service."

How Twitter Defines Usability

The section that follows doesn't contain rules, exactly; rather, it describes a series of guidelines that (if followed) will ensure you don't earn any ire from Twitter's platform folks. It might seem draconian of them to dictate how your app should operate, but it's in the best interest of users, some of whom will be confused if your app does things with the platform that other Twitter apps don't. In that spirit, Twitter asks that you adhere to the following:

- **Don't surprise users:** Don't misuse Twitter functionality or terminology:

  - **Maintain the integrity of Tweets. There is a lot of information packed into Tweets, even though they are just 140 characters long. See Chapter 13 for Twitter Visual Design guidance.**

---

[1] https://groups.google.com/forum/#!topic/twitter-development-talk/yCzVnHqHIWo/discussion

- Don't edit or revise user-generated content delivered through the API.

- Always show the user that authored or provided a Tweet.

- **Don't create or distribute spam:** Get a user's permission before you do any of the following:

  - **Send Tweets or other messages on her behalf. The fact that a user authenticates through your application does not constitute consent to send a message on her behalf.**

  - Modify her profile information or take account actions (including following, unfollowing, and blocking) on her behalf.

  - Add hash tags, annotations data, or other content to a user's Tweet. Show the user exactly what will be published.

- **Don't make placeholder apps for the sake of name-squatting.**

- **Respect user privacy:** You need to utilize proper security standards such as 0Auth, as discussed in Chapter 2. You should also do the following:

  - Respect the privacy and sharing settings of Twitter Content.

  - Promptly change your treatment of Twitter content as changes are reported through the Twitter API.

  - **Always show users a privacy policy for your service. You should also clearly disclose what you are doing with information you collect from them.**

  - **Clearly disclose when you are adding location information to a user's Tweets, whether as a geotag or annotations data.**

  - Do not solicit another developer's consumer keys or consumer secrets if they will be stored outside of that developer's control.

  - Do not facilitate or encourage the publishing of private or confidential information.

- **Be a good partner to Twitter:** You need to follow all the rules described in this chapter, including the following:

  - **Don't use business names and/or logos in a manner that can mislead, confuse, or deceive users.** For more information on the use of Twitter Marks, see the trademark rules later in this chapter.

  - Try not to confuse or mislead users about the source or purpose of your application.

  - Don't link to malware.

> ▦ **Don't replicate, frame, or mirror the Twitter website or its design.**

> ▦ Don't misuse the API to impersonate others on Twitter.

Login and Identity

Twitter also has some guidelines pertaining to login and identity:

> ▦ You must present users with the option to log into Twitter via the OAuth security protocol, as discussed in Chapters 2 and 5 of this book.

> ▦ **You should give end users without a Twitter account the opportunity to create a new Twitter account.**

> ▦ You must display the Connect with Twitter option at least as prominently as the Facebook Connect button, or any other social Web login option.

> ▦ You must do the following once an end user has authenticated via Connect with Twitter: clearly display his Twitter avatar, his Twitter user name, and the Twitter bird graphic.

Displaying Content Correctly

Here are the guidelines that cover displaying Twitter content correctly:

> ▦ You should have all URLs referencing content in a Tweet direct users back to the page where that content is displayed, and not to any intermediate pages.

> ▦ You must show Tweets that reference Twitter as the source if your service displays updates commingled with Tweets.

> ▦ Don't put pornography in user profile images or backgrounds.

> ▦ **Only surface actions that are organically displayed on Twitter.** For example, when a user executes the unfavorite or delete actions, you should not do something Twitter doesn't, such as publicize that a Tweet was deleted.

> ▦ Do not falsely report an account as Verified.

Monetizing Your App

You should adhere to the following guidelines when attempting to monetize your app. One of the most important aspects of this is to respect user content:

> ▦ Tweets may be used in ads, but not *as* ads.

- You must get permission from the user that created a Tweet if you want to use it on a durable good, or if you're implying the sponsorship or endorsement of that user.

Twitter Ads

Twitter may serve advertising in your app via its APIs (i.e., Twitter Ads); however, Twitter will share a portion of advertising revenue with you if you contact it.

Advertising Around Twitter Content

You are allowed to advertise inside your own Twitter API app, but there are (of course) rules about this, too:

- **You must pay Twitter a cut of your revenue if the "primary basis" of your advertising deal is Tweets. If you think your ad deal may fall under this rubric, email Twitter at** `partner@twitter.com`. **This includes things like custom visualizations.**

- **You cannot put ads in the Twitter timeline or in any other message else that might reasonably be confused by users as a Tweet. For example, ads cannot have Tweet actions like ReTweet, Favorite, and Reply.**

- You must generally maintain a clear separation between Twitter content and your advertisements.

New Rate Limits and the End of Whitelisting

Until early 2011, Twitter had a *whitelist* of developers it allowed to exceed the hourly rate limit of API calls. The concept of the whitelist was a hold-over from the early days of the REST API, when Twitter had few bulk request options, and the Streaming API wasn't public yet.

Since then, Twitter has added more efficient tools for making bulk requests: lookups, ID lists, authentication, and the Streaming API. Still, now that all whitelist requests are being denied, some app projects that might have been ingenious back in 2010 won't be viable today.

If you're planning to do advanced research and analytics, you'll need to buy data through a reseller of Twitter data like Gnip.

The real change, however, comes a bit later in Sarver's announcement, when he notes that "there are going to be some things that developers want to do that just aren't supported by the platform." Instead of granting whitelisting to make advanced research and analytics possible, writes Sarver, Twitter now asks that developers contact Gnip, currently the primary reseller of Twitter data.

REST API Rate Limiting

Twitter places a limit of 150 requests per hour on API calls. For OAuth calls, the limit is 350 per hour. As we said previously, Twitter won't let you whitelist your way out of this rate limit. You can buy bulk data from a reseller, but at the time of writing, the only such reseller is Gnip. But others may follow, and a market for Twitter data may emerge. In any case, many developers report negative experiences trying to work with unstructured dumps from Twitter's firehose.

Assuming you're interested in the particulars of Twitter's rate limits, we've summarized its allowances here:

- Authenticated calls are measured against that user's limit, while unauthenticated calls are deducted from the allowance of the host. Hosts are permitted 150 requests per hour.

- OAuth calls are permitted 350 requests per hour.

You can find the complete document that spells out these limits at this URL:

`http://dev.twitter.com/pages/rate-limiting#rest`

As with most social platforms, Twitter's API places no rate limits on HTTP POSTs; however, the company has said it may consider limiting POSTs in the future. Methods that include limits are called out in the document at this URL:

`http://dev.twitter.com/pages/rate-limiting#rest`

> **NOTE:** API methods that are not directly rate-limited are still subject to organic (and therefore unpublished) limits.

If you think your app may be close to exceeding rate limits, you can monitor its status by inspecting the HTTP response headers that are returned. With the default rate limit headers, these response headers will also show the following:

- X-FeatureRateLimit-Limit

- X-FeatureRateLimit-Remaining

- X-FeatureRateLimit-Reset

You'll know you've hit a rate limit when you get back HTTP 400 response codes.

Facebook: Mind Your Manners

Facebook's rulebook is slightly less imposing than Twitter's, and it's more interested in guiding developers than scaring them straight. In the sections that follow, we'll explain some of Facebook's usability principles. Consider these to be the foundation for the personality of your app.

The Lowdown on Platform Policy

You can find Facebook's complete, unedited platform policies at this URL:

http://developers.facebook.com/policy/

Creating a Great User Experience

Facebook has provided the following guidelines for creating a terrific user experience:

- **Build social and engaging applications:** What does this mean? Well, the best Facebook API projects in the App Store prioritize communication and interaction with other users. More passive, consumption-oriented apps (like a News Feed reader) aren't right for Facebook, but make more sense on Twitter.

- **Give users choice and control:** Facebook's API has a dizzying number of objects, relationships, and actions. And while many of them seem insignificant, it's crucial that you adequately inform the user when something is going to be posted or shared with others.

- **Help users share expressive and relevant content:** Ideally, Facebook would have you build an app that doesn't merely access its Social Graph; it would also like your app to contribute new content to it. Apps that upload user photos, videos, and links from the Web are considered better citizens than those that don't.

Be Trustworthy

Like Twitter, Facebook asks that you respect a user's privacy, eschew spam, and avoid any other unscrupulous activity. And like Twitter, Facebook doesn't want developers competing with its own internally created iOS app. However, Facebook is more diplomatic about the way it explains its wishes, and it seems lax about forcing developers to abide.

Specifically, Facebook says you must not make derivative use of Facebook icons. Similarly, you cannot use terms for Facebook features and functionality that make it sound like a stand-in or replacement for the official Facebook app. However, one look in the App Store shows that many developers have copied Facebook's blue-and-white color scheme and made generous use of some Facebook iconography and terminology. But while Facebook shows lenience today, Twitter's example has demonstrated that platforms can decide to create or enforce their developer terms as they please. Know that if you decide to mimic Facebook's theming and its characteristics, your app may eventually earn the ire of the platform regulators. It will also look indistinguishable from dozens of apps in the App Store.

Rate Limits

Facebook imposes rate limits on users and API calls. For an authenticated user, the limit is 5 million. API calls are limited to 100 million. Perhaps to preclude any major competitor from using Social Graph data to compete with Facebook for ad dollars, Facebook limits your app to 50 million impressions per day.

For Your Privacy Policy

Facebook asks that you tell users what user data you are going to use and how you will use, display, share, or transfer that data in your app privacy policy. It also wants you to include your privacy policy URL in the application. To read more about privacy, review Chapter 2 (on privacy) and Chapter 5 (on OAuth and safe account management).

Other Stuff

Facebook has other rules about the use of its API, but thankfully its rules are more succinct than Twitter's:

- **Don't sell data:** If you are acquired by or merge with a third party, you can continue to use user data within your application; however, you cannot transfer data outside your application.

- **Delete your old projects:** If you stop using the Facebook API or Facebook disables your app, Facebook asks that you delete all the data you've received through the API (unless it is basic account information or you have the consent of the user to retain information on him).

- **Don't use a user's friend list outside of your application:** Even if a user consents to such use, this isn't allowed. But you can use connections between users who have both connected to your application.

- **Always provide a function in your app that allows people to access their Facebook data from the app.**

Rules About Content

Facebook's platform police hold you accountable for all content in your app, *including* user-generated content. This means you're responsible for policing (or creating a policing mechanism like a "flagging" function) in your app to ensure that your users don't post any of the following content to Facebook:

- Alcohol-related content

- Nudity

- Tobacco-related content

- Content featuring firearms or graphic violence

- Content that infringes upon the rights of any third party (such as intellectual property rights)

- Gambling-related content

- Illegal contests like pyramid schemes, sweepstakes, or chain letters

- Content that is hateful, threatening, defamatory, or pornographic

While Facebook might not be too aggressive in enforcing some of its design and functionality terms, it's actually very strict about violations to its content policy. The community and its moderators have been known to flag and remove pictures many of us might find rather innocent, such as an image of a mother breast-feeding her child. Still, keep your users' content PG or it will be quickly removed.

Other Odd Rules About How Facebook Apps Must Work

You will also want to keep the following rules in mind when working with Facebook APIs:

- Do not pre-fill your text fields with certain kinds of data, unless the user specifically asks you to create this kind of post. Rules against pre-filling fields apply to Stream stories (i.e., the `user_message` parameter for `Facebook.streamPublish` and `FB.Connect.streamPublish`, as well as the message parameter for `stream.publish`), photo captions, video descriptions, Notes, Links, and Jabber/XMPP.

- Adhere to Facebook's restrictions on your choice of advertising partners. A list of approved companies appears within the Apps section of Facebook.com.

- You must ask a user for permission every time your app posts something on his behalf after he grants you publishing permission.

- You must provide users with an obvious way to *skip* agreeing to the terms of a Facebook social channel.

- **You must *not* give users the option to publish more than one post at a time in your app.**

- You must not include platform integrations in your advertisements, including social plugins such as the Like button. If you want to do this, you have to get Facebook's written permission. You can contact the company on this page:

    `http://developers.facebook.com/policy/contact/`

- **Do not use Facebook messaging as a channel for your app to communicate directly with users; Facebook messaging (i.e., email sent to an @facebook.com address) is designed for communication between users.**

The Principles in Action

Facebook's rules seem to be motivated by very specific behaviors it hopes to discourage. The company's platform documentation provides pages and pages of specific examples with visual aids that explain the difference between compliant and non-compliant apps. We've summarized Facebook's ideas about compliancy here, so that you can digest them quickly and move on.

Photos

Facebook has several guidelines you should follow when working with photos:

- Never have your app automatically tag a user or her friends in a photo.

- Tag a photo only with the expressed consent of the user on whose behalf you are doing the tagging. Also, you must only tag images when the tag accurately labels what is depicted in the image. In other words, Facebook wants you to tag only human faces whose names you know.

- Don't tag a series of photos of a person in a row; you want to avoid creating a *banner* effect at the top of her profile.

The Like Button

The only unexpected rule here is that you must not automatically reward users for Liking your Page. If you want to reward people somehow for their fandom, you should make it clear that Liking your page allows fans—both new and existing—to become eligible for current and future rewards; however, the reward can't be immediate or automatic.

Advertising

Twitter and Facebook rules diverge somewhat radically on the subject of advertising. Twitter has a series of very specific guidelines about discussing its features in your app. For example, as you'll learn in Chapter 13, its guidelines ask that developers capitalize the word Tweet when they discuss Twitter content.

By contrast, Facebook's policy asks that you completely avoid Facebook logos, trademarks, and site terminology. Facebook is also quite adamant that its site features must not be emulated in your app. In other words, if your app looks too much like Facebook property and works too much like Facebook.com (or touch.facebook.com), you'll probably hear from Facebook.

If you'd like to read Facebook's ad guidelines in their entirety, visit this URL:

`http://www.facebook.com/ad_guidelines.php`

Using the Social Stream

Facebook also has several rules that govern how you interact with the Social Stream. The emphasis here is on authentic sharing of user-generated, user-authorized content:

- You should always ask a user whether he wants to publish a Feed story, rather than do it automatically. Also, you should offer to do so only after the user has taken a genuine action that may be associated with an award.

- You must not pre-fill any of the fields associated with the following products (unless the user manually creates the content):

  - Stream stories (i.e., the `user_message` parameter for `Facebook.streamPublish` and `FB.Connect.streamPublish`, as well as the `message` parameter for `stream.publish`)

  - Photo captions

  - Video captions

  - Notes

  - Links

  - Jabber/XMPP

Button Text

Here are a few examples of button text that are permitted for developers:

- Post

- Share

- Publish

- Add to Profile

And here are a few examples of button text that are too vague to incorporate into your app, in Facebook's opinion:

- Ignore

- OK

- Share & Continue

- Request

App Gallery

Now that we've spent some time telling you what you cannot build, we'd be remiss if we didn't show you some really excellent apps that are (more or less) within the bounds of the Twitter and Facebook platforms. There may be boundaries, but there's still plenty of space for developers to play in this sandbox.

Twitter Apps

In the authors' opinions, the best apps that use the Twitter API do the following:

- Combine Twitter's API with your own (or another) API to provide existing Twitter users a convenient way to add value to their existing Twitter service.

- Prioritize either (a) the consumption of Tweets or (b) the creation of Tweets. Traditional Twitter client apps, for example, prioritize the timeline and make it easy to browse through the content of other users. However, an RSS reader might have no provision at all for viewing your Twitter timeline, opting instead to provide only one button that Tweets an article.

Begin by recalling the Twitter design principles mentioned earlier in the chapter:

- **Don't surprise users:** Don't misuse Twitter functionality or terminology.

- **Respect user privacy:** You need to utilize proper security standards such as OAuth.

- **Be a good partner to Twitter:** You need to follow all the rules described in this chapter.

What follows are some apps that work creatively with the Twitter API and satisfy the aforementioned design principles.

Remember The Milk

Remember The Milk (or RTM, as it's abbreviated) gets a lot of love from its users. It's a productivity app that uses Twitter integration (among other tricks) to make itself behave more flexibly than a simple to-do list (see Figure 11–1).

Figure 11–1. *Remember The Milk uses Twitter as a backbone for a kind of remote command system.*

RTM uses Tweets and direct messages to create and edit items on a to-do list that is hosted elsewhere. Note that, while Tweets and direct messages are core Twitter functions, they are being used in a novel way and in conjunction with other backend software belonging to the RTM developers. In a nutshell, that's the kind of app that Twitter prefers developers to create: it adds a new layer of usefulness and functionality on top of the existing Twitter infrastructure.

Adding Tasks

By adding @RTM as a Twitter contact, users can Tweet to-do items for themselves and watch them appear later in in Remember The Milk's task queue. To get items into their to-do list (along with due dates and other task properties), users direct message @RTM with their task in plain text. Here are some typical sample messages:

- "pick up the milk": Adds a new task with that name to your to-do list.

- "call jimmy at 5pm tomorrow": Adds a new task with the specified name and due date to your to-do list.

- "return library books in 2 weeks": Adds a new task with the specified name and due date to your to-do list.

- "take out the trash monday at 8pm *weekly #errand": Adds a new task with the specified name and due date. It also marks it as a repeating task with the #errand tag. RTM calls this *Smart Add*.

Sending Tasks to Other Twitter Users

You can also use RTM to send tasks to other Twitter users. For example, tweeting "@username pick up the milk" sends the task to the specified Twitter username, assuming this user is also signed up for Remember The Milk.

Updating Tasks

To modify tasks that already exist in your to-do list, users can Tweet @RTM commands like the following:

- !complete call jimmy (shortcut: !c): Completes the specified task.

- !postpone call jimmy (shortcut: !p): Postpones the specified task.

You can also get new tasks:

- !today (shortcut: !tod): Gets tasks due today.

- !tomorrow (shortcut: !tom): Gets tasks due tomorrow.

- !getdue friday (shortcut: !gd): Gets tasks due on the specified date—Friday, in this case.

- !getlist personal (shortcut: !gl): Gets tasks from the specified list—personal, in this case.

- !gettag call (shortcut: !gt): Gets tasks with the specified tag—call, in this case.

- !getlocation office (shortcut: !go): Gets tasks at the specified location—the office, in this case.

Changing Preferences

Remember The Milk also lets you change settings by Tweeting commands. Some example commands you can Tweet include the following:

- !on – Enables task reminders.

- !off – Disables task reminders.

- !confirmon – Enables confirmations (task actions, such as adding tasks via Twitter, will be confirmed).

- !confirmoff – Disables confirmations (task actions, such as adding tasks via Twitter, will be confirmed).

- !help – Gets help info.

- !tips – Gets a list of commands.

Evernote

Evernote is a very popular cross-platform note-taking app for iOS, Android, Mac, PC, and other mobile and desktop platforms (see Figure 11-2).

Figure 11–2. *Evernote is a cross-platform notetaking app that allows you to submit notes by at-replying @MyEN.*

Evernote uses Twitter in much the same way that Remember The Milk does; however, Evernote emphasizes the use of SMS messaging as a way of accessing Twitter. Because Twitter can translate text messages into Tweets, it's frequently used by developers as a way of adding universal mobile phone functionality to apps that might see especially broad adoption outside the iOS ecosystem.

Like Remember The Milk users, Evernote users can compose a public Tweet or a direct message @myEN to have the body of the Tweet sent to an Evernote notebook (as seen in Figure 11–3).

Also like RTM, Evernote uses Tweets and direct messages, just as any other app would; however, Evernote messages don't add anything to the user's Tweet. Instead, they use the bot @myEN to determine how to process and file incoming notes. The result is a seemingly magical system that recognizes your submissions and files them correctly.

Figure 11–3. *Tweeting @MyEN*

SMS notes

Thanks to Twitter's built-in SMS support, Evernote users can send notes to Evernote from mobile phones operating in most countries worldwide. In the United States, the Twitter short code is 40404. Composing a message to 40404 containing the command d myEN tells Twitter to create a direct message @myEN, just as you would from a Twitter client. The text accompanying the command is entered into a new note in your default notebook.

Figure 11–4. *Adding Evernote content via Twitter's SMS support*

Adding TwitPics

Evernote also makes it easy to append pictures to your Evernote-bound Tweets. To do this, Evernote supports TwitPic URLs. If you compose a Tweet @myEN that contains a TwitPic URL, a thumbnail of the photo will show up in Evernote, along with a TwitPic link in the body of the note that links to the full-sized image.

Waze

Because iOS has no pre-loaded turn-by-turn navigation apps, apps that promise driving directions are an open market. One of the best of the lot is Waze, which takes a somewhat sillier approach to navigation than some of its competitors (see Figure 11–5). Waze puts a kind of game layer over your highway map, awarding you points as a way of encouraging you to report accidents, new roads, hazards, speed traps, and other ever-changing road features.

Figure 11–5. *Waze is a popular traffic app for iOS that uses Twitter as its notification infrastructure.*

Prior iterations of Waze allowed users to Tweet their traffic woes, collecting them in near real-time to create a dynamic map of road conditions. Now, Waze scans all of Twitter's data for traffic jam information, whether or not the person who composed the Tweet has a Waze account. This means that, even if a non-Waze user Tweets that he is stuck in construction traffic, your Waze app will show that person's warning on a map (assuming the user attached his location to the Tweet). People who already use Waze are encouraged to Tweet their updates with the hash tag #wazelive to make sure the system catches it.

This is what Twitter means when it says apps should strive to use data culled from the Twitter API to build new experiences. You won't find a Twitter timeline or list of followers and followees anywhere in Waze. Instead, the app uses search and messaging to create a real-life map of Twitter users in traffic in your area.

Waze also integrates Facebook and Foursquare APIs, letting you see if you have friends in the area you're driving through. You can also check in at your destination venue from inside the app, if you're so inclined.

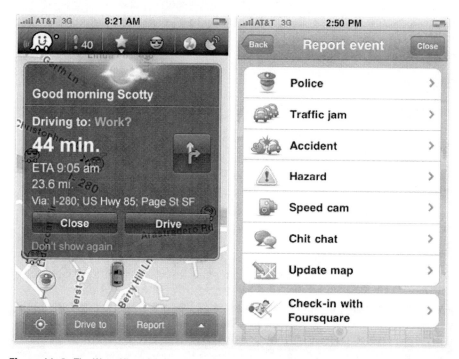

Figure 11–6. *The Waze UI, which barely betrays any sign of the Twitter or Facebook APIs*

Facebook Apps

Making a useful app that integrates the Facebook API is somewhat harder than one that integrates with Twitter, if only because Facebook's popularity and its well-documented APIs have made it such a popular choice with developers. Still, some apps stand out from the crowd; and even if they're not perfect, they embody the things that Facebook says makes a great API integration.

Let's begin by reiterating the Facebook design principles from earlier in the chapter:

- **Build social and engaging applications:** In other words, prioritize communication and interaction with other users.

- **Give users choice and control:** Be sure to adequately inform the user when something is going to be posted or shared with others.

- **Help users share expressive and relevant content:** Apps that upload user photos, videos, and links from the Web are considered better citizens than those that don't.

Fone

Fone isn't a perfect app, but it's a relatively simple project that does something the Facebook app doesn't excel at. Fone takes the instant messaging and voice calling feature from Facebook and puts it on the iPhone, creating a Facebook alternative to the system-standard Phone app (see Figure 11–7). (There is no voice calling from inside the official Facebook app.)

Figure 11–7. *Fone isn't a perfect app, but it adds some value to the Facebook chat experience—in the form of voice calls—and more or less avoids looking too Facebook-like.*

Because it's meant to connect users with other users, this app adheres to Facebook's usability principles. It also does a good job of using visual assets to communicate its function (see Figure 11–8). The blue colors harken back to Facebook, but the iconography lets people know that this app makes calls. Despite being a predominantly blue app, there isn't much evidence of any Facebook branding here. The typography alone makes it rather clear to users that they aren't inside a Facebook-branded app, as does the card interface (inspired no doubt by the preloaded iOS Weather app).

Figure 11–8. *Fone does a good job of communicating its function.*

Flipboard

Flipboard is a popular reader app for the iPad (see Figure 11–9). It operates under the supposition that much of the content you add to your Facebook profile or Twitter timeline comes from online sources like blogs, magazines, and the Social Graph. The app puts its focus on content, allowing you to read your RSS feeds, Facebook and Twitter news, and your favorite online magazines. It also makes it easy for people to take that content and share it with their network of friends.

Figure 11–9. *Flipboard, the popular news reader app for the iPad, integrates Facebook APIs nicely.*

Flipboard allows users to post Status updates, Tweets, and photos from anywhere within the magazine (see Figure 11–10).

Figure 11–10. *Flipboard allows you to consume your Facebook news feed in a different format than any of the Facebook sites or apps.*

Flipboard's Founder and CEO, Mike McCue, made a succinct explanation of what makes a good social API project at the release of the latest iteration of the app, when he said[2]:

> *"The people you're connected to via your social networks are becoming curators of the news and information that matters to you, an important principle we are increasingly seeing in Flipboard. Many of our readers use Google Reader and Flickr for news and photos curated by people they trust. The full integration of these social networks takes us another step toward realizing our vision of a social magazine that puts everything you care about in one place."*

In other words, the Flipboard app isn't just a one-way reader app. It allows you to consume and produce content in the same place, and do it around content you're pulling in from elsewhere. In short, it's apps like Flipboard that get fresh air into the Facebook arena and keep our news feeds from becoming mundane.

Conclusion

There are probably more rules around Twitter and Facebook API integration than you foresaw; some of them certainly surprised us. While you probably won't incur any legal trouble from violating most of these rules, Twitter and Facebook will probably get in

---

[2] http://flipboard.com/press/flipboard-new-edition

touch with you if you don't follow their rules, asking that you redesign your app or lose access to their APIs. Since the preceding pages have been rather dense, we've produced a cheat-sheet that you can use while vetting ideas for your app.

First, here is a major rules cheat sheet for Twitter:

- Don't use the Twitter API for purposes of monitoring the availability, performance, or functionality of any of Twitter's products and services.

- Don't use Twitter Marks in a manner that creates a sense of endorsement, sponsorship, or false association with Twitter.

- Use or access the Twitter API to aggregate, cache (except as part of a Tweet), or store place and other geographic location information contained in Twitter content.

- Don't have your client frame or otherwise reproduce significant portions of the Twitter service. You should display Twitter content using the Twitter API. (i.e., don't create new Twitter clients that operate like the Twitter app).

- Maintain the integrity of Tweets. There is a lot of information packed into Tweets, even though they are just 140 characters long. See Chapter 13 for Twitter Visual Design guidance.

- Always get permission before sending Tweets or other messages on a user's behalf. The fact that a user authenticates through your application does not constitute consent to send a message on his behalf.

- Always display a privacy policy with your service. Clearly disclose what you are doing with information you collect from users.

- Clearly disclose when you are adding location information to a user's Tweets, whether as a geotag or annotations data.

- Don't use business names and/or logos in a manner that can mislead, confuse, or deceive users. For more information on the use of Twitter Marks, see the trademark rules later in this chapter.

- Give end users without a Twitter account the opportunity to create a new Twitter account.

- Only surface actions that are organically displayed on Twitter.

- Don't let your advertisements resemble or be reasonably confused by users as a Tweet. For example, ads cannot have Tweet actions like ReTweet, Favorite, or Reply.

And second, here is a major rules cheat sheet for Facebook:

- Focus on authentic sharing of user-generated, user-authorized content.

- Always ask users whether they want to publish a Feed story; don't do so automatically. Also, offer to publish a story only after the user has taken a genuine action that may be associated with an award.

- Never pre-fill any of the fields associated with the following products, unless the user manually generated the content earlier in the workflow: Stream stories (the user_message parameter for Facebook.streamPublish and FB.Connect.streamPublish, as well as the message parameter for stream.publish), Photos (caption), Videos (description), Notes (title and content), or Links (comment).

- Don't use Facebook messaging as a channel for applications to communicate directly with users.

- Don't automatically reward users for Liking your Page. If you want to reward people somehow for their fandom, you should make it clear that Liking your Page allows fans—both new and existing—to become eligible for current and future rewards.

- Never have your app automatically tag a user or his friends in a photo.

- Tag a photo only with the expressed consent of the user on whose behalf you are doing the tagging. Note that you must only tag images where the tag accurately labels what is depicted in the image.

- Don't provide users with the option to publish more than one Stream story at a time.

Chapter 12

UI Design and Experience Guidelines for Social iOS Apps

In the last chapter, we talked about all the rules and regulations that Facebook and Twitter have conceived in the name of "protecting the user experience." Of course, those guidelines only address things that could reflect poorly on the platform. This chapter offers a little guidance on how to make something that doesn't merely satisfy the letter of the law: an app that is actually intuitive to use.

If this is your first time designing an iOS app, this section is required reading. It will address several sections of Apple's Human Interface Guidelines (HIG), which are especially important for social apps. It will also tell you how you can use visual and interaction design correctly, avoiding both user confusion and trademark conflicts. Follow these rules, and you'll get great feedback from users—and no hassling from the Twitter and Facebook platform reps.

We, the authors, believe the best iOS apps generally follow Apple's HIG, except where they purposely diverge to make an improvement upon the interface. In other words, we believe the best design should win, and developers can and should replicate each other's best interactions in the hopes of creating organic UI standards.

What we're really saying here is that learning the rules is crucial if you're going to be empowered to break them. If you've designed apps before, then this chapter is optional. However, you may want to page through it briefly to review certain paradigms.

UI Basics for Facebook and Twitter

This chapter begins with some very basic advice about social app design on iOS. The official Twitter and Facebook apps (and their legions of existing app developers) have standardized the interaction and visual design of these apps, so users have very high expectations for any UI you design. Following the advice of this chapter will help you do right by the user and avoid the wrath of all the rules we discussed in Chapter 11.

To start, here are two essential pieces of advice:

■ Be careful how you handle accounts upon setup.

■ Allow users to sign up, sign in, and sign out from your app with both Twitter and Facebook API integrations.

We'll begin by looking at how you handle accounts when you set them up. Showing users an error or a blank view simply because they haven't logged in yet fosters a bad user experience. We hate to pick on anybody, but here is an anonymous Twitter app we found on the App Store. At startup, it looks like the image shown in Figure 12–1.

Figure 12–1. *An error should never be the first thing a user sees in your app.*

Showing the user an error that says "Warning" when first starting up is a lame way to introduce the user to your app. It gets worse. If you click OK and fail to enter your account information in this app (buried in More ➤ Config, in this case), you simply get a blank timeline the next time you start the app. This is also not a great way to handle user accounts.

A better approach to the startup sequence can be seen in Twitterific (see Figure 12–2). This app also happens to be a good segue into our second, perhaps insultingly basic piece of advice.

Figure 12–2. *Twitterific's signup screen presents itself nicely.*

That is, you should allow users to sign up, sign in, and sign out from your app with both Twitter and Facebook API integrations. Both platforms ask that you do this, and it's only fair to users to follow through on it. Similarly, your app should be equipped to handle a scenario where the phone is offline upon launch or where the network connection fails during sign-in.

Attention to Detail: Start with the Icons

Design is paramount on iOS, so your attention to the detail of visual assets should be scrupulous. We'll begin by making sure you know the appropriate dimensions for iconography. This is your app's calling card to the world, so it must have the correct dimensions if it's going to look good on a Retina display.

Here are the proper icon sizes for both the iPhone and iPod:

- iPhone 4 icon: 114x114px (the old standard iPhone icon resolution was 57x57, which is the minimum acceptable size).

- App Store icon: 512x512px

- Spotlight Search: 29x29px

- iPhone 4 Spotlight: 58x58px

Apple's required icon sizes in a table below.

Table 12-1. *Apple's required icon sizes*

Image	Size for iPhone, iPod Touch (pixels)	Size for iPad (pixels)	Guidelines
Application icon **(required)**	57 x 57 114 x 114 (high resolution)	72 x 72	"Application Icons"
App Store icon **(required)**	512 x 512	512 x 512	"Application Icons"
Small icon for Spotlight search results and Settings (recommended	29 x 29 58 x 58 (high resolution)	50 x 50 for Spotlight search results 29 x 29 for Settings	"Small icons"
Document icon (recommended for custom document types)	22 x 29 44 x 58 (high resolution)	64 x 64 320 x 320	"Document Icons"
Web Clip icon (recommended for web applications and websites)	57 x 57 114 x 114 (high resolution)	72 x 72	"Web Clip Icons"
Toolbar and navigation bar icon (optional)	Approximately 20 x 20 Approximately 40 x 40 (high resolution)	Approximately 20 x 20	"Icons for Navigation Bars, Toolbars, and Tab Bars"
Tab bar icon (optional)	Approximately 30 x 30 Approximately 60 x60 (high resolution)	Approximately 30 x 30	"Icons for Navigation Bars, Toolbars, and Tab Bars"
Launch image **(required)**	320 x 480 640 x 960 (high resolution)	Portrait: 768 x 1004 Landscape: 1024 x 748	"Launch Images"

The largest visual asset you'll need to make here is 512 x 512 pixels. This is the graphic that is displayed when the app is being viewed in iTunes Cover Flow or when it's on a banner atop the App Store. In general, start all your icon designs at 512 pixels and adjust them to the required size. Simply scaling down a single icon to other sizes will result in blurry icons.

NOTE: PNG format is recommended for all images and icons. The standard bit depth for icons and images is 24 bits (8 bits each for red, green, and blue), plus an 8-bit alpha channel. Although you can use alpha transparency in the icons for navigation bars, toolbars, and tab bars, do not use this feature in app icons. You do not have to restrict yourself to Web-safe colors.

Here are the iPad standard app sizes:

- Application icon: 72x72px

- App Store icon: 512x512px

- Spotlight Search: 50x50px

- Settings icon: 29x29px

NOTE: The App Store only accepts applications with PNG files for icons.

You don't have to add gloss to your icons; it happens automatically. There's a Boolean switch you can use to toggle the glossy effect, if you want the unvarnished look.

The same goes for the rounded corners on app icons: leave your graphics with perpendicular corners and they'll automatically be rounded.

Show All Kinds of Feedback

Feedback is defined as any sound, vibration, or visual indicator that some process is under way. Showing feedback is important, especially on a touch device where there is no tactile sensation to manipulating on-screen objects. It's also important to show feedback when your app is doing something of its own volition, such as automatically loading new Tweets.

Apple says that every user action should show some perceptible change on the screen—even if it's just a shadow on a depressed button. Apple also wants you to show an activity indicator when an operation takes more than a few seconds.

Another kind of feedback is animation. Twitter says that animations can help "enhance readability," and Apple's HIG says that those animations should be "subtle and appropriate," and should serve one of the following purposes:

- Communicate status.

- Provide useful feedback.

- Enhance the sense of direct manipulation.

- Help people visualize the results of their actions.

Apple warns you to use animations conservatively because they have a tendency to feel annoying when used gratuitously. One other thing: Apple says you should strive to make animations consistent with those in built-in iOS apps.

However, in practice many developers break from Apple's use of animations in order to make what they consider to be improvements upon a given interaction. One example—pioneered by the official Twitter app's developer—is the pull-to-refresh indicator, which has been copied over and over by developers (including those at Facebook). You can see it in action in Figure 12–3.

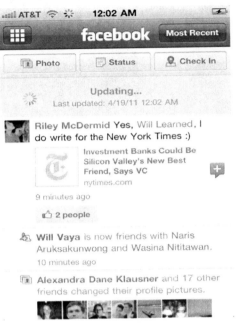

Figure 12–3. *The Facebook app shows users when it's loading new information.*

Note that it's unusual for a single developer's innovation to spread so widely, so you're very unlikely to make your mark in the annals of iOS design by upending some very common system animation. But if you feel strongly that your app justifies a departure from the HIG and from the App Store's design elite; then, by all means, give it a shot and see what kind of feedback you get during testing.

Also note that the *updating* indicator isn't the same as the activity indicator the app uses to show a Wall Post is in progress (see Figure 12–4). In the latter case, a simple iOS activity indicator is used to show the pull-and-release Refresh control has been activated and that posts are refreshing. (You can read about what your app should do if the phone is offline in Chapter 8.)

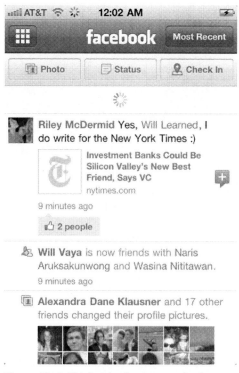

Figure 12–4. *The Facebook progress wheel*

In iOS, sound is a second-class medium for feedback because Apple believes there are too many scenarios where the feedback can't be registered because the environment is too loud. Vibration is a more reliable feedback mechanism, but it should only be used for the most important notifications. They can't be too frequent, either. And users must be able to turn them off.

Facebook gives you the option of using both sound and vibration. It also uses the phone's accelerometer input with the Shake to Reload feature (see Figure 12–5).

> **NOTE:** Facebook follows Apple's design guidelines by keeping these feedback preferences in a pane in the system Settings app. For more about preferences, see the "Present Settings in the Standard Way" section later in this chapter.

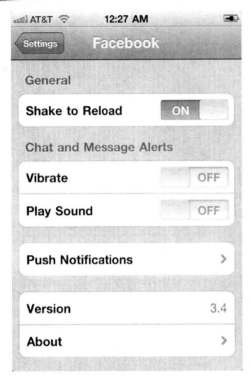

Figure 12–5. *Facebook keeps a few set-and-forget preferences in the system Settings app.*

Touch Targets and Text

The minimum size of a touch target in iOS is 44 x 44 pixels. Be sure to leave adequate padding between controls; and, as we said in the preceding section, don't crowd the screen with controls. For example, we like the way TwitHit situates its core task right in the middle, as shown in Figure 12–6.

Figure 12–6. *TwitHit makes the main task obvious.*

Remember to make all your controls tappable and to pay attention to their labels. You can find guidance on labeling—and the use of trademarks and iconography—in the sections that follow.

Prototype and Test

Apple heavily recommends user testing before submitting your app to the App Store. This is especially vital in social app design. If you're building apps with Facebook or Twitter, be sure to download other apps that use the APIs (many of which we've discussed in this book already). See how they handle certain operations and how they distinguish themselves visually. Also, ask your friends and colleagues what they like about various other apps, and then let their feedback inform your design process. Xcode is very flexible when it comes to fine-tuning apps, and it's easy to iterate a few times to get things right.

What the User Wants from Your App

Here are seven essential areas that you should prioritize when you're designing your app:

- Content
- A logical path
- Obvious settings
- Branding
- Brevity
- A license agreement
- Appropriate iPad design

In the sections that follow, we'll take a look at each of these design principles and how you can leverage them in your app.

Content

Facebook and Twitter both revolve around two core tasks: consuming and creating content in the broad *social graph*.

If your app can post, it should present users with a clean, spacious interface for entering text or media, without a lot of other controls in or around the text box. Although it's not a totally minimalist design, we like the way TweetBot presents the creation of a Tweet.

If your app pulls in information from either of the Facebook or Twitter APIs, it should be presented in appropriate way. For photos, this means your app should be shown full-screen with controls that are translucent and disappear when they're not being used. For text, this means legible typefaces.

A Logical Path

The official Twitter and Facebook apps can feel labyrinthine in their complexity; however, they manage it well. Twitter manages its complexity with a dynamic application bar, whereas Facebook does so with its "grid" UI. But, as we'll discuss later in this chapter, you can't replicate either of these strategies if your app is complex. Read on to learn how to design interactions around Twitter and Facebook content.

Obvious Settings

Apple says developers should avoid putting their app's settings inside the app itself; rather, they should opt for a pane inside the system Settings app. However, many popular apps that use both Facebook and Twitter APIs don't follow this convention, often because they find the System Settings API too limiting. Our suggested compromise: Pick set-it-and-forget-it options, stick them in the Settings app, and put more commonly used options inside your app. Many users will get impatient if they have to leave your app to edit their account information or play with visual display options.

The official Facebook app actually follows the convention we just described, whereas the Twitter app handles all its settings over a couple of screens inside the app (see Figure 12–7).

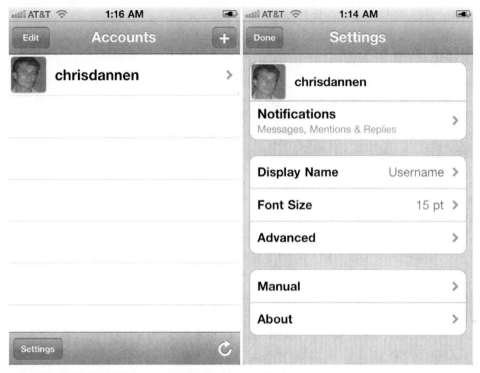

Figure 12–7. *Twitter handles its preferences inside the app.*

Branding

You should use colors, styles, and customized art and animation to create a look and feel that is unique to your app. This is how users distinguish you from other developers and your app from those of your competitors.

Brevity

Label things with short, specific terms. If you can't think of a reasonable label for a control, consider using one of Apple's system icons or a symbol that users will understand from either the Facebook or Twitter platforms. Also, consider a license agreement or disclaimer.

A License Agreement

Okay, maybe users don't want a license agreement. But both Twitter and Facebook say they require developers to show users a license agreement. For the record, Apple says it's optional, so we say play it safe and write one. If you do include a EULA, don't ask users to agree to it upon first launch. (Do ask for permissions for the use of their location and Push notifications upon first launch, however.) Instead, you should give users a chance to use the app before asking them to accept your terms and/or put them in the Settings pane of your app.

Appropriate iPad Design

If you're developing for iPad, remember to avoid the temptation to create complex hierarchies or nested headings in your app's navigation stack. Also remember to use the Popover control for modal tasks and to move toolbar content to the top of the screen.

Make Usage Easy and Obvious

As we said in the introduction to this chapter, iOS design should always give primacy to ease of use and learning. According to Apple, you can ensure you adhere to this principle by doing the following:

- Reduce the set of controls to only the most common and useful set. For additional options, use a More button or system-standard Actions button.

- Use standard controls and gestures appropriately and consistently, so that they behave the way people expect them to.

- Label controls clearly, so that people understand exactly what they do.

In iOS apps, this is trickier than it seems. Users are already accustomed to dozens of different UI paradigms from using the official Twitter and Facebook apps. When they arrive in yours, they have certain expectations for what controls are called; the nomenclature of the labels; and the core capabilities of your app.

Therefore, it's important that you strive to use terminology correctly and avoid deviating from standardized interactions. In Chapters 13 and 14, we'll delve deeper into the proper use of terms, trademarks, and other branding.

Conclusion

Now that we've reviewed the foundation of what makes a good social app design, you may consider flipping through the rest of Apple's Human Interface Guidelines if you've never read them.

Once you're ready, proceed to the next two chapters, which you can think of as Human Interface Guidelines for Twitter and Facebook, respectively.

Chapter 13

Twitter UI Design

Because so many Twitter clients already exist on iOS, there are already a number of design paradigms out there that you should be aware of when you create your app.

This section will discuss the visual, navigational, and interactional paradigms that we believe you should avoid, revise, or pay homage to.

Usability Priorities

If you're going to design a Twitter API project with an adequate user experience, you should get your priorities on paper first. For most Twitter API projects, this means putting the most time and energy into the following:

- *Loading and scrolling*: What is today the official Twitter app for iOS began as Tweetie, a one-man project devoted to one key feature: fast-scrolling Tweets. Since Tweets are a centerpiece to most Twitter apps, you should make lists, content, and Tweets load as quickly and smoothly as possible.

- *Using images, URL shorteners, and Geo-tagging*: If your app creates Tweets, these three features have become standards and are expected anywhere a Tweet is made.

- *Keeping users inside your app*: Tweets are attached to schemas of actions and content: pictures, contacts, URLs, Retweets, @replies, and so on. Try to handle all relevant operations inside your app, without resorting to Web views or launching one of the system apps. Ejecting users from your app is confusing and it slows them down.

- *Honoring privacy first and foremost*: Don't print Tweets without permission from the author. Use real Tweets from real accounts that are operated internally or that you have permission from the user to display. When showing example content, always use screenshots of your own Twitter profile (with your own Tweets).

Anatomy of a Tweet

Twitter is supremely specific about how it wants Tweets displayed. In fact, it has even specified that we should capitalize *Tweet* when writing a book like this. You can see how Twitter expects Tweets to be displayed in its "Anatomy of a Tweet" graphic, which is from the following URL (see Figure 13–1):

```
http://dev.twitter.com/pages/display_guidelines
```

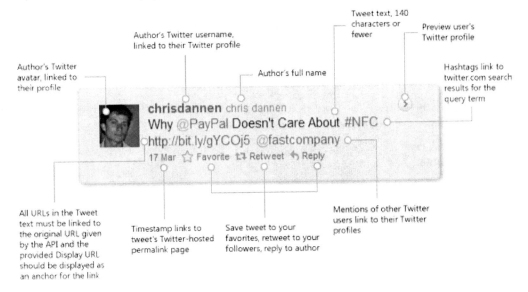

Figure 13–1. *The "Anatomy of a Tweet," according to Twitter's official design guidelines*

Let's examine all the elements shown in Figure 13–1 in greater depth:

1. *Tweet Author*: Twitter says you must present the handle of a user's Tweet; however, displaying a user's real name next to her handle is optional. Tapping the username should link to the user's Twitter profile, preferably within your app. Twitter design guidelines dictate that the username and the real name (if you show it) should be in different styles. Don't put an @ symbol in front of a user's handle.

2. *@mentions*: Mentions of other Twitter users inside a Tweet should be linked to their user profile. Tapping that username should lead to the profile of that user, preferably within your app.

3. *Hashtags*: If a user includes a hashtag in a Tweet, it should link to a Twitter.com search for that query term inside your app.

4. *URLs*: URLs in a Tweet should be presented as tappable hyperlinks to the location passed through the API.

5. *Branding*: If your app shows a single Tweet outside a Twitter timeline or other relevant context, Twitter asks that you put the Twitter wordmark or Twitter bird somewhere on the image. If you are showing a group of tweets outside a Twitter timeline or other relevant context, Twitter asks that you put the words "Content From Twitter" nearby. You will learn more about the Twitter bird and wordmark later in this chapter.

Note that Twitter says it can make exceptions to these rules if you email it to seek approval. Email your requests to trademarks@twitter.com.

When composing a Tweet, you should be aware that there are a few additional elements not pictured:

1. *Tweet box*: A view for composing a new Tweet should always be presented with the "What's Happening?" prompt above it.

2. *Tweet button*: If your app is posting content only to Twitter, the button that executes the task should be labeled, "Tweet." If the post is being pushed to another service in addition to Twitter, label the button, "Update."

3. *Character count*: Every blank Tweet should have a character counter in view that counts down from 140 characters to show how many characters are still available.

Suggested Components

In addition to the preceding "requirements," Twitter also has a bunch of suggested design guidelines that you may (or may not) want to follow. The following section reproduces Twitter's official suggestions, and balances them with examples from apps that ignore these suggestions for the better:

- *Avatar and alignment*: Twitter likes developers to display the user's avatar on the left side of the Tweet. Other Tweet content is then supposed to be aligned left, immediately to the right of the avatar. The avatar links to the user's Twitter profile at http://twitter.com/username.

    - *Counterpoint*: Tweetbot, one of the most visually distinctive Twitter clients in the App Store, chooses to put the avatar below the Tweet (see Figure 13–2). It works.

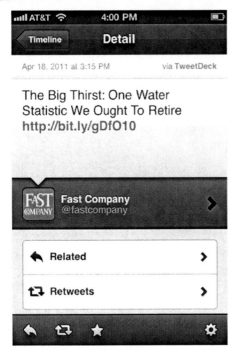

Figure 13–2. *Tweetbot presents Tweet details in a non-conventional way, and we think it works nicely.*

- *Timestamp and Permalink*: "This information can be shown either relative, e.g. '2 minutes ago,' or absolute, e.g. '8:45 AM, Jul 8th'). The timestamp should be on its own line after the Tweet text and styled differently to be less prominent than the Tweet text (lighter color and/or smaller size). The timestamp should also link to the Twitter hosted permalink page for the individual Tweet."

    - *Counterpoint*: Twitterific technically adheres to this suggestion (see Figure 13–3), but only barely: the typeface on the timestamp is only about 1pt smaller than the typeface of the Tweet itself. However, the padding between the timestamp and the Tweet accounts for enough of a distinction. Putting the timestamp above the Tweet puts context first.

Figure 13–3. *Twitterific presents Tweet details in a conventional way.*

- *Tweet Actions*: "Reply, Retweet, and Favorite actions should always be available from a Tweet, and should be displayed with their respective action icons. They should be arranged left to right as Reply, Retweet, Favorite."

    - *Counterpoint*: Almost every app that features the Twitter API presents these Tweet actions in a different way. We like Twitter's suggestion, but sometimes hiding less-used controls makes for a cleaner interface. Both Tweetbot and Twitterific do this in Figures 13–2 and 13–3, respectively.

- *Source*: "Along with the timestamp and permalink, you may choose to display the client or means by which the Tweet was posted (e.g. 'from web' or 'from Twitter for iPhone'). If client is supplied, please make sure it links to the source page URL provided."

    - *Counterpoint*: This is only relevant if your project is Twitter-centric. If your app is more interested in the content of certain Tweets (as opposed to the full Twitter experience), you probably don't need to append the client to a Tweet. Tweetbot does (see Figure 13–2), whereas Twitterific does not (see Figure 13–3).

■ *Multiple Tweets*: "If showing multiple Tweets at once, they can be visually separated by horizontal lines, empty spaces, or alternate background colors. The empty space should be proportional to the overall height of the Tweet itself."

   ■ *Counterpoint*: In our opinion, this guideline shouldn't be optional. It's hard to think of a context where it would be fitting to present Tweets as anything but a list of discrete items. Twitterific presents Tweets nicely (see Figure 13–4).

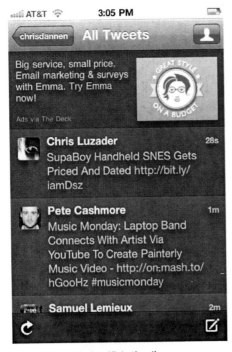

Figure 13–4. *Twitterific's timeline*

■ *Chronological order*: "It usually makes sense for Tweets to be ordered in reverse chronological order (latest first), but we understand that this might not always be the most relevant way to arrange Tweets. When shown as search results or other criteria (keyword, user, or other editorial constraints) Tweets may be ordered by those criteria."

   ■ *Counterpoint*: Actually, it's hard to find a Twitter API project on the App Store that orders Tweets by any criteria other than by how recent Tweets are. Search is the only salient exception.

(Not) Using Twitter Colors

Colors are a major way that users will identify functionality in your apps. They're also an intuitive way to associate yourself with the Twitter platform. However, Twitter really wants you to minimize the extent to which you use its color palette and its trademarked logos, buttons, terms, and icons.

As a result, designers of Twitter API projects are less slavish to the Twitter color scheme than Facebook developers are to their platform's color scheme. Perhaps in the hopes of avoiding Twitter's ire, Twitter API apps tend to be more diverse in their iconography and logos.

For reference, you can find some examples of Twitter's own typography and logo art in Figure 13–5. These buttons are fine for use on the Web, but don't use them in your iOS app—unless they link back to Twitter.com or are used to indicate compatibility with Twitter. If you disregard these requests (which are summarized in the section below entitled "Using the Twitter Trademark"), you may end up in some trouble. If you want to use a bird theme or related assets, you'll have to design or provide them yourself.

Figure 13–5. *You can use Twitter's web buttons in a website—but not in your iOS application, unless under specific circumstances*

Create Theme Elements

Depending on how reliant your app's functionality is on the Twitter API, you may find yourself in a position where your app looks too much like the official Twitter app.

That's why Twitter gives designers this pointer: you should design your site with unique branding and logos.

Twitter also asks that you adhere to the following:

- **Don't** copy the Twitter look and feel.

- **Don't** use anything other than the most current versions of the Twitter logos, where appropriate.

- **Don't** use any other artwork from the Twitter site without explicit permission.

- **Do** create your own buttons or marks using Twitter's logos.

For reference, Figure 13–6 shows the various aspects of the official Twitter app, including the timeline (leftmost image), a Tweet (center image), and a user profile (rightmost image). You need to create your own visual designs and design interactions that don't mimic the ones shown in this figure.

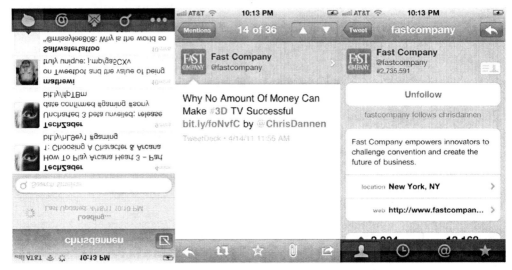

Figures 13–6. *The official Twitter app UI, which you are not supposed to imitate*

Using the Twitter Trademark

Twitter has published a list of dos-and-don'ts regarding its trademarks for developers using the Twitter API.[1] What follows is a summary and analysis of the relevant points.

You *may* do the following:

- Use the current Twitter logo or current Twitter bird mark as a link to the Twitter service.

- Use the current Twitter logo or current Twitter bird mark to show that your product is compatible with Twitter.

- Make sure that you include a direct reference to Twitter when mentioning *Tweet* (for instance, "Tweet with Twitter") or display the Twitter marks with the mention of *Tweet*.

- Manipulate the logos, unless it is necessary due to color-related restrictions inherent in your app, like the black and white iOS toolbar.

You *may not* do the following:

---

[1] http://support.twitter.com/entries/77641

- Use the marks in a way that might imply a false sense of partnership with or endorsement of your brand.

- Distort or alter the Twitter marks in any way.

- Use the marks in a way that confuses the Twitter brand with another brand.

- Use the Twitter bird as a spokesperson to carry your logos or messaging.

Advertising in the App Store

Twitter also has the following guidelines about advertising in the App Store:

- *Do* use screenshots of the logged-out Twitter home page, the Twitter About Us page, or even the @twitter profile page.

- *Don't* use screenshots of other people's profiles or Tweets without their permission.

We Don't Know You

Twitter also asks that you adhere to the following guidelines:

- Refer to *Twitter* when talking about the Twitter service or company, and use *Tweets* (with a capital *T*) when talking about the messages or updates on its service.

- Don't make inaccurate statements about the Twitter service. (Duh!)

- Don't refer to Twitter in a way that implies partnership or endorsement.

Twitter Navigation Paradigms

Loren Brichter, the creator of Tweetie, the predecessor to today's official Twitter app, first conceived of his project as a simple scrolling project. As he said in 2009, he didn't do anything special with Tweetie except to make it fast and in keeping with the spirit of Apple's Human Interface Guidelines (which had not been updated with iOS guidelines at that time):[2]

> It was around the same time that his Verizon Wireless contract expired and he finally got an iPhone. He started scouring the App Store. "I realized there are no good Twitter apps," he recalls. "But there are a billion bad ones." He figured he could probably write a better app. "What triggered me to do it? I was

---

[2] *iPhone Design Award Winning Projects* by Chris Dannen, p.4 (Apress, 2009)

playing with Twitterific, which I used, and everybody used. I thought: I wonder why the scrolling is so slow? I wonder if I can make it faster." In an hour, he had built a prototype of a list of fast-scrolling tweets. Then, after a two-week paroxysm of coding, he had built Tweetie, pictured in Figure 2-1, which is as of this writing the most popular mobile Twitter client on any platform, and the most popular Twitter app for iPhone.

The problem isn't with how the other apps used Twitter's API, it's with the way they interacted with the iPhone OS," he says. "Either they were doing something completely custom, or completely wrong." His antipathy wasn't even aimed at Twitterific, though it was the immediate catalyst for Tweetie. "To tell you the truth, I didn't have a lot of beef with Twitterific," he says. "They were the ADA winner from the year before, and everyone loved the app. It just didn't jive with the way I used Twitter."

When he rebuilt Tweetie as Tweetie 2 from the ground up, he completely re-thought the UI. One surprising addition was the inclusion of a dynamic application bar at the bottom of the screen. You can see this application bar change between the views in Figure 13–7.

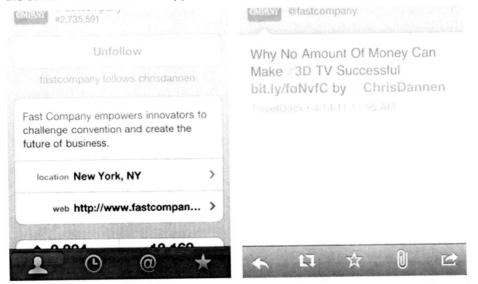

Figure 13–7. *Twitter's dynamic toolbar goes against iOS conventions. On the left, you see the bar as shown in a user profile; on the right, you see the bar as shown when viewing a Tweet.*

Unlike in preloaded iOS apps, the application bar in Tweetie 2—which would become the official Twitter app—had icons that would change, depending on what the user was viewing. When asked why he departed from Apple's precedent in Tweetie 2, Brichter said:[3]

---

[3] Ibid.

Having an application-global tab bar is extremely limiting. In Tweetie 2 I'm optimizing for navigation stack *depth*. By having a screen-specific bottom bar that morphs depending on current context you can expose a massive wealth of information without requiring the user to deal with excessive drill-down.

Apple doesn't do this. In fact, they don't recommend doing what I'm doing. While I think Tweetie 2 is a great example of an iPhone-ish iPhone app, I'm bucking the HIG because I think Apple's recommendations are too confining. A shallow app can get away with an application-global tab bar. A deep, rich app can't. And Tweetie 2 is deep.

The tricks in Tweetie 2 let you explore massive amounts of information without the tap... tap... tap... of pushing tons of view controllers onto the navigation stack. As a quick example, say I'm looking at a tweet in my timeline. A user is asking the Twitterverse a question. I want to check out responses. I can swipe the tweet, tap the user details button, then tap the @ tab of the pushed user-details screen. I'm viewing the responses to this user from everyone, and I'm only a *single* view controller away from where I started.

Tweet list -> Recent user mentions

Without optimizing for navigation stack depth, imagine if I had to push a new view controller for each navigation action:

Tweet list -> Tweet details -> User details -> Recent user mentions.

This stinks.

I don't use a normal tab bar in Tweetie 2 for these context-specific tab bars. I draw them with custom code. I wanted them to be familiar, but different enough that users didn't expect the standard application-global tabs.

Although Brichter's way is now standard in the official Twitter app, he doesn't recommend that most Twitter API projects follow this lead. It's only because Tweetie was attempting to duplicate all the functionality of the Twitter website (and then some) that it became complex enough to warrant a dynamic application bar. Now that broad duplication of Twitter functionality is against Twitter's developer terms, Brichter says it's likely that you won't need to follow this paradigm in your app:

I don't recommend everyone follow my lead. Twitter is *incredibly* rich with information. Chances are most other apps are shallow enough and will be good enough using an application-global tab bar or just simple drill-down.[4]

---

[4] Ibid.

Twitter Logos and Icons

Twitter offers the following logos and icons for download, so that you can accurately display Twitter branding in your app, where appropriate. (The rules and guidelines regarding the use of Twitter branding materials are discussed in the preceding sections of this chapter.) You can download the graphics shown in Figure 13–8 at this URL:

`http://twitter.com/about/resources/logos`

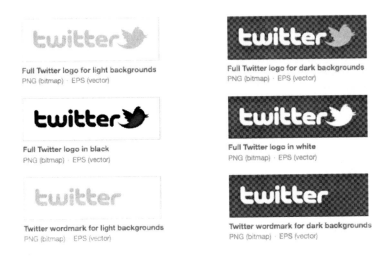

Full Twitter logo for light backgrounds
PNG (bitmap) · EPS (vector)

Full Twitter logo for dark backgrounds
PNG (bitmap) · EPS (vector)

Full Twitter logo in black
PNG (bitmap) · EPS (vector)

Full Twitter logo in white
PNG (bitmap) · EPS (vector)

Twitter wordmark for light backgrounds
PNG (bitmap)   EPS (vector)

Twitter wordmark for dark backgrounds
PNG (bitmap) · EPS (vector)

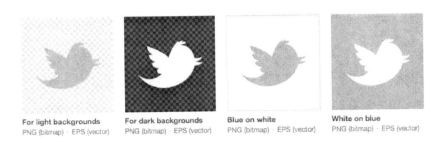

For light backgrounds
PNG (bitmap) · EPS (vector)

For dark backgrounds
PNG (bitmap) · EPS (vector)

Blue on white
PNG (bitmap) · EPS (vector)

White on blue
PNG (bitmap) · EPS (vector)

Figure 13–8. *Twitter logos and icons, which you're meant to use sparingly*

As discussed previously, Twitter strongly discourages the use of its colors and logos in third-party apps. This fact has left a lot of developers struggling to somehow make their icons reminiscent of Twitter without actually directly referencing the company. Various birds have become the standard fare for Twitter clients (see Figure 13–9); but now that no new clients are permitted by Twitter's new terms, Twitter will have an even smaller visible presence in the App Store. In keeping with these guidelines, make your Twitter iconography unique and match it to the visual designs for your app.

Figure 13–9. *The Twitter brand, as paid homage to by various icons in the App Store*

Splash Screens

Splash screens aren't really necessary on today's iOS devices, which load apps quickly. However, you should test your app on multiple generations of devices. If an older iOS device experience lags, see what you can do programmatically to improve load times. If there's nothing to be done under the hood, consider adding a splash screen to your app to welcome waiting users. It passes the time, and it offers you a second to present your branding and make a good impression. If more than a moment or two is required to load your app, consider moving out of the splash screen briskly and presenting a reduced-functionality view of your app's interface. Also, continue to show that your app is loading information, and be sure to inform the user if there is a break in connectivity.

Visual Assets (a.k.a., the Exceptions)

The visual indicators shown in Figure 13–10 are available for download and allowed for use in your app, per the guidelines discussed in this chapter. PNG versions, which are preferred for iOS, are also available as *sprites*. To download these graphics, go to the following URL:

```
http://dev.twitter.com/pages/image-resources
```

Birds

Icons

Sprites (available in .png)

Figure 13–10. *Twitter's sprites, which are available for use in your app*

Naming Your Project

Twitter has compiled a list of dos-and-don'ts for referencing Twitter when you name your project, which we'll cover in this section.[5]

Do the following when naming your project and referencing Twitter:

---

[5] http://support.twitter.com/entries/77641

- Name your website, product, or application with something unique. Uses of *Tw-* and *Twit-* are generally okay.

- Feel free to include language on your site explaining that your application is built on the Twitter platform, so people understand your product.

- Use *Tweet* in the name of your application only if it is designed to be used exclusively with the Twitter platform.

Don't do the following when naming your project and referencing Twitter:

- Use *Twitter* in the name of your website or application.

- Use *Tweet* by itself or in conjunction with a simple letter or number combination (e.g., *1Tweet*, *Tweet*, or *Tweets*).

- Register a domain containing *twitter* (or misspellings of twitter).

- Apply for a trademark with a name that includes *Twitter*, *Tweet*, or similar variations thereof.

- Use *Tweet* in the name of your application if used with any other platform.

Offline Display Guidelines

If you are making some kind of Twitter visualizer or plan for your app to be viewed on a larger display via the iPad, then you should follow the offline display requirements outlined in this section.

For example, you are permitted to do the following:

- Include the Twitter logo in close proximity to Tweets for the duration that Tweets appear in a broadcast.

- Make sure that the Twitter logo is a reasonable size in relation to the content.

- Include the username with each Tweet. If you have concerns about user privacy or broadcast standards, please contact Twitter regarding exceptions, unless you have a prior agreement with Twitter.

- Use the full text of the Tweet. If privacy or broadcast standards are concerned, please contact Twitter regarding exceptions, unless you have a prior agreement with Twitter.

And here are some things you should not do: delete, obscure, or alter the identification of the user. You may show Tweets in anonymous form in exceptional cases, such as concerns over user security. Showing unattributed data in aggregate or visualized form is permitted, but you must still include the Twitter logo.

To see Twitter's complete list of offline display and broadcast media guidelines, go to the following URL:

http://support.twitter.com/entries/77641

Working with Notifications

Until Spring 2011, the official Twitter app dealt with notifications conservatively: it only delivered a Push alert if you were pinged by an @reply or a direct message. Generally, the authors agree this is really all the notifications a Twitter app requires.

However, in March 2011 Twitter introduced something called the *QuickBar*, which was supposed to be a way for the editorial powers at Twitter to introduce a trending topic (or, ahem, paid promotional Tweets) to the top of users' timelines. Instead, it became a raging source of user ire and is commonly nicknamed the *Dickbar*.

On an app that is a veritable godfather of iOS design, this was a major blunder. Outlets everywhere panned Twitter's folly, and they pummeled the company until it erased the QuickBar from a subsequent update.[6] Mac developer Marco Arment's reaction on his blog was particularly articulate and provided a sense of what's so important about good iOS apps: the clarity of purpose that underpins every screen.

Note that near the end of his rant, he evaluates the QuickBar against three criteria:

- Am I supposed to Tweet about this?
- Am I supposed to save this search?
- Am I supposed to read these Tweets?

These are the core functions of Twitter, so any feature that uses the API should be in some way related to at least a couple of them. An edited version of Arment's post follows:[7]

> Twitter's official iPhone app, formerly Loren Brichter's Tweetie and an otherwise awesome client, got a lot of negative reactions from the recent addition of the QuickBar, a mandatory trending-topics banner on top of the tweet list. A lot of people really hate it, calling it the "dicker" and often abandoning the Twitter app entirely because of it.
>
> Its initial implementation as a floating overlay over anything you were doing in the app was far worse. Now, it's just at the top of the main timeline, and it scrolls with the list. But it's still offensive to most people who hated its debut,

---

[6] http://blog.twitter.com/2011/03/so-bar-walks-into-app.html

[7] http://www.marco.org/2011/03/20/why-the-quick-bar-dickbar-is-still-so-offensive

because making it scroll with the list didn't solve the problem of it being there and being mandatory.

The reason Twitter added the QuickBar was, presumably, to be able to feature ads, which show the "Promoted" badge.

If it only ever showed ads like this, I don't think the response would be so negative. The bigger problem is that it's showing a random "trending" topic or hash-tag most of the time. Here are a few of the topics I've seen in the last 24 hours:

LovatoAndGomez
ChrisBrownFAMEAlbum
Gus Johnson
#100factsaboutme
Wolverines
Cingular
GSM
#michigan

*It's a news ticker limited to one-word items, lacking any context, broadcasting mostly topics that I don't understand. What's worse is that it's shown in a context—my Twitter timeline—that otherwise **contains only content that I've (indirectly) chosen to put there.** (I've chosen who to follow based on what I want to see in my timeline.) I'm not interested in sports or celebrities or middle-school survey trends, so I don't follow people who overwhelm my timeline with those unwanted topics.*

Content that I've chosen to follow, and... Michigan. I don't even know what that's supposed to mean. Presumably, there's some bit of news happening that's relevant to the state of Michigan, and Twitter wants users to tap on this disembodied word for a reason that's not made clear to us.

So I tapped on it.

I see, from top to bottom: intentional spam, unintentional spam, and a random person's frivolous, meaningless tweet about sports that I don't care about. (I scrolled down and it only got worse.) I guess "#Michigan" is a trending topic because something important happened with a Michigan sports team.

What am I supposed to do with this information?

Am I supposed to tweet about it? If so, why doesn't the interface encourage that? Even if I hit the (effectively invisible) New Tweet button from this screen, my tweet isn't prepopulated with "#michigan", so whatever I say in response won't be included here.

Am I supposed to save this search, which the interface does encourage, so I can see this topic again in a few days or weeks or months, when it's presumably no longer coherent or useful? (Ignoring, for the moment, that it's neither coherent nor useful now.)

Am I supposed to read these tweets? If so, why haven't stronger anti-spam methods or human filtering mechanisms been employed to keep the stream somewhat readable? As-is, it's a huge and easily exploited spam target, and it shows.

We don't know Twitter's true reason for adding the QuickBar. Presumably, it's part of a longer-term strategy. But today, from here, it looks like an extremely poorly thought-out feature, released initially with an extremely poor implementation, with seemingly no benefits to users.

This is so jarring to us because it's so unlike the Twitter that we've known to date. Twitter's product direction is usually incredibly good and well-thought-out, and their implementation is usually careful and thoughtful.

And in the context of this app, most of which was carefully and thoughtfully constructed by Loren Brichter before Twitter bought it from him, we're accustomed to Brichter's even higher standards, which won Tweetie an Apple Design Award in 2009. (I suspect he had little to no authority in the QuickBar's existence, design, or placement, and it's probably killing him inside.)

The QuickBar isn't offensive because we don't want Twitter making money with ads, or because we object to changes in the interface.

It's offensive because it's deeply bad, showing complete disregard for quality, product design, and user respect, and we've come to expect a lot more from Twitter.

Design Tricks from the Web App

There are some things about Twitter's touch-oriented mobile Web app that put its native iOS app to shame. We like the way it presents options to take Tweet actions (like Retweet, Reply, and Favorite) without the need to slide aside the Tweet. It's also cool that composing a Tweet requires no buttons to operate: you simply place the cursor and start Tweeting. Figure 13–11 shows the mobile Web app (left) and the native iOS app (right) side-by-side.

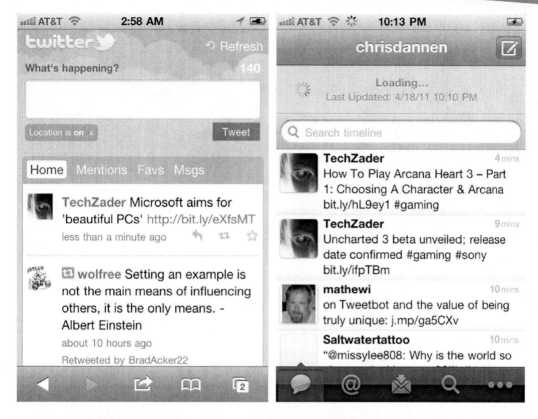

Figure 13–11. *Twitter's mobile web app (left) compared to its iOS app (right)*

Conclusion

Twitter's zeal for rules and regulations is an understandable, if annoying, byproduct of its emerging role as a kind of information infrastructure. And while that has severely limited the way you can build your own Twitter experience, it has also opened up the possibility for apps that do more than just display a rushing timeline. Unfortunately, this means that a good Twitter API project might involve more sweat equity than it did when Loren Brichter built Tweetie 1.

Next, we'll discuss Facebook design conventions.

Chapter 14

Facebook UI Design

The Facebook app is one of the App Store's most unusual; it is also the most capable client on any platform for the world's largest social network. If it looks like an iPhone within an iPhone, it's because the Facebook platform is just as formidable as iOS. Figure 14–1 shows the Facebook app's iOS-like grid UI.

Figure 14–1. *Facebook was the first major platform to reproduce the iOS "grid" UI inside an app.*

Usability Priorities

Facebook API projects should have slightly different priorities than Twitter projects. Those priorities should include the following:

- *Looking people up*: Users query other users more frequently on Facebook, and there is more information to surface, so give these tasks primacy.

- *Contacting and being alerted of contact*: The Facebook app sends you a push notification and/or a vibration for up to nine alerts. By contrast, Twitter does two. Facebook is a lean-forward app with a highly active user base. These users are used to being notified promptly and communicating with alacrity. Figure 14–2 shows Facebook's Push notification options.

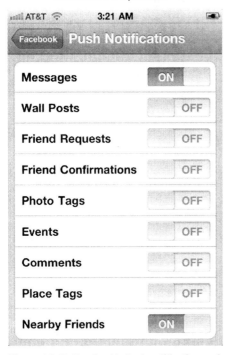

Figure 14–2. *Facebook's Push notification preferences are quite granular and let users interact quickly with each other.*

- *Giving users context*: Facebook is such a powerful platform that many apps only reproduce select parts of the Web app's functionality. This may lead users to expect some tasks that aren't present in your app. You can ameliorate this by picking a descriptive name for your app and by arranging core controls in a way that the user understands its functionality intuitively. This is especially important to posting: users must know where an item is going and who will see it. If you must, use help prompts; however, use them inside the app, not as a pop-up dialog box, as the MyPhone+ does (see Figure 14–3). For the record, we also don't recommend telling users to reboot after installing.

Figure 14–3. *Don't do this.*

Create Your Own UIAs we discussed in Chapter 11, Facebook's terms make the following stipulation (see Figure 14–4):

"Facebook site features cannot be emulated."[1]

If your app looks too much like Facebook and works too much like Facebook, you'll probably hear from respresentatives of Facebook. However, you might be interested to know that the reasons for this actually benefit the user, as well as Facebook. Joe Hewitt, the original developer of Facebook for iOS, explained Facebook's reasoning:

> *The first version of the app did have the tab bar at the bottom, but I took it out because I feel like Facebook is a platform in itself, and each of the tabs were almost like apps in and of themselves that really called for use of the full screen.*
>
> *I had to look forward; we have a lot of new apps coming down the pipe, and I felt like the model Facebook works on lends itself better to sort of being a 'phone' in and of itself. Facebook has its own chat, phone book, mail, photos, and applications, so squeezing it all into tabs made it feel*

---

[1] http://developers.facebook.com/policy/

too limited. Going with this model—it's a home screen just like the iPhone home screen—will let it grow and become full-featured. It also gives us room to add more apps within our app.

I haven't really seen other apps that do [the grid], and I wouldn't really recommend that anyone else do it. Facebook is kind of unique in its breadth and the amount of stuff people do on it. I really hesitated to build in the grid for a while, but as I kept moving things around and trying to make it all fit into the tab bar, I just felt like this was the best solution. I was expecting more people to complain about it, but it seems to have worked out pretty well.

Economy [of taps] is always a motivating factor, but the grid adds an extra tap [because you need to press the grid button] versus the full-time tab bar. That was a compromise I felt was necessary. There's always that balance between screen clutter—adding tabs—and the number of taps.

What went into creating Facebook's view controllers?

I did a lot of custom stuff. The app is built on an open source framework I created called Three20, and it uses its own view controllers, all of which I had to write. I had to try to reinvent the Apple photo browsing app and the Apple Mail composing tool, among other stuff.[2]

FACEBOOK LOADING PROJECT[3]

This project shows how the Facebook app caches old information and checks for available services before posting. Hewitt explained it like this:

Everything in the app works that way. There's a disk cache so if you load events, notes, or requests, it's cached so when you go back to the app, and we show the cached version. And as we show it, we try to load the latest version. If it's a week old—or some number of days, I forget the exact number— the app will just show you "loading" and clear the old stuff.

---

[2] /iPhone Design Award-Winning Projects/ by Chris Dannen (Apress, 2009)

Before that system was in place, you were constantly looking at a little spinner wherever you went—loading, loading, loading. I think it feels nicer to see something right away that you can interact with while the new stuff is coming in.

The code that follows is an excerpt of the Facebook app's disk cache framework, which serves as a replacement for Cocoa's classes for fetching network data (in this case, from Facebook's servers). Hewitt has written the Three20 framework to allow the cache to be stored on disk. In Apple's framework, RAM would be required. Here is the code itself:

```
- (NSData*)generatePostBody {
  NSMutableData* body = [NSMutableData data];
  NSString* beginLine = [NSString stringWithFormat:@"\r\n--%@\r\n", kStringBoundary];

  [body appendData:[[NSString stringWithFormat:@"--%@\r\n", kStringBoundary]
    dataUsingEncoding:NSUTF8StringEncoding]];

  for (id key in [_parameters keyEnumerator]) {
    NSString* value = [_parameters valueForKey:key];
    // Really, this can only be an NSString. We're cheating here.
    if (![value isKindOfClass:[UIImage class]] &&
        ![value isKindOfClass:[NSData class]]) {
      [body appendData:[beginLine dataUsingEncoding:NSUTF8StringEncoding]];
      [body appendData:[[NSString
        stringWithFormat:@"Content-Disposition: form-data; name=\"%@\"\r\n\r\n", key]
          dataUsingEncoding:_charsetForMultipart]];
      [body appendData:[value dataUsingEncoding:_charsetForMultipart]];
    }
  }

  NSString* imageKey = nil;
  for (id key in [_parameters keyEnumerator]) {
    if ([[_parameters objectForKey:key] isKindOfClass:[UIImage class]]) {
      UIImage* image = [_parameters objectForKey:key];
      CGFloat quality = [TTURLRequestQueue mainQueue].imageCompressionQuality;
      NSData* data = UIImageJPEGRepresentation(image, quality);

      [self appendImageData:data withName:key toBody:body];
      imageKey = key;

    } else if ([[_parameters objectForKey:key] isKindOfClass:[NSData class]]) {
      NSData* data = [_parameters objectForKey:key];
      [self appendImageData:data withName:key toBody:body];
      imageKey = key;
    }
  }

  for (NSInteger i = 0; i < _files.count; i += 3) {
    NSData* data = [_files objectAtIndex:i];
    NSString* mimeType = [_files objectAtIndex:i+1];
    NSString* fileName = [_files objectAtIndex:i+2];

    [body appendData:[beginLine dataUsingEncoding:NSUTF8StringEncoding]];
    [body appendData:[[NSString stringWithFormat:
                        @"Content-Disposition: form-data; name=\"%@\";
filename=\"%@\"\r\n",
```

```
                        fileName, fileName]
        dataUsingEncoding:_charsetForMultipart]];
  [body appendData:[[NSString stringWithFormat:@"Content-Length: %d\r\n", data.length]
        dataUsingEncoding:_charsetForMultipart]];
  [body appendData:[[NSString stringWithFormat:@"Content-Type: %@\r\n\r\n", mimeType]
        dataUsingEncoding:_charsetForMultipart]];
  [body appendData:data];
}

[body appendData:[[NSString stringWithFormat:@"\r\n--%@--\r\n", kStringBoundary]
                dataUsingEncoding:NSUTF8StringEncoding]];

// If an image was found, remove it from the dictionary to save memory while we
// perform the upload
if (imageKey) {
  [_parameters removeObjectForKey:imageKey];
}

TTDCONDITIONLOG(TTDFLAG_URLREQUEST, @"Sending %s", [body bytes]);
  return body;
}
```

Figure 14–4. *Facebook would prefer that you not crib from its visual designs, but lots of developers do it, anyway. This is yet another reason to avoid doing so yourself.*

Themes and Icons

According to Facebook, you're not supposed to mimic Facebook visual design or its iconography. However, that obviously doesn't stop many developers from doing exactly that. So what's a new Facebook developer to do?

In our opinion, there are circumstances where a color scheme reminiscent of Facebook's is highly appropriate. If your app is going to provide extensive Facebook functionality (in addition to other stuff, of course), then it might be instructive to users to be in an environment that smacks of (but doesn't replicate) Facebook (see Figure 14–5).

Third Party Resources

Figure 14–5. *If you must take inspiration, consider Facebook's interaction design and its design conventions, and try to pay homage to those.*

Figure 14–5 shows a third-party set of Photoshop images. They're free to use. They're also meant for Web designers, but don't let that stop you. These visual designs should help you mock up your app or borrow certain aspects of the Facebook UI that you like. Remember not to borrow too liberally because reproducing the Facebook UI in your app is against the API's terms and conditions.

You can download this free Facebook UI kit from Surgeworks at the following URL:

http://surgeworks.com/blog/design/facebook-gui-free-psd-resource

Create Theme Elements

To the extent that you're capable of doing so, develop your own color scheme, branding, logos, and iconography.

Not only does Facebook discourage developers from using its blue-and-white color scheme, but common sense does, too. There is a dearth of quality iOS applications in the App Store that use the Facebook API—but there is a wealth of awful ones. Most of the bottom-feeding apps shamelessly mimic Facebook's colors and iconography. Copying Facebook isn't just against the rules; it's also a little low-end.

Fortunately, Facebook is still useful without the sanitary style sheet. Hootsuite, a social aggregator, and Taptu, a reader app, are two applications that present Facebook content in a unique way, using unique color palettes and branding.

Hootsuite

As you can see in Figure 14–6, Hootsuite's teal color scheme looks more like Twitter than Facebook. But its visual elements and its application bar are more like a weird hybrid of the two social networks—and less like a copy of either one.

Figure 14–6. *Hootsuite combines Facebook and Twitter colors and conventions, which is its way of avoiding looking too much like either.*

Taptu

Taptu is an app for the iPhone and the iPad that funnels RSS feeds, social news, and other content into *streams* that are easier to read than traditional readers. As you can see in Figure 14–7, the Facebook feed gets packaged just like any other feed, with Status Updates (and their author and timestamp) presented in a chronological timeline, vaguely Twitter-style. This is another hybrid design that satisfies the design guidelines of its platform.

Figure 14–7. *Taptu's interpretation of the News Feed*

Rules for Facebook Art

As we said at the outset of this chapter, Facebook doesn't have nearly the elaborate set of rules that Twitter does for trademarks and visual assets. That might be one reason that so many app developers borrow freely when they create their app icons and interfaces.

The previous section instructed you to create your own theme elements. When you do so, you'll need to keep a few brief guidelines in mind, according to Facebook:

- Your advertisements must not include or be paired with any platform integrations, including social plugins such as the Like button, without Facebook's written permission.

- Developers aren't allowed to market themselves in a way that implies the participation or endorsement of Facebook.

- Developers should also avoid using Facebook logos, trademarks, or site terminology. These include but are not limited to Facebook, The Facebook, FacebookHigh, FBook, FB, Poke, Wall, and other company graphics, logos, designs, or icons).

If you'd like to read Facebook's ad guidelines in their entirety, visit this URL:

`http://www.facebook.com/ad_guidelines.php`

Button Text

Here are a few examples of button text that are permitted for Facebook developers:

- Post
- Share
- Publish
- Add to Profile

Here are a few examples of button text that are too vague to use, in Facebook's opinion:

- Ignore
- OK
- Share & Continue
- Request

Facebook Navigation

Because of its grid UI, the official Facebook app sets some strange navigational paradigms. In fact, it borrows a lot from Android and a little from webOS. The Facebook app does the following:

- Uses tap-and-hold to mimic iOS's app icon "jiggling" effect.
- Uses a status bar that rises up from the base of the screen, similar to Android, for notifications.
- Has "apps" within it, just like the iOS UI.
- Animates a glimmer when you tap the titlebar, similar to the HP webOS.

CAUTION: Don't copy Facebook's UI and navigation.

We like all these little quirks, and we wouldn't want the official Facebook app to work any other way. But we don't advise that you imitate any of these paradigms. They're not at home on iOS (at least, not yet?), and they will only confuse your users.

Showing Progress

As we discussed earlier in this chapter, showing the user progress is a vital part of your app's feedback. In the official Facebook app, the user is never presented with an empty News Feed; if a network connection can't be found, the app displays recent updates it's cached behind the scenes. Facebook users are doubtless accustomed to the speed and efficiency of Facebook's iOS and Web apps, so you'd do best not to keep them waiting.

If you must, use the activity indicator and consider showing users a warning message if the operation is going to take a substantial amount of time; however, an activity indicator should never prevent the user from switching tabs or composing other content. The Facebook-integrated MyPhone+ app only has one main task, and it's a big one. The app handles this task nicely, as you can see in Figure 14–8.

Figure 14–8. *MyPhone+ displays a progress indicator for its central task, which is only a good idea under certain circumstances.*

Essential Three20 Components

As you learned in Chapter 10, the Three20 project is Facebook iOS developer Joe Hewitt's gift to the Facebook developer community: an entire framework he built himself for the Facebook app for iOS.

It's open source, and it's comprised of several of the constituent parts of the Facebook app. These parts are the photo viewer, the message composer, the Web image view, and other goodies. You can find their Git addresses at this URL:

http://joehewitt.com/post/the-three20-project/

Here are some of the components you will want to be aware of as you design your app and Joe's descriptions of each one:

- *Photo Viewer*: "TTPhotoViewController emulates Apple's Photos app with all of its flick'n'pinch delight. You can supply your own "photo sources," which work similarly to the data sources used by UITableView. Unlike Apple's Photos app, it isn't limited to photos stored locally. Your photos can be loaded from the network, and long lists of photos can be loaded incrementally. This version also supports zooming (unlike the version in the current Facebook app).

  "This has probably been the single biggest timesink in the whole Facebook for iPhone project for me, so if I can help anyone else save that time I will sleep better."

- *Message composer*: "TTMessageController emulates the message composer in Apple's Mail app. You can customize it to send any kind of message you want. Include your own set of message fields, or use the standard To: and Subject:. Recipient names can be autocompleted from a data source that you provide."

- *Web image views*: "TTImageView makes it as easy to display an image as it is in HTML. Just supply the URL of the image, and TTImageView loads it and displays it efficiently. TTImageView also works with the HTTP cache described below to avoid hitting the network when possible."

- *Internet-aware table view controllers*: "TTTableViewController and TTTableViewDataSource help you to build tables which load their content from the Internet. Rather than just assuming you have all the data ready to go, like UITableView does by default, TTTableViewController lets you communicate when your data is loading, and when there is an error or nothing to display. It also helps you to add a "More" button to load the next page of data, and optionally supports reloading the data by shaking the device."

- *Letter Text Fields*: "`TTTextEditor` is a `UITextView` which can grow in height automatically as you type. I use this for entering messages in Facebook Chat, and it behaves similarly to the editor in Apple's SMS app."

  "`TTPickerTextField` is a type-ahead `UITextField`. As you type, it searches a data source, and it adds bubbles into the flow of text when you choose a type-ahead option. I use this in `TTMessageController` for selecting the names of message recipients."

Design Tricks from the Web App

Facebook's touch Web app is arguably as well designed as its iOS app (see Figure 14–9). Although it has all the limitations that come with being in the browser, there are nevertheless some good design paradigms here that you can actually borrow from (unlike the grid).

Figure 14–9. *Facebook's home page for Mobile Safari users*

The Tabbed Approach

Tabs were used in the first versions of the Facebook for iOS app, but they quickly became cluttered as the app became more robust. The Web app held onto tabbed browsing longer, but its developers recently revised the app's navigation bar to contain only four items:

- Profile

- Messages

- More (Friends, Photos, Places, Groups, Events, Notes, Notifications, Settings, and Logout)

- Search button

We'd say the contents of these tabs reflect the Facebook usability priorities we established at the beginning of this section:

- Looking people up

- Contacting people

- Context

And with that, this discussion has come full circle!

Conclusion

This is a time after a rush. Web developers have flocked to the Twitter and Facebook APIs, and iOS developers are following after them. But the influx has caused the management of these platforms to become conservative as they try to protect and sustain their growth. No one wants to derail a good thing, and the platforms have constructed a schema of rules and terms that ensure no one can sully their name but themselves.

This is not a death sentence for the creativity of developers and designers. Rather, it forces them to create apps that add real value to the platform. We encourage you to think of ways to use Facebook and Twitter that haven't been done—or haven't been done right, previously. And when you hit upon a unique experience with an audience you know, you need to design visual assets that reflect the personality of your app. In the App Store, looks aren't everything. They're merely *almost* everything.

Index

B

J, K

L

N

CPSIA information can be obtained at www.ICGtesting.com
Printed in the USA
237358LV00010B/1-92/P

9 781430 235422